Debating Swaraj

Debating Swaraj

Edited by

Dhananjay Rai

Orient BlackSwan

DEBATING SWARAJ

ORIENT BLACKSWAN PRIVATE LIMITED

Registered Office
3-6-752 Himayatnagar, Hyderabad 500 029, Telangana, India
e-mail: centraloffice@orientblackswan.com

Other Offices
Bengaluru, Chennai, Guwahati, Hyderabad,
Kolkata, Mumbai, New Delhi, Noida, Patna

First published 2025

ISBN 978-93-5442-827-2

040885

Typeset in
Adobe Jenson Pro 11.5/13.5
by Manmohan Kumar, Delhi

Printed in India at
Avantika Printers Private Limited, New Delhi 110 020

Published by
Orient Blackswan Private Limited
3-6-752 Himayatnagar, Hyderabad 500 029, Telangana, India
e-mail: info@orientblackswan.com

To

Papa

Contents

Abbreviations

BHU	Benaras Hindu University
CAGR	compounded average growth rate
ECAAR	Economists Allied for Arms Reduction
GDP	gross domestic product
INC	Indian National Congress
WTO	World Trade Organization

Preface and Acknowledgements

Debating Swaraj invites attention to the constant endeavour to improve associational life, either by enhancing the framework or envisioning an alternative framework in which heterodoxy is deliberately proposed, critically analysed, and reflectively implemented.

In addition to challenging orthodoxy, debating *swaraj* is crucial for understanding the challenges and limits of heterodoxy as well. Is the theory of heterodoxy sufficient for transformation, or should thinkers also be contemporaries while outlining the act of transformation? Contesting or moving beyond hagiography is critical for contemporising and actualising ideas, all the while being careful not to dehistoricise the ideas.

This reasoning also invites us to abandon the hierarchical and, to some extent, artificial division between theory and thought, which claims the former as superior and the latter as bereft of theory. Even when these two are treated as analytical categories, there is an overlap between and transgression of boundaries. Reading this way is a serious challenge, that is, to read intentionally or with theoretical integrity while contributing profoundly to a contemporaneous reading.

This book debates M. K. Gandhi and the idea of *swaraj* for contemporary, historical, and transformative values. *Debating Swaraj* draws attention to the need to debate the idea of *swaraj* for associational life in an egalitarian manner.

This book is the culmination of a decade-long debate on Swaraj. The year 2015 remains a critical point at which the idea of debating *swaraj* originated. It was galvanised by select speakers at the international conference on 'Debating Swaraj after Hundred Years of Gandhi's Return to India from South Africa', organised on 4–6 October 2015 by the Central University of Gujarat, in collaboration with the Indian Council of Social Science Research (ICSSR), New Delhi. I am very grateful for this conference. Colleagues, researchers, and students from the Department of Gandhian Thought and Peace Studies and the Central University of Gujarat were vital in organising the workshop and offered numerous opportunities to develop ideas.

The process of thinking and deliberating on *swaraj* continued after the seminar, in the academic ambience of the university and beyond.

Discussions continued with the contributors to this volume. The centrality of Gandhi/*Swaraj* remained an important conjuncture, while the points of analysis varied, making this volume vivid and necessary. I am immensely grateful to the contributors for patiently tolerating my incessant emails and communications.

A series of intermittent engagements galvanised the process, moving it from debating to publishing. At Orient BlackSwan, Roopa Sharma, Sunaina Mathur Dalaya, Proteeti Banerjee, and Nilanjana Majumdar played vital roles in publishing the book.

I am also grateful to Professor R. K. Kale (former Vice-Chancellor, Central University of Gujarat), Professor S. A. Bari (former Vice-Chancellor, Central University of Gujarat), and Professor Rama Shanker Dubey (Vice-Chancellor, Central University of Gujarat) for encouraging a slew of academic activities and enabling this work. I am also grateful to Professor Rama Shanker Dubey for all the academic encouragement and suggestions.

I am grateful to the following interlocutors who facilitated discussions on multiple occasions at multiple sites: Dr Akash Thakur, Professor Akhil Ranjan Dutta, Dr Amarendra Pandey, Dr Bhavna Harchandani, Dr Binayak Roy, Professor Dharmendra Kumar, Dr Debajyoti Biswas, Professor E. V. Ramakrishnan, Professor Hilal Ahmed, Dr Indrajeet Jha, Professor Janak Singh Meena, Dr Jyotsna, Dr Jyotasana, Professor Kamal Nayan Choubey, Professor Lajwanti Chatani, Mahendra Parmar, Dr Manas Kandi, Professor Manindra Nath Thakur, Professor Manoj Rai, Professor Manoranjan Mohanty, Dr Mohammad Naushad, Professor N. Rajaram, Professor Om Prakash Dwivedi, Dr Pawan Kumar, Professor Prem Anand Mishra, Dr Rityusha Tiwary, Professor Sadan Jha, Professor Satish Kumar Jha, Professor Savita Singh, Dr Siba Mohanty, Dr Smruti Ranjan Dhal, Professor Tapas Kumar Dalapati, Dr Vikas Kumar, Dr Vikas Pathe, Dr Vikram Amarawat, and Dr Vivek Rai.

My interactions with Deependra Baghel were highly beneficial during my journey with this book. His passing away in 2024 was a great loss to academia. He was almost a living encyclopaedia of critical theory and thought. His keen interest in this work and the collective project was invaluable. He taught us that knowledge is important, and not merely its personification. He avoided the limelight and promoted discursive debates. He referred to reading as an act of self-consumption, and we greatly benefitted from those readings. I miss his presence immensely.

I am grateful to Aanya and Rityusha for forgiving my multiple absences. Rityusha's comments helped clarify a slew of ideas. Before the book could be published, my father, Captain Ramayan Rai, passed away. I dedicate this book to his loving memory.

Needless to say, I remain responsible for any errors left out unknowingly.

Introduction

Debating Swaraj

Dhananjay Rai

Debating Swaraj sets out to re-envision the idea of political community, juxtaposing the excruciating suzerainty of the state/government with the increasingly blurred distinction between peoples' participation and decision-making on behalf of the people. Reading *swaraj* (literally, self-rule) as a political community based on egalitarian principles presupposes certain caveats, which this volume attempts to navigate. Swaraj cannot be delimited either by historical frigidity or geographical rigidity. It cannot be treated as a mere historical subject, delinked from contemporary space. It cannot be remembered in a postcolonial sense alone or as a reproduction of relevance in the Indian context. Swaraj cannot be treated as a defence of mere indigeneity. Instead, this volume attempts to read M. K. Gandhi's rendition of swaraj as a 'living alternative', i.e., an alternative which is liveable. This living alternative of swaraj becomes the edifice of a re-envisioned political community that problematises contemporary reality. The chapters in this volume that engage with the political community or swaraj highlight certain concrete aspects of Gandhi's swaraj.

Rethinking State/Government

Rethinking state/government engenders the significance of *debating* the contours of swaraj for the arrival of the political community. Both are intertwined, as the problematique of the first is answered and filled by the second. Rethinking state/government is a prerequisite since its 'terms and scope' are reduced to a hegemonic consensus towards an uncritical acceptance of the 'sovereign'. The accountability of the people to the sovereign is enshrined, delineated and absolute, but the sovereign ceases to be accountable towards the people. In the body politic, two determinants ('on behalf' and 'delegation'), *inter alia,* have become the standard norm and permanent fixtures by converting people into residual therein. The liberal model of 'on behalf' and 'delegation' not only centralises decision-making but also paves the way for *depeopleisation,* i.e., decisions being made for people *without* people. Depeopleisation (an outcome of the 'on behalf' and 'delegation' axioms) is augmented and cemented through specialisation and technolisation of decisions. If classical capitalism needed a polity to endorse decisions 'on behalf' of the people, thereby ensuing a method through delegation, neoliberal capitalism abandons polity through privatisation of decisions and decision-making bodies. The artefact of 'on behalf', 'delegation' and 'depeopleisation' reduces people to being governed subjects. Unlimited exploitation and quadrupled violence against people are increasingly justified in the name of governing norms that have technical legitimacy through 'on behalf' and 'delegation' principles.

Rethinking state/government must be supplemented by *thinking* about the political community. A brief description of the 'terms and scope' of the political community will suffice here. A detailed discussion covers the topic ahead. The foundational premise of the political community is 'ontological reminder', which is based on associational norms. Associational norms do ask the questions why ('Why to associate?' principle) and how ('How to associate?' principle) we are associated with each other. The questions 'Remind whom?' and 'For what purpose?' need certain explication. 'Remind whom?' pertains to each other as a horizontal group. 'For what purpose?' entails the egalitarian arrival of the associational principle. The political community backed by ontological reminder rejects 'ontological indifference', which is a foundational norm of the state/government. The ontological indifference is based on the governing principle of *people to be governed.* Ontological indifference, by the state/government attacks the ontological reminder of the political community. The ontological indifference (people to be governed) is a rejection of the ontological reminder ('Why to associate?' and 'How to associate?'). The assertion of ontological reminder is moving beyond the state-/government-led governing norms.

Reading swaraj as a political community is also an attempt to transcend the limitation and *fait accompli* of the state/government.

Swaraj, Ontological Indifference and Competing Claims

Colonialism is one of the worst forms of 'ontological indifference'. In colonialism, rejection and reduction are co-partners serving imperialism. Besides economic exploitation, the two quintessential features of colonialism are 'rejection of a being' and 'reduction of people to be governed'. Therefore, a being is reduced to be governed in the absolute sense. The existence of a being is negated, converted into a lifeless subject.[1] There is complete unanimity between the 'main texts' and 'a footnote' of British imperialism with regard to 'rejection' and 'reduction'. James Mill represents the main text through his 'critical history' of India. 'A critical history is ... a *judging* history' (1817: x). Mill, however, had 'never been in India' (ibid.: xii). This was not required because 'a man who is duly qualified may attain more knowledge of India, in one year, in his closet in England, than he could obtain during the longest life, by the use of his eyes and his ears in India' (ibid.: xv). In colonialism, the othering is an epithet for 'barbarian', which then supports the arrival of 'civilizational modus vivendi'. Therefore, a being becomes a barbarian (a phrase used for anything unfamiliar from the days of Socrates) and can be corrected by civilised governors. A being is accused of 'criminality, debauchery, and unnatural sexual appetites'. Therefore, '[h]is book ... [advocates] ... for a despotic style of British Rule in India, in which Indians ... [will have] ... as little share as possible' (Bagchi 2008: 215). Regarding 'civilized and barbarian', 'James Mill ... endorsed the duty of the civilized to rule the barbarian until the latter became capable of self-government' (Jones 2005: 182–83).

J. S. Mill adds a required texture to the main text. Eileen Sullivan highlights a significant difference between early liberals (Jeremy Bentham, James Mill) and J. S. Mill. '[T]he liberal tradition inherited by J.S. Mill was dominantly anti-imperialist. The basic liberal argument was that England did not benefit, economically or politically, from the retention or expansion of empire' (Sullivan 1983: 605). In the case of Ireland and India, where imperialism was condoned,

> the argument was that England had no choice but to sustain the loss for political or humanitarian reasons. And, above all, the two instances of

> English imperialism were seen as truly exceptional cases; neither James Mill nor Bentham saw Ireland or India as models for England to follow elsewhere. (Sullivan 1983: 605)

On the economic front, for J. S. Mill, 'imperialism ... [was] ... an economic advantage for both England and her colonies and dependencies'. These 'uncivilized dependencies also benefited from the order and security, the trade which England provided' (ibid.: 609–10).

However, Sullivan herself provides 'rejection' and 'reduction' formulations which bring J. S. Mill closer to James Mill. On the cultural front, '[l]ike his father, he assumed that there was a readily available scale of civilization upon which peoples could be ranked. He was quite certain that the English were civilized and that the peoples of Asia, Africa, and Ireland were uncivilized and barbarous' (Sullivan 1983: 610). J. S. Mill

> asserted that with the power and prestige gained from imperialism, England could intervene more successfully in international affairs. He believed England to be the most civilized nation on earth, 'incomparably the most conscientious of all nations ... the only one whom mere scruples of conscience would ... deter'. (ibid.)

Therefore, the separation between Empire and colonies was rejected, which would compromise the prestige of the former: 'any separation [from our colonies] would greatly diminish the prestige of England, which prestige I believe to be, in the present state of the world, a great advantage to mankind' (ibid.: 612). How 'ontological indifference' is associated with J. S. Mill remains a puzzling question in the context of his defence of both liberty and imperialism. Responding to a few critics of J. S. Mill (e.g., Chakrabarty [2000]; Chatterjee [1986]; Dossa [2002]; Lal [1998]; Mehta [1999]; Parekh [1995]), Mark Tunick finds 'tolerant imperialism' in Mill. He 'defends interference in India to promote the protection of legal rights, respect and toleration for conflicting viewpoints, and a commercial society that can cope with natural threats' (Tunick 2006: 586). This remains an untenable position due to the sheer insistence of 'ontological indifference' in J. S. Mill, as stated above.

Another main text, 'Proclamation by the Queen to the Prince, Chiefs and the People of India, November 1, 1858', is categorical about even rejecting 'tolerant imperialism':

> we hereby call upon all our subjects within the said territories to be faithful, and to bear true allegiance to us, our heirs and successors, and to submit themselves to the authority of those whom we may hereafter, from time to time, see fit to appoint to administer the government of our said territories, in our name and on our behalf. (Ellam 1984: 227)

Interestingly, there is an uncanny resemblance between the main text of imperialism and a footnote of imperialism towards absolute ontological difference, leaving hardly any space for even 'tolerant imperialism'. A book-length response by Captain J. E. Ellam, *Swaraj: The Problem in India*, suggests that any violation of such a proclamation and ruling of British colonialism (or violation of the main texts) must invite serious repercussions and even expulsion. 'The Andamans ... might very well be utilised as a Swaraj "reserve"' (Ellam 1984: 275). Since he remains doubtful of such actions by 'sentimentalists' at home in England, the outcome could be disastrous. 'The alternative is, as Mr. Gandhi expressed it, "red ruin, a revolution, the breaking-up laws"' (ibid.). A Foreword by Lord Brentford of Newick, P.C. to the book endorses perpetual governing: 'India has proved herself quite unfit for democratic self-government, and that she must, for some generations, in her own interests, be governed and controlled by Great Britain, and by that wonderful Civil Service which has done so much for India, and of which we are all so proud' (ibid.: vi). These comments of forgotten footnotes might appear trivial or irrelevant in the history of British imperialism. However, the point is that even this marginal and obscure footnote encapsulates sheer ontological indifference through an absolute focus on construction, endorsement and the implementation of 'subject', 'faithful', 'true allegiance', 'unfit for democratic self-government', and 'governed and controlled'. Even the minor (footnote) is frightening.

Overall, 'ontological indifference' remains absolute, as does the absolute presence of pauperisation serving imperialism. This became the backdrop to the emergence of competing claims through swaraj. It is *not* the rejection of 'ontological indifference' during colonialism that makes the competing claims significant, but rather their competing hypotheses of eventual replacement or the anatomy of the future (which can be traced in the contemporaneity). Interestingly, the etymology of swaraj in the form of 'self-government', 'self-rule', 'independence' or 'home rule' is a gluing factor, but divergences ensue as soon as the political philosophy of swaraj is charted. There are both minimalist and maximalist explanations. The minimalist explanation finds no problem in engaging with the rejection of ontological indifference. It highlights the brazenness of even a footnote of imperialism causing severe plundering. The maximalist explanation demands a clarificatory note about an alternative to colonial rule or an alternative way of political association.

There have been four standpoints, *inter alia*, with regard to swaraj. In the first, the minimalist explanation (that is problematic of colonialism) is present, but swaraj as a future hypothesis is probably absent. Dadabhai Naoroji figures herein. He accepted the minimalist explanation but did not comment on the maximalist explanation.

> Naoroji redefined the goal of the Congress in deliberately ambiguous terms: 'Self-Government or Swaraj like that of the United Kingdom or the Colonies'—there would remain considerable difference between the political systems of Britain and the colonies or Dominions till at least the Statute of Westminster of 1926. (Sarkar 1989: 136)

Tilak defined swaraj as home rule without categorical delinking from the British Empire. His swaraj, i.e., home rule, was located in the Empire. 'Tilak wanted to keep the word Swaraj undefined' (Keer 1959: 350). 'To put it briefly, the demand that management of our affairs should be in our hands is the demand for Swaraj ... We want to remain ... under the sway of this rule' (ibid.: 352).

If Tilak wanted an undefined swaraj, Bhagwan Das defined it as 'Swaraj qua Higher Self'. Das proposes the meaning of swaraj elaborately in the absence of it in 1921. Before defining swaraj, Das envisaged it as a form of parliamentary government in which elected representatives would be retired from a competitive active professional life, or the business of making money, who would not represent any particular interest but would be benevolent towards the interests of all. 'Subject to the above principles, India's *Swaraj* may be within an India-British Federation or Commonwealth wherein the Head of the Executive (Governor-General or Viceroy) may be a member of the British Royal family or such other person as the King of Great Britain may nominate' (Das 2011: 89). The definition of swaraj is needed to remove 'misunderstandings'. The Parliament of England, which created and governed the Government of India, was representative of the capitalists and the landed gentry of

England. The twofold evils identified in India are different than in the West: between bureaucracy and people, not between capitalists and labour. The secondary form of evil is between rich and poor, which, because of a rooted brotherhood in India, could not become more acute. True swaraj is a government of the higher self while rejecting government by a lower self. A government of the lower self is government by 'another'. The lower self-government is foreign and tyrannical due to the focus on self-interest. 'To secure true Self-government, true *Swaraj*, means, then, to ensure purity and wisdom of head and heart in its legislators by wise election' (ibid.: 93). In this swaraj, the work of 'men of thought' (legislatures) and 'men of action' (executive) is not blurred. As informed by the ancient indigenous tradition, the four departments of the government are the educational, the protectional, the economic and the recreational (ibid.: 87–89).

The second standpoint, according to K. C. Bhattacharyya, advocates swaraj as 'indigenous universalism'. Both 'ontological indifference' and 'ontological reminder' are addressed through 'ideas'. Ontological indifference is construed as 'western universalism' and ontological reminder as 'indigenous universalism'. He explores 'svaraj in ideas'. In the political sphere, domination appears in the outer sphere and is therefore recognisable. In the cultural sphere, there is subtler domination of swaraj in ideas. This is what Bhattacharyya calls cultural subjection.

> There is cultural subjection only when one's traditional cast of ideas and sentiments is superseded without comparison or competition by a new cast representing an alien culture which possesses one like a ghost. This subjection is slavery of the spirit; when a person can shake himself free from it, he feels as though the scales fell from his eyes. He experiences a rebirth, and that is what I call *Svaraj* in Ideas. (Bhattacharyya 2011: 105)

To explain cultural subjection, Bhattacharyya intertwines knowledge with universalism. According to him, Western education is responsible for cultural subjection through the creation of universalism without any knowledge of the indigenous culture. There is the imposition of Western culture with our consent and no resulting creativity from this assimilation. In fact, in the absence of our standpoint, we fail to understand the inwardness of our culture. Since Western universalism is our universalism, we lack our own estimation of Western literature, culture and thought. There is no Indian standpoint on Western philosophy. Indian philosophy becomes important for discovering the soul of India. Our education therefore has created a shadow mind without roots in either the past or the present. A strange mishmash of regional/vernacular and English languages to express a hybridisation of ideas is not helpful because of our negligence of expression in the regional/vernacular language. The problem of hybridisation is 'translation'. 'No idea of one cultural language can exactly be translated into another cultural language. Every culture has its distinctive "physiognomy" which is reflected in each vital idea and ideal presented by the culture' (Bhattacharyya 2011: 106).

In spiritual life, our ideas cannot be compromised. A patchwork of ideas or ideals without adjustment or with mechanical adjustment, complacently accepted, is evil. We have to be serious about ideas for them to even conflict with other ideas. We may respect new ideals without accepting them and we may also attempt a synthesis without compromise. However, a 'synthesis' of ideas/ideals should not be attempted in every case. Some foreign ideals have an affinity with our own and are really alternative expressions of them in a foreign idiom that has no sacredness for us; and then there are others which have no real application to our conditions. The rationalism of 'efflux of reverence' is crucial for a traditional institution in place of the rationalism of 'not essential' in which sentiments are rejected. Foreign ideals that have an affinity to us are acceptable. The only universalism is the universalism of our ideas. Our educated men suffer more from 'rootless' universalism than from clinging to particularism because of the way history, philosophy and moral sermons with a propagandist character are imparted and learned. Therefore, our role should be of 'critical reverse' rather than 'docile acceptance'. Imposition is not possible in mathematics and natural sciences in the absence of 'valuation'. Bhattacharyya believes that 'docile acceptance without criticism is slavery'. There is a need for genuine translation of foreign ideas into native ideas. We must think within the context of our cultural concepts. In politics, there is a realisation that power is not for good, but is instead used for evil. This can be changed with peoples' participation.

In another field, there is insufficient realisation in this regard, particularly in the sphere of ideas. Bhattacharyya would like us to think in terms of indigenous ideas. Western education creates a new caste, which is more intolerant than the traditional caste: '[L]et us come back to the cultural stratum of the real Indian people' (Bhattacharyya 2011: 111).

As a representative of the third standpoint, minimalist and maximalist explanations become complex in Aurobindo Ghose. His rejection of ontological indifference gets resolved in the form of cultural nationalism. In other words, the colonial projection of a being and governed people finds resolution in the form of cultural nationalism in a binary sense. In a talk delivered in Nasik on 24 January 1908, Ghose dwelt on 'The Meaning of Swaraj'. In a departure from Dadabhai Naoroji, he defines swaraj as follows: 'Swaraj means administration of affairs in a country by her people on their own strength in accordance with the welfare of the people without even nominal suzerainty, which is the object which we wish to attain' (Ghose 1977: 2). He further said: '*Swaraj* is life, it is nectar and salvation. *Swaraj* in a nation that is the breath of life. Without breath of life a man is dead. So also *Swaraj* being the life of a nation it is essential for it' (ibid.: 2–3).

For Ghose, swaraj must be gained through our own effort. He distrusted help from the neighbourhood and the English government in this regard. 'We should, therefore, be prepared to undergo hardships in the struggle for swaraj, as there is no other alternative. We want *swaraj* which means independence, but independence cannot be had unless we are independent' (ibid.: 3). Thereafter, Ghose adds a theological touch to his definition of swaraj. 'Our idea of the struggle for *swaraj* is that it is the commandment of God, which we must obey. To oppose it is not in our power' (ibid.: 4). As he was delivering this lecture in Maharashtra, he appealed to the inhabitants of Maharashtra and to Bengalis, both being 'sons of Aryabhumi, let us all jointly set ourselves to the task of bringing about a state of things in accordance with the commandment of God' (ibid.: 4). The process of achieving swaraj drives his efforts towards cultural nationalism. While his cultural nationalism transcends colonial beings and colonial political subjects, it situates them within the dominant cultural system, defying logical and ontological reminders. His apotheosis ultimately manifests as 'ontological indifference'.

The Empire is perceived as 'alien' and 'indigenous' in both a minimalist and maximalist sense. Swaraj shifts the focus towards 'nation' and thus generates cultural swaraj or cultural nationalism. From both minimalist and maximalist standpoints, Ghose's use of certain categories needs explication. With regard to ontological indifference and the hypothesis of the future, a pamphlet, 'Bhawani Mandir', provides ample clues. 'Bhawani Mandir' is 'for revolutionary preparation of the country' (Ghose [1970] in Minor [2003: 92]). India is identified as 'the mother'. The mother is, therefore, 'the goddess in all her power and strength'. This strength is required to wipe out barbarism and Aryanise India (ibid.).

So, barbarianism is to be replaced by Aryanisation and the *Bhagavad Gita* becomes a text of violence. Whether the *Bhagavad Gita* is violent or not violent is not important. Instead, the issue is why the idea of redemption in implementing the said purpose is attached to the text and therefore justifies a theological violence. Ghose explains it thus:

> Under certain circumstances, a civil struggle becomes, in reality, a battle and the morality of war is different from the morality of peace. To shrink from bloodshed and violence under such circumstances is a weakness deserving as severe a rebuke as Sri Krishna addressed to Arjuna when he shrank from the colossal civil slaughter on the field of Kurukshetra. (Ghose 1970: 98)

Ghose did not change his opinion with regard to intertwining the relationship between the text and violence, and the place of the former in life. 'Even after retiring from active nationalism, Aurobindo would never give up the sense that the *Bhagavad Gita* was speaking of violence. Violence, he would say in his nonpolitical, yogic period, was an important element in the evolution of the eternal spirit to higher levels of consciousness'. For Ghose, destruction and nature are intertwined. 'Destruction in itself is neither good nor evil. It is a fact of Nature, a necessity in the play of forces, as things are in this world' (cited in Minor [2003: 94]).

The fourth standpoint becomes crucially important as it is related to swaraj and Gandhi, but is not limited to him. However, the focus is on Gandhi and swaraj because of the specific nature of the engagement. Here, the religious vocabulary and texture need to be suspended since initial legitimacy was intertwined with an invocation of religious words. Ontological indifference and ontological reminders can be seen in Gandhi's attempt at envisaging the political community. This was not an insulating event. Swaraj *per se* was unfolding in everydayness. Swaraj discourses shaped Gandhi and Gandhi in turn shaped the swaraj discourse. Naoroji, Tilak and Ghose were formidable challengers to this discourse. Gandhi's proactiveness, for example, in outlining swaraj in *Hind Swaraj* (1909), promising 'swaraj within one year' (*Young India*, 22 September 1920; Sarkar 1989: 197), passing the resolution of *Poorna Swaraj* at the

1929 Lahore session of the Indian National Congress and the passing of resolutions on Fundamental Rights and Duties, Labour, Economic and Social Programme at the 1931 Karachi session of the INC to make Swaraj Government (Sitaramayya 1946) assured the irrelevance of the aforementioned two standpoints.

Gandhi responded to the rejection of being and the reduction of people to governed subjects or the complete rejection of ontological indifference by proposing a definition of swaraj. On these two points *Hind Swaraj* is very categorical. On the rejection of being, Gandhi suggests that '[s]waraj has to be experienced by each one for himself[herself]'. On reduction, he points out, '[i]t is Swaraj when we learn to rule ourselves' (Gandhi 1997: 73). In the years that followed, Gandhi elaborated on swaraj further, and this thoughts were later compiled into *Village Swaraj* (1962). Herein, swaraj or self-rule means both internal and external control. It must be linked with 'rejection of rejection of being'. 'The word Swaraj ... [means] ... self-rule and self-restraint' (ibid.: 12). Self-rule is crucial and must arrive through the recognition of being and not in the absence of it. Colonialism makes self-rule absent. Self-restraint must be understood as non-violation or the creation of dependent relations. Colonialism is therefore rejected for its rejection and reduction of a being. This has been the minimalist position so far. The maximalist position offers a complete break and an alternative. There is also a methodological twist. Gandhi's tone may be religious in the minimalist position, but when defining swaraj he does not enforce indigeneity.

In Gandhi's swaraj, the inclusionary apotheosis is as follows:

> By Swaraj I mean the government of India by the consent of the people as ascertained by the largest number of the adult population, male or female, native-born or domiciled, who have contributed by manual labour to the service of the State and who have taken the trouble of having registered their names as voters. (ibid.)

Therefore, real swaraj is resistant to the rule of a few, thus paving the way for people to realise their own capacity. Real swaraj will come not by the acquisition of authority by a few, but 'by the acquisition of the capacity by all to resist authority when it is abused. In other words, Swaraj is to be obtained by educating the masses to a sense of their capacity to regulate and control authority' (Gandhi 1962). 'Swaraj is to be for all, including the farmer, but emphatically including the maimed, the blind, the starving toiling millions' (ibid.: 17). Swaraj is not majoritarianism; it is rule by the people for justice. 'It has been said that Indian Swaraj will be the rule of the majority community, i.e. the Hindus. There could not be a greater mistake than that ... for to me Hind Swaraj is the rule of all people, is the rule of justice' (ibid.: 18). The political community envisaged by Gandhi focuses on ontological reminders, one of the crucial pointers of which is interdependence.

Three critical questions regarding Gandhi's swaraj forces the anatomy of swaraj into an open-ended endeavour and the possibility of constant engagement. In 1921, S. A. Dange 'visualized a Swaraj which would nationalize big factories, impose a ceiling on and redistribute zamindari land among peasants' (Sarkar 1989: 213). In 1922, just before the Gaya session of the INC, C. R. Das was 'emphasizing that Swaraj must be for the masses and not for the classes' (ibid.: 227). In the 1930s, B. R. Ambedkar reminded us succinctly: 'Tell me what share I am to have in the Swaraj' (Bandyopadhyay 2008: 356). These questions must be seen in the context of the epistemological expansion of the idea of swaraj, which is also a need for the constant evolution of swaraj as a political community. One of the problems vis-à-vis Gandhi and swaraj has been its treatment as a closed concept or *a priori* practices. Therefore, Gandhi's political community must not be seen as a closed concept that does not need constant revision. These questions are foundational to the political community and cannot be treated as aberrations.

Political Community, Ontological Reminders and Swaraj

Against the backdrop of minimalist and maximalist explanations and explication of standpoints on swaraj, it becomes important to delineate the contours of the political community. The political community is inclusive of state/government. Conversely, the state/government does not necessarily constitute a political community. There are two fundamental differences between political community and state/government: 'ontological reminder' and 'ontological indifference'. In the political community, ontological reminders remain the fulcrum and comprise the associational norm, which functions by way of two interrelated axioms. The first reminds us about the existence of the relationship. This can be called the 'Why to associate?' principle. The political community is all about people's eagerness to live collectively and interdependently. This interdependence is the negation of class control, caste rules and gendered relations. The political community as interdependence is arrived at after serious contemplation. The political community may be an idea before an actual materialist transformation or *post facto* an actual practice.

In either case, the central point is that people do not want to be associated with each other for some unknown factors, or factors explained in terms of class, caste and gender, which are dependent-relations. Class prepares the foundation for the arrival of the social (caste, gender) while making the latter autonomous, eventually, without a complete disconnect from the former. Class and social categories are not separate. The dependent (class) and autonomous-dependent (caste and gender) relations remain antithetical to interdependence. Class is crucial to explaining caste or gender for it avoids relapsing into a theological explanation. The class question negates a theological explanation while reinforcing the material existence of caste and gender. Envisaging a political community or its materialisation must elicit deliberation on interdependence while rejecting dependence and autonomous-dependence. The ontological reminder through the 'Why to associate?' principle rekindles such questions to remind us that these are not closed concerns.

The second axiom (How to associate?) takes the question 'Why to associate?' further into the inviolability of interdependence. There cannot be anything voluntary about this. There must be guiding norms that do not highlight the structural presence of the interdependence question, but rather focus on its absence. 'How to associate?' attempts to eradicate dependence and develop interdependence. One of the quintessential features of capitalism is envisaging a system dependent on class exploitation and the perpetuation of autonomous-dependent relations. The entire process of exploitation and accumulation causes deprivation. Social systems/relations codify everydayness, which leads to inverse social practices. Accumulation and inverse practices become a major challenge for guiding norms. Since the political community keeps asking and reminding us why we have been associated with each other, guiding norms necessarily become an encapsulating conveyance. Therefore, the disjuncture between 'Why to associate?' and 'How to associate?' is jettisoned in the political community. This jettisoning is not the only important feature in politics; the fact that the first axiom informs the second is another.

The political community expedites interdependence through associational norms. The state/government, which does not function as a political community, acts conversely. Transformation (or regression) from the political community to mere state/government can be proved empirically through the presence of a dependent-relation and autonomous-dependent relation. In this process,'ontological indifference' plays a crucial role.

In state/government sans political community,'ontological indifference' becomes a vantage point for the art of rule. 'Ontological indifference' eclipses 'ontological reminder'. 'Ontological indifference' is the removal of commitment from a political community with regard to the 'Why to associate?' principle. The transformation (or regression) from political community (associational norm) into mere state/government (governing norm) changes the contour of the discourse on moving from ontological reminder to ontological indifference. The focus shifts towards the teleological pursuit of the'governing norm'.'Ontological indifference' is the absolute prioritisation of teleological pursuits over foundational principles of the political community. Once the teleological pursuits normalise, the foundational principles of the political community are ignored by the state/government. For example, for a capitalist state, the pursuit of surplus accumulation by abandoning the foundation principles of the political community is a priority.

For the state and government, governing norms become an '*end*'-pursuing entity. Their invocation becomes a *fait accompli* towards telos. Legitimacy is accrued in the name of telos. The 'legitimacy to use violence' and the 'legitimacy to rule' are both attributed to the state/government, generating a complex scenario wherein the associational norm is omitted for the governing norm. The framework is constituted accordingly, wherein peoples' participation is sought in order to continue the rhythm of the monopoly of actions and legitimation.

Therefore, swaraj as a political community must be treated as an antithesis to ontological indifference, which then heralds the arrival of ontological reminder. For this, swaraj must not be treated as an extension of state/government. Locating swaraj within the paraphernalia of state and government gives a fillip to the structural purpose of the latter. Swaraj can be situated in or construed as a political community. Conceptually, the political community is a living entity wherein 'ontological reminder' is a perennial pursuit.

Given this, the associational norm surfaces often. In a democratic society, the question of 'we' in the associational norm must be answered in a non-hierarchical manner. 'We' represents a democratic and equal association, any violation of which makes the 'we' infructuous. Thereafter, the norms of the association are envisaged. In a state and government partnership, the governing norm is delinked from the associational norm. It therefore becomes easier to abandon the latter so the ruling classes can ask: 'Why are we associated?'. The promise at the foundation (that is, an ontological reminder) is continually kept in abeyance to fulfil the structural and material needs of the ruling classes.

In the associational norm of the political community, the 'why' and 'how' are linked, with the former being given priority over the latter. In other words, in the political community, the question 'Why are we associated?' is a constant reminder of 'How are we associated?'. This helps non-deviation in the second question, which is an actual materialisation of the first. Defining swaraj in the form of political community wherein ontological reminders take precedence over the ontological indifference of the state/ government not only helps to question institutional injustices and violence, but is also a reminder that people are at the centre of discourse.

Such a definition also helps to overcome two widely accepted prevalent mechanisms within capitalism and the corresponding liberal political theory and institutions: conservative adjustment and welfare adjustment. These operate within a liberal framework wherein political equality and economic inequality are non-negotiable. There may be a slight variance in the two mechanisms due to a democratic surge, which does not, however, blur the foundational difference between the two. Conservative adjustment and welfare adjustment (and their variance) do respond to dependent-relations and autonomous-dependent relations amidst the division between political equality and economic inequality.

Conservative adjustment renders futile the first question 'Why are we associated' while paving the way for the categorical division and championing of political equality and economic inequality.[2] Even the right to vote (political equality) is used to sustain glaring economic inequality. How the rights to resources, health, education, dignity and respect are distributed depends on the associational norm. The governing norm (which is rejuvenated and legitimised through political equality) atrophies questions related to distribution and dignity. Conservative adjustment generates two separate realms (political equality and economic inequality) which are united by the state/government.

Welfare adjustment is a moderate response within the prevalent liberal discourse on state/government and has been construed as a radical intervention. Welfare adjustment attempts to bridge the neat division between political equality and economic inequality. Among the slew of reforms it brings about, the most important is 'care'. This 'care' is construed as emphatic intervention by the state/government or as the state/government 'reaching out to people as an emphatic caretaker of people'. Some of the reforms have been important interventions like the rejection of pre-capitalist exploitation and discrimination. These became unacceptable theoretically due to their loss of validity in a capitalist formation. Unacceptability, however, is not eradication. Therefore, within the capitalist formulation, there is always the possibility of a resurrection of the 'unacceptable' because of its immanent tendency. So, a radical reform today may appear normal in the future and eventually fade into insignificance. In the absence of continuous evolution and rupture, today's radical reform may also appear regressive.

Welfare adjustment creates a complex paradox. The 'care' attempts to bring back an ontological reminder of the political community while trying to achieve 'care' empirically in the state/government, which has disjointed from the former long ago. In other words, due to constant social and political churning and movements along with widespread dissatisfaction because of inequality and violence, a political structure is forced to ponder over the 'why' principle. Thinking about the 'why' principle is a different pursuit altogether than conjoining with the 'how' principle. For example, the promise made at the beginning (ontological reminder) can be implemented only when structural changes are achieved. Most of the ambitious care programmes fall flat because of the glaring gap between 'Why are we associated?' and 'How are we associated?' and the complete detachment of the latter from the former.

The construal of swaraj as a political community calls for a definite departure from the state/government formulation. The political community is a shared responsibility for collective living, arrived at through equal relations and equal partnership. Shared responsibility is a constant reminder of 'Why are we associated?', thereafter constantly evolving terms and ethics in the form of 'How are we associated?'. The political community does not abandon the ontological reminder by developing ontological indifference. Ontological indifference not only deters the state/government from revoking ontological reminder but also deters it from developing a system in which 'Why are we associated?' is completely detached from 'How are we associated?'. Shared responsibility for collective living takes care of everyday participation and stands firm against accumulation and violence. People's agency is empowered through the politics of equalness, which is not just the empirical verification of reality but a long-term approval of concerted living and acting.

Intimacy, Anonymity and Abstract Space

The political community must engage with three spaces (intimate, anonymous, abstract) in order to *absent* ontological indifference. For swaraj to be a 'living concept', the three spaces are crucial for the non-arrival of *partial* swaraj. For the arrival of ontological reminder, or concretisation of swaraj and rejection of ontological indifference, the question of intimacy remains an unaddressed domain in swaraj. Intimacy has invited considerable attention in social and behavioural sciences. Erik Erikson (1968) understands intimacy in the context of the individual development of identity. Unlike Edmund Husserl's idea of intimacy, which is linked with one's interiority and states that people could know only indications of interiority but not interiority, Jacques Derrida believes that intimacy

> is not self-presence, a relation of presence to self, but rather one of the otherness and self, non-presence and presence. Intimacy is the inhabitation of the other in the same. What is more, intimacy is the welcome extended by the other to the same, by the foreigner to the native, the outsider to the insider. Not vice versa. Such is Derridean intimacy, which is intimacy tout court. (Dutoit 2004: 16)

For Lynn Jamieson, self-intimacy (intimacy to self) is vital for intimacy with others (Jamieson 1998: 154). Anthony Giddens links intimacy with dialogical act and democracy in non-public life (e.g., husband-wife, parents-children, androgyny). According to him, '[i]ntimacy means the disclosure of emotions and actions which the individual is unlikely to hold up to a wider public gaze' (1992: 138). For the democratisation of personal life, '[t]he possibility of intimacy means the promise of democracy. ... We can envisage the development of an ethical framework for a democratic personal order ...' (ibid.: 188). Giddens envisages intimacy as a democratic space without which democracy in public life is not tenable.

Niklas Luhmann construes intimacy as 'interpenetration' while warning us that '[i]ntimacy is also not understood to be a relationship based on exchange' (1986: 57). Zygmunt Bauman highlights the complexity of the intimate relationship. 'In a liquid modern setting of life, relationships are perhaps the most common, acute, deeply felt and troublesome incarnations of ambivalence' (2003: viii). The biggest casualty comes from consumerism.

> The fading of sociality skills is boosted and accelerated by the tendency, inspired by the dominant consumerist life mode, to treat other humans as objects of consumption and to judge them after the pattern of consumer objects by the volume of pleasure they are likely to offer, and in 'value for money' terms .... In the process, the intrinsic value of others as unique human beings (and so also the concern with others for their own, and that uniqueness's, sake) has been all but lost from sight. Human solidarity is the first casualty of the triumphs of the consumer market. (ibid.: 75–76)

The aforesaid rich contribution to intimacy needs further expansion. Intimacy itself is not a sovereign body or realm. It has a serious impact through a slew of social/political/economic structures. Quite contrary to understanding intimacy as an insulated and benign realm, it also reflects control and possession. In other words, the more intimate the relationship, the more the control and possession. Intimacy can be sustained by controlling and possessing people. Intimacy, being familiarity itself, paves the way for structural control of the state/government/communities. In fact, to jettison ontological indifference, one of the factors, i.e., 'intimacy', needs significant attention. To put it differently, is a political community possible where 'intimacy' is profound? Intimacy remains problematic due to the reproduction of relations for control and possession. For instance, caste is an intimate control and gender is an intimate possession. The politics of intimacy needs to be broken in the political community to ward off the reproduction of control and possession.

An articulated challenge to the politics of intimacy can be fathomed in Ambedkar's rejection of it through his allusion to villages in India. The village is a cynosure of the politics of intimacy. The village per se cannot be an approximation of the idea of a republic. 'The village is the very negation of a republic. If it is a republic, it is a republic of the Touchables, by the Touchables and for the Touchables' (Ambedkar 2006: 330). For Ambedkar, 'villages were "cesspools" that harboured caste oppression and social and economic backwardness ... a "very dangerous system ... the bane of public life in India" ... because their "local patriotism" left no room for national identification or civil consciousness'. Omvedt argues that 'for the Depressed Classes, village society meant dependence' (Omvedt 2004: 55). Therefore, the politics of intimacy has no place in the political community.

If 'the realm of intimacy' begets the presence of exploitation, control and possession, 'the realm of anonymity' also invites attention, which is associated with urbanisation and its political economy. The political economy of the city has invited significant attention amidst massive urbanisation. In fact, in the contemporary debate, the city has turned into a cynosure. 'The right to the city' has become a crucial concern in theory (Harvey 2008; Lefebvre 1996) and urban social movements in the form of politics of encounter (Merrifield 2011). Henri Lefebvre envisages the city as '"oeuvre", a feature which contrasts with the irreversible tendency towards money and commerce, towards exchange and products. Indeed, the oeuvre is use value and the product is exchange value' (1996: 66). For him, '[t]he right to the city cannot be conceived of as a simple visiting right or as a return to traditional cities. It can only be formulated as a transformed and renewed right to urban life' (ibid.: 158). Moreover, 'priority of use value, inscription in space of a time promoted to the rank of a supreme resource among all resources, finds its morphological base and its practico-material realization' (ibid.). For David Harvey, '[t]he right to the city is far more than the individual liberty to access urban resources: it is a right to change ourselves by changing city' (2008: 23). Military expenditure and urbanisation are outcomes of the absorption of the surplus of capitalism (ibid.: 25). Urban transformation, based on surplus absorption, 'has entailed repeated bouts of urban restructuring through "creative destruction", which nearly always has a class dimension since it is the poor, the underprivileged and those marginalized from political power that suffer first and foremost from this process' (ibid.: 33). Andy Merrifield takes the discussion from 'the right to the city' (an earlier assertion of Lefebvre) to 'the right to encounter' (a later assertion). In other words, '[a] major motif of Lefebvre's right to the city is, of course, "the right to centrality"; ... a right to participate in life at the core, to be in the heat of the action' (Merrifield 2011: 475). The politics of encounter is not about space or centrality but decentralisation of resistance. 'For in any politics of encounter, it's not in space that people act: people become space by acting' (ibid.: 480).

The city as a consumerist space sustained through sheer depoliticisation activates its consumer aspect while deactivating the political aspect. It proposes the political structure through the politics of anonymity wherein ontological indifference is in practice. The political structure is governed by rules and regulations where individuals live anonymous lives. In other words, a consumerist remains bereft of political ambitions, in turn demanding an unconcerned state. In this context, anonymity entails an unconcerned state or government. Normatively, the state regulates in place of care. For the politics of anonymity, urban spaces become an ideal space and one which generates urbanity. This urbanity rejects rusticity and thereafter urbanity and anonymity become synonymous. The state/government would take considerable action on regulation and less on care. The procedural regularity absents humanistic concern. The right to live is a constitutional matter in place of associational matter. Regulations create subjects and further the gap between different 'subjects'. State and subject are related, but subject and subject are unconnected. The creation of subject and unconcerned subjects are features of the politics of anonymity. Thus, urbanity and anonymity become a powerful feature of the existence of state/government per se. And consumerist individuals and regulated individuals do combine in each other through the politics of anonymity.

Gandhi's rejection of urban, urbanity and anonymity must be understood against these backdrops. Urbanity and anonymity must be used interchangeably. Gandhi is categorical that cities are bad for both England and India. The latter is exploited by the former through cities. And cities have exploited Indian villages.

> The blood of the villages is the cement with which the edifice of the cities is built. I want the blood that is today inflating the arteries of the cities to run once again in the blood vessels of the villages .... Village life must not become a copy or appendage of city life. The cities have to adopt the pattern of life and subsist for the village. (Gandhi 2002: 362–63)

Therefore, he 'would say that, if the village perishes, India will perish too' (ibid.: 369). The anonymous political life is antithetical to Gandhi's political community.

At this juncture, a clarificatory note is required. Ambedkar's rejection of intimacy is not the acceptance of anonymity. Gandhi's rejection of anonymity is not the acceptance of intimacy. This can only be done when both Ambedkar and Gandhi are read as a critique of existing political structures, and not through categorical binaries of 'either/or'. Their engagement with the nature of the political community should invite more attention than the competing lexical priorities that pit them against each other.

The politics of intimacy and politics of anonymity must be understood comprehensively, but the two are not insulated from the abstract space of global capital which has now reached into both intimate and anonymous spaces. Global capital has reached every sphere, and this has been achieved by, in the terminology of Henri Lefebvre, the abstract space (Lefebvre 1991). This space is the space of capitalism (ibid.; Wilson 2013: 364). 'Abstract space is thus repressive in essence and *par excellence*—but thanks to its versatility it is repressive in a peculiarly artful way: its intrinsic repressiveness may be manifested alternately through reduction, through (functional) localization, through the imposition of hierarchy and segregation' (Lefebvre 1991: 318). According to him, abstract space is created by capitalism and neo-capitalism. The abstract space includes

> the 'world of commodities', its 'logic' and its worldwide strategies, as well as the power of money and that of the political state. This space is founded on the vast network of banks, business centres and major productive

> entities, as also on motorways, airports and information lattices. Within this space, the town—once the forcing house of accumulation, fountainhead of wealth and centre of historical space—has disintegrated. (ibid.: 53)

There are three crucial developments to be addressed by swaraj as a political community due to the creation of abstract space. First, the arrival of a neoliberal economy, which does, *inter alia*, two things. One, it commodifies every possible article or item. Two, the commodification takes place through the withdrawal of the state. Second, this also generates a 'neoliberal polity'. This neoliberal polity creates institutions known as independent regulatory institutions. These are not statutory institutions, but independent institutions from 'polity'. There is a clear disjuncture between polity and policy. The polity will have no accountability towards policies. These policies will be regulated by independent regulatory bodies. Third, neoliberal economy and neoliberal polity engender the neoliberal self. The neoliberal self becomes apolitical and competes against itself. Since it withdraws from the polity, it recognises the existence of the self only. This self is against the self in swaraj, which recognises the existence of multiple selves for the arrival of the political community of interdependence.

II

Debating Swaraj is concerned with *both* the churnings of state/government and *thinking* about the (alternative) political community. Both churning and thinking are constituents for the apotheosis of contestation and an alternative *Weltanschauung*. Churning about (rejection of) ontological indifference culminates in the assertion of ontological reminder in which the 'rejection of being' and the 'idea of governed subject' are both negated. For swaraj to continuously evolve as a living concept, spheres of intimacy, anonymity and the abstract must be interrogated. The chapters in this volume not only substantially outline the premise of Gandhi and swaraj, but they also detail specific advancements that are quintessential for a just, egalitarian and thinking community. The chapters ensure enriching debates on swaraj by highlighting it, *inter alia*, as unalienated life (Chapter One: 'Gandhian and the *Mentality* of *Swaraj*'), common people/

civil society over sovereignty (Chapter Two: '*Swaraj* and Sovereignty'), non-violent society (Chapter Three: 'Gandhi's *Swaraj*: A Revisit'), and political community (Chapter Four: '*Hind Swaraj*: Metaphors of Political Community'). Chapter Five ('Gandhi, Economics and Welfare') is concerned with the political economy and discusses how Gandhi overcame the dichotomy between the economic agent and the political citizen. Gandhi's emphasis on 'knowledge with experience' (Chapter Six: 'Spinning the *Swaraj*: Technology, Science and Experience in the History of the Spinning Wheel') and *Nai Talim* as the labouring body for swaraj, along with its limitations (Chapter Seven: '*Swaraj* and *Nai Talim*: Notes on Self-sufficiency'), are a crucial concern in swaraj. The Gandhi and Ambedkar debate in the discourse on swaraj is crucial for limitation and advancement. Therefore, a methodology for hermeneutic engagement between Gandhi and Ambedkar becomes crucial (Chapter Eight: 'Reading Texts and Traditions: The Ambedkar–Gandhi Debate'). Moreover, in the debate on swaraj, and as the chapters in this volume do concomitantly, both theoretical complacency and rigidities of social-political and economic orders need to be unsettled by deliberating on alternity.

According to Akeel Bilgrami (Chapter One), *Hind Swaraj* presents diverse themes which require a proper historical and interpretative framework, 'a genealogical reading of the text', which allows a complete understanding of Gandhi's philosophical and political motivations. In the first decade of the twentieth century, Gandhi did not agree with the inevitability of the trajectory of the political economy of Europe. His scepticism helped save his country and its people from a future this method envisioned. Here, it is important to understand the genealogy of 'cast of mind', which considers such a future inevitable. The metaphysical basis upon which Gandhi's economic and political themes were integrated was arrived at by asking a question: 'How and when did the concept of nature get transformed into the concept of natural resources?' For Gandhi, nature was not only an ecological issue but encompassed a 'whole range of relations with its inhabitants and a tradition and history that grows out of these relations'. For Bilgrami, Gandhi's genealogical question is a larger one: 'When and by what conceptual transformation did the "world" cease to be a place merely to live in and become instead a place to master and control?' He narrows down the scope of Gandhi's inquiry to locate him in the tradition that not only illuminates his thought but also expands it.

Thereafter, Bilgrami assiduously unravels, *inter alia*, the nature of science, early modernity in Europe, being a detached observer *vs.* an agent, disenchantment, desacralisation of nature (freeing nature for extraction by capital), and the suppression of dissenting traditions/scientific dissenters by the Royal Society and its alignment with powerful interest groups, the development of a predatory commercial attitude towards culture and its impact on democratic culture (development of alliances among the scientific establishment, the Anglican Church, commercial interests and oligarchies), and development of courtly civilities. An enchanted world is a precondition to possessing both agency and living an unalienated life. Integrating Gandhi with the early dissenting tradition of the Radical Enlightenment leads to understanding 'at home in the world', the most fundamental form of an unalienated life. This is the most cherished ideal which politics must strive for.

Anuradha Veeravalli (Chapter Two) distinguishes between Gandhi's swaraj and sovereignty in the context of the modern nation-state. Gandhi's swaraj offers a fundamental and systematic critique of sovereignty. Gandhi maintained that there were two important questions: 'Who has the authority to rule?' and 'Who has the supreme authority to rule?'. Gandhi's swaraj offers a different theory of sovereignty with regard to the relationship between civil society and the state. In post-Enlightenment theories, sovereignty is defined by 'supreme authority within a territory'. In the sovereignty of the modern nation-state, the supreme authority and territory are constitutive principles. In the social contract theories, either civil society or state remains a source of authority. In either postulation, society is an artificial construct of individuals under the social contract; the state is vital, and society and state come into existence simultaneously; both are therefore two faces of the same thing. However, in modern political theory, there is room only for the state and the individual. Veeravalli cites the example of statutory laws that recognise criminal cases (state *vs.* individual) and civil cases (individual *vs.* individual). There is no room for civil society to represent either the voice of the individual or the collective. In other words, there is no space for civil society in the formulation between the state and the individual. Moreover, territoriality, and thereafter the separation of one nation-state from another, becomes an important component of sovereignty. This also means that the state and its law and order paraphernalia encroaches on the realm of civil society. Gandhi's contribution to swaraj takes the form of the rejection presupposition of the state and its laws in the following ways: non-violence is not a personal or private virtue, but the law of our species-being; dualism is not between the individual and the collective as a social contract, but between common people/society and the state. Gandhi's theory of sovereignty is based on the separation between the state and civil society on their origin, constitution and method. Gandhi's swaraj is categorically different from the modern theory of sovereignty on the following grounds: (a) civil society is different from the state with regard to origin and constitution; (b) self-reform or freedom from the other, or rather, no control over the other, is a constituent of sovereignty; (c) territory as relationships/frontiers (not boundaries) between different nations and self and the other.

Sudarshan Iyengar (Chapter Three) points out that Gandhi's going to South Africa was 'a chance occurrence'. In South Africa, a slew of circumstances transformed him from householder to *mumukshu* (seeker of spiritual knowledge) along the path of political and social service of the community which he adopted. The concept of swaraj inculcated a sense of duty. For Gandhi, swaraj was the formation of a non-violent society and the unit was the individual. Therefore, swaraj had to first be achieved at the individual level while simultaneously working to achieve political, social and economic swaraj for society. Iyengar unravels Gandhi's swaraj in two intertwined parts. In the first part, he explains Gandhi's initial take on swaraj soon after his return from South Africa to India. Embedded in his return was a commitment to work towards his vision. Integration of all communities and religions was an essential component of Gandhi's work. For a nuanced understanding of Gandhi's vision, mission and position, Iyengar analyses three of his speeches, at the opening of the Banaras Hindu University (BHU) (4 February 1916), in Madras on *swadeshi* (14 February 1916) and at Muir Central College, Allahabad on Economic v. Moral Progress (22 December 1916). Gandhi's return to India highlighted his commitment towards the self and the nation. The self, regulating the self and achieving home rule are intertwined in Gandhi's vision of swaraj. In the second part, the relevance of Gandhi's return in the context of his thoughts and philosophy of swaraj is delineated. The importance given to the lowest unit (i.e., the village), a decentralised production system, society as an oceanic circle, individuals as a centre, non-violence based on soul force–truth-force–love force can all be seen in Gandhi. The 'return' of Gandhi must be read in the context of asserting the need for an autonomous moral agent 'by way of rejecting the economic agent'.

In Chapter Four, Dhananjay Rai explains *Hind Swaraj* as the embodiment of twenty metaphors of the political community. Methodologically, Rai reads Gandhi's three books (*Hind Swaraj* [1909], *Satyagraha in South Africa* [1928] and *An Autobiography or the Story of My Experiments with Truth* [1927/29]) together while reversing their chronological order. Gandhi and the political community are discussed through an analysis of significant markers of Gandhian scholarship. Thereafter, both epistemological and methodological problems are highlighted when reading the three texts together for the arrival of the political community. Reading them in reverse order also provides an effective method to comprehend the political community in the context of its evolution and advance arguments in the context of epistemological and methodological problems. The three texts are construed as a narration of the human condition, the transformation of the human condition and foundational principles of the political community. Metaphors for the political community are explored in each chapter of *Hind Swaraj*.

Prabhat Patnaik (Chapter Five) examines the concept of 'economic agent', a core concept in economics (excluding Marxism), and its rejection by Gandhi, which leads to the overlapping of the Gandhian problematique and the Marxist problematique despite well-argued differences. The twin principles of self-interest promoting individual welfare and the protraction of own welfare contingent on acquiring maximum goods produces two conundrums: in the realm of the economy, individuals remain self-centred entities; in the realm of polity, the same individuals are supposed to improve the distribution of the total bundle of goods/services produced in the aggregate among all individuals. Mainstream economics produces a split personality within each member of society in the form, simultaneously, of 'self-absorbed being and self-transcending being', 'unconcerned being and concerned being' and 'economic agent and political citizen'. The debate between civil society (self-seeking individuals) and state (rectification of ills in civil society) is representative of this dichotomy and writ large in the work of Alfred Marshall and the economists (A. C. Pigou and J. M. Keynes) of the Cambridge School.

Patnaik adds that 'economic agent' is an outcome of the capitalist mode of production, which is linked with alienation and not recognised by mainstream economics. Gandhi recognises this alienation through his critique of material civilisation, greed, exploitation of the weak, and his debates with Tagore over the replacement of labour by machines. In the context of the Gandhi–Tagore debate, Patnaik substantiates Gandhi's standpoint by highlighting the impact of deindustrialisation on peasants' income. Despite two interpretations of well-being—conformity to an ethical life or a life linked with the well-being of neighbours—Patnaik argues that Gandhi overcomes the dichotomy between economic agent and political citizen in mainstream economics. Neighbours/neighbourhoods are linked with a geographical area or self-sufficient economic unit in which all are gainfully employed without exploiting outside units. Additionally, the *charkha* must be treated as a metaphor for non-capitalist development. The last section in this chapter shows the difference between the Gandhian problematique and the Marxist problematique with regard to the notion of the individual's 'welfare function'.

Sadan Jha (Chapter Six) underlines the centrality of the spinning wheel in the Gandhian model of swaraj or self-rule. He reminds us that for Mahatma Gandhi, the spinning wheel was not a mere tool of political emancipation; it was also a metaphor for both ancient work ethics and a socioeconomic reaction to British rule. Jha approaches the performative nature of this symbol through four historical moments: the pre-colonial lives of this symbol, as a mythical Gandhian symbol, as a Gandhian symbol visualised by rural womenfolk, and as a postcolonial symbol amidst the appropriation of cultural economics of corruption, caricature and high culture. He provides several pointers to help understand the spinning wheel. It is important to locate the economics of Gandhian symbols in the Gandhian notion of Indian life and vision for India's well-being. Gandhi had rejected the difference between economics and ethics, a moment of departure between himself and Tagore. It is also important to remember that Gandhi's reading of tradition takes place in its displacement from colonialism. Gandhi did not invent anything new but reworked old symbols after careful selection and by giving them new meaning, vitality and life, thus politicising Indian life. Moreover, the khadi movement helped Gandhi broaden his mass base and organisational strength, which not only challenged colonial economics and culture, but also offered an alternative to 'colonial science' and 'colonial knowledge systems'. Therefore, the khadi movement's response was both cultural and technological. Gandhi can therefore not be construed as anti-science and technology. The charkha/khadi movements must not be understood in isolation, but by placing them amid Gandhian metaphors and economic philosophy. At the end of the chapter, Jha highlights that spinning is not separated from other experiences. This embeddedness—not the separation of science and art, economics and ethics, scientists and satyagrahis, and knowledge and experience—is crucial to discovering the truth. To arrive at the truth and politics of knowledge in Gandhi, embeddedness in one another and primacy of experience over knowledge supported by the specific history of science is crucial.

Deeptha Achar (Chapter Seven) highlights both the value of *Nai Talim* and its limitations. The Wardha Resolution of 1937 introduced a new category known as 'craft' in school education. It was a radical entry into the discourse on education in India. Achar's chapter explores how swaraj is built into the Gandhian scheme of education and its implication for the imagination of the nation. In Gandhi's swaraj, there is a shift from government to self and the body becomes an important site of self-government. A slew of initiatives like diet and *brahmacharya* indicate the arrival of the new value of the body. The 1937 resolution greatly impacted provincial Congress governments. In both Gandhi-led craft-based education and the Report of the Zakir Husain Committee, a mass education around manual work, embodied as a craft, became vital. Gandhi's idea of Nai Talim went against the nationalist position on education wherein children were becoming self-sufficient by selling their craft and using the proceeds to sustain their education. Craft denotes a democratic principle that transcends hierarchy, while linking intellectual pursuit with a skill that extends dignity to labour and builds human solidarity. This is a radical way of bridging the gap between physical and intellectual activity, countering the colonial idea of separating childhood from the sphere of work and breaking urban-centric education by giving primacy to village craft and working-class competencies over textbook learning. The labouring body of the child came to be governed by swaraj, which would then also contain the soul force offering satyagraha. Craft-based education, however, failed to address caste oppression due to an emphasis on the practice of a craft, which was imposed in the form of exploitation.

Valerian Rodrigues (Chapter Eight) outlines the conceptual framework of Ambedkar and Gandhi before sketching the hermeneutic engagement between the two. Ambedkar proposes a new world while stressing on a correct hermeneutic perspective. Gandhi revisits traditions differently; his critical vantage points and vision of a new future not only for India but also for the world make him different from 'articulate contemporaries and epigones'. Ambedkar and Gandhi read texts and traditions differently while constituting different outlooks. Despite disagreements, deciphering their hermeneutic engagement is a privileged site which shows the unity between the two on certain issues, concerns and substantive positions. Ambedkar's conceptual framework, largely influenced by the European Enlightenment paradigm, includes the modern as the triumph of reason, radical secularity, the centrality of human agency, and an interrogation of the culture sphere. The Gandhian paradigm includes ideas of the self and transcendence, religion and morality, the modern world and its other, reason and action, and moving beyond reason. For Rodrigues, Ambedkar's engagement with modernity and Gandhi's engagement with tradition was not an innocuous intervention, but a complex process that also brought about changes in both spheres. In the section titled 'Gandhi–Ambedkar Hermeneutic Engagement', Rodrigues points out how both men considered the hallowed texts important due to the normative design and constitution of communities. All authoritative interpretations, however, were contested. Methodologically, Rodrigues dwells on both interface and confrontation by making Ambedkar an interlocutor and Gandhi the proponent with regard to their disagreements and the range of texts and traditions both read. Do they have a coherent theory of interpretation? They certainly employed a coherent body of the idea while dealing with texts and traditions. Ambedkar did not reject Gandhi's yardsticks of interpretation, but preferred to chart out his own paradigmatic and methodological project.

This book highlights collective diversity that points towards a better alternative world in which differentiation, discrimination and exploitation are constantly negated by reviewing everydayness. The reviewing of everydayness becomes a significant component when debating swaraj due to the stress on a thinking being and political community.

Notes

1. The colonial construction of people attempts this. However, people's resistance continues to defy this colonial construct at an unprecedented scale. In fact, co-option and resistance remain a continuous process within the edifice of colonialism.

2. E. M. Wood (1981) had originally offered this argument.

References

Ambedkar, B. R. 2006. 'Untouchability: Outside the Fold'. In *The Essential Writings of B. R. Ambedkar*, ed. Valerian Rodrigues, 323–31. New Delhi: Oxford University Press.

Bagchi, A. K. 2008. *Perilous Passage: Mankind and the Global Ascendancy of Capital*. New Delhi: Oxford University Press.

Bandyopadhyay, S. 2008. *From Plassey to Partition: A History of Modern India*. Hyderabad: Orient BlackSwan.

Bauman, Z. 2003. *Liquid Love: On the Frailty of Human Bonds*. Oxford: Polity Press.

Bhattacharyya, K. C. 2011. 'Svaraj in Ideas (1928)'. In *Indian Philosophy in English: From Renaissance to Independence*, ed. N. Bhushan and J. L. Garfield, 103–11. New York: Oxford University Press.

Chakrabarty, D. 2000. *Provincializing Europe: Postcolonial Thought and Historical Difference*. Princeton, NJ: Princeton University Press.

Chatterjee, P. 1986. *Nationalist Thought and the Colonial World*. Minneapolis: University of Minnesota.

Das, B. 2011. 'The Meaning of Swaraj or Self-government (1921)'. In *Indian Philosophy in English: From Renaissance to Independence*, ed. N. Bhushan and J. L. Garfield, 87–99. New York: Oxford University Press.

Dossa, S. 2002. 'Liberal Imperialism? Natives, Muslims, and Others'. *Political Theory* 30 (5): 738–45.

Dutoit, T. 2004. 'From Esthetics of Intimacy to Anesthetics in Extimacy: The Examples of Jacques Derrida'. *L'Esprit Créateur* 44 (1): 9–26.

Ellam, J. E. 1984. *Swaraj: The Problem of India*. Delhi: LOGOS Press.

Erikson, E. H. 1968. *Identity: Youth and Crisis*. New York: W. W. Norton & Company.

Gandhi, M. K. 1962. *Village Swaraj*. Ahmedabad: Navajivan Publishing House.

Gandhi, M. K. 1997. *Hind Swaraj and Other Writings*. Edited and with an introduction by Anthony Parel. Cambridge: Cambridge University Press.

——. 2002. 'All-round Village Service'. In *The Mind of Mahatma Gandhi*, ed. R. K. Prabhu and U. R. Rao, 365–71. Ahmedabad: Navajivan Trust.

Ghose, A. 1970. *Sri Aurobindo Birth Centenary Library*. Pondicherry: Sri Aurobindo Ashram.

——. 1977. 'Nasik Speech'. *Sri Aurobindo: Archives and Research* 1 (1): 2–6.

Giddens, A. 1992. *The Transformation of Intimacy: Sexuality, Love and Eroticism in Modern Societies*. Stanford: Stanford University Press.

Harvey, D. 2008. 'The Right to the City'. *New Left Review* 53 (September–October): 23–40.

Jamieson, L. 1998. *Intimacy: Personal Relationships in Modern Societies*. Cambridge: Polity Press.

Jones, H. S. 2005. 'The Early Utilitarians, Race, and Empire: The State of the Argument'. In *Utilitarianism and Empire*, ed. B. Schultz and G. Varouxakis, 179–87. Oxford: Lexington Books.

Keer, D. 1959. *Lokamānya Tilak: Father of our Freedom Struggle*. Bombay: S. B. Kangutkar.

Lal, V. 1998. 'Organic Conservatism, Administrative Realism, and the Imperialist Ethos in the "Indian Career" of John Stuart Mill'. *New Quest* 54 (January–February): 54–64.

Lefebvre, H. 1991. *The Production of Space*. Trans. D. Nicholson-Smith. Oxford: Blackwell.

——. 1996. 'The Right to the City'. In *Writings on Cities: Henry Lefebvre*. Ed. E. Kofman and E. Lebas, trans. J. Gaines and D. L. Jones. Cambridge, M.A.: Wiley-Blackwell.

Luhmann, N. 1986. *Love as Passion: The Codification of Intimacy*. Cambridge: Polity Press.

Mehta, U. S. 1999. *Liberalism and Empire: A Study in Nineteenth-century British Liberal Thought*. Chicago: University of Chicago Press.

Merrifield, A. 2011. 'The Right to the City and Beyond: Notes on a Lefebvrian Re-conceptualization'. *City* 15 (3–4): 473–81.

Mill, J. 1817. *The History of British India*. Vol. 1. London: Baldwin, Cradock, and Joy.

Minor, R. N. 2003. 'Sri Aurobindo's Dismissal of Gandhi and his Nonviolence'. In *Indian Critiques of Gandhi*, ed. H. Coward, 87–106. New York: State University of New York Press.

Omvedt, G. 2004. *Ambedkar: Towards an Enlightened India*. New Delhi: Penguin Books.

Parekh, B. 1995. 'Liberalism and Colonialism: A Critique of Locke and Mill'. In *The Decolonization of Imagination: Culture, Knowledge and Power*, ed. J. N. Pieterse and B. Parekh, 81–98. London: Zed Books.

Sarkar, S. 1989. *Modern India: 1885–1947*. New York: Palgrave Macmillan.

Sitaramayya, B. T. 1946. *The History of the Indian National Congress: Volume I (1885–1935)*. Bombay: Padma Publications.

Sullivan, E. P. 1983. 'Liberalism and Imperialism: J. S. Mill's Defense of the British Empire'. *Journal of the History of Ideas* 44 (4): 599–617.

Tunick, M. 2006. 'Tolerant Imperialism: John Stuart Mill's Defense of British Rule in India'. *The Review of Politics* 68 (4): 586–611.

Wilson, J. 2013. 'The Devastating Conquest of the Lived by the Conceived: The Concept of Abstract Space in the Work of Henri Lefebvre'. *Space and Culture* 16 (3): 364–80.

Wood, E. M. 1981. 'The Separation of the Economic and the Political in Capitalism'. *New Left Review* 1 (127): 83–86.

One

A Genealogical Reading of Gandhi's Critique of Modernity

Akeel Bilgrami

I

Modern life is beset with *distinctive* anxieties. That, if true, suggests that the *Early* Modern period of history and intellectual history is an appropriate focus for a *genealogical* diagnosis of the conditions in which and with which we now live and cope. This is a methodological instinct shared by thinkers and sensibilities as diverse as J. J. Rousseau, Karl Marx, T. S. Eliot, and M. K. Gandhi.

I look to Gandhi among these for my initiating framework because the *seemingly miscellaneous* themes that I want to *integrate* in this chapter are all present with something approximating the requisite integrity in Gandhi's ideas. By comparison, Eliot's interests are far too narrow, Rousseau has no real grasp of the colonial condition, and though all the conceptual elements are certainly there in Marx, the abiding disservice done by Louis Althusser's distinction between an early and late Marx makes miscellaneous the very things I want eventually to integrate. But I am getting ahead of myself; at this point, I merely want to briefly motivate my interest in Gandhi's ideas and the urge in him to give them some genealogical depth.

Although *Hind Swaraj* presents a critique of what Gandhi summarised in such portentous terms of generality as 'modern Western civilization', its themes are very diverse and range vastly over (to name just a few): the political economy of capitalism; the deracination of education in India from its roots in living and making to a set of intellectually distanced cognitive enterprises (what came to be called 'disciplines'), pursued not just in an imposed natural language but an imposed ideological repertory remote from the *conceptual* vernacular; the social effects of the introduction of railways in India; the transformation of the public aspects of moral life into a lawyer's professional domain; the effects of modern medicine in shifting the notion of the body into a site not of health understood as an equilibrium of meaning and emotions, but in purely corporeal terms of near-forensic diagnosis and detached treatment and cure (Gandhi 1997). The relation between the general nature of the critique and this diverse thematic breakdown needs to be put in a proper historical and interpretative framework before it can be philosophically understood and politically motivated. And this, I believe, eventually requires, as I stated above, a genealogical reading of the text, which I try and provide, leaving a detailed analysis of the text itself to another occasion.

Let me begin with a frameworking interpretative remark.

In the first decade of the last century when Gandhi wrote *Hind Swaraj*, he was convinced that (a) 'modernist' ideological voices (like the Hindu ideologue V. D. Savarkar's, for instance) were wrong to think that there was something inevitable about the idea that India must go down the path of nationalist modernity set by the post-Westphalian ideal in politics and, equally, that (b) all the voices of the Right and Left around him in the Congress party and beyond were wrong to think that there was something inevitable about the path that political economy in Europe in the late seventeenth century was on. There was passion in his scepticism regarding all these voices as well as a quiet desperation about not losing his people and his country to the future they envisioned.

All this makes poignant his intellectual efforts to understand the cast of mind that made such a future seem inevitable. He wished for an exorcism of such a cast of mind, but for that to happen we first need to come to some genealogical understanding of it. In Gandhi's view, India, in his time, stood at the sort of cusp that an accurate genealogy would trace back to and properly identify with our term '*Early* Modernity', if it was not so laden with the air of forward historical movement towards a teleological end. Were it possible to speak that term in an entirely innocuous and neutral tone, as a pure descriptor of a time in Europe that left it entirely open which way things would turn out, then Indian society was indeed properly describable by the term in the much later chronological time in which he lived.

His own approach to such a genealogy was to ask a question of profound importance, a question whose central theme, he thought, provided the metaphysical basis upon which his more specific economic and political themes were to be integrated: How and when did the concept of *nature* get transformed into the concept of *natural resources?*

The precise idiom in which I have posed this question is mine, not Gandhi's. For complicated and ambitious intellectual reasons, he would ask it differently. Like Martin Heidegger, he preferred to talk of the 'world' rather than of 'nature'. And though, like Heidegger, he must have known that the word 'world' was a term of art, he did not want it to be more abstract and rarefied than is found in our most *ordinary* talk about the world. That is to say, in a crucial commitment, perhaps more Ludwig Wittgenstein's than Heidegger's, he was drawn to the idea of, as Wittgenstein would put it, '*leaving the world alone*'.

That last phrase (and thought) needs elaborate interpretation and, in a way, the rest of this chapter will obliquely be devoted to it. At first sight, the phrase might give the impression of quietism. That impression would be wrong. Quite apart from the fact that (far from quietist) Gandhi was an *activist* of unique genius, his view of what the phrase might mean amounted to a wholesale resistance to many of the admired orthodoxies of the Enlightenment.

Let me explain.

It is well known that Gandhi showed a studied indifference[1] to the familiar principles and codes and rights that defined the Enlightenment. Commentators often ask why this was so and give a disappointingly insufficient answer, drawn from a cursory look at some of his least interesting writings. Their answer to his indifference is that those things are alien to Indian culture and society.

The real grounds for Gandhi's indifference went much deeper because, in his view, all these principles and codes and rights stand supported by a much deeper and more underlying commitment that is usually unspoken. Indeed, I would go so far as to say that it may be the deepest commitment of the Enlightenment: that even though we are capable of bad things, the bad in us can be constrained by *good politics*. Gandhi simply did not believe this.[2]

It was the scepticism, really the pessimism, of an essentially religious person. He thought that it must be the passing of something akin to religion, the relaxing of the rigours of devotion, that allowed us the false optimism by which we could believe that something as shallow as the political forms that were generated in Europe and America less than 200 years ago could be enough to make us better; to believe, in other words, that being good *citizens* would set us on a path to being good *people*. And it is not merely that he thought this form of politics to be inadequate in this way; he thought its very aspiration to shape us, hitherto merely people, into citizens of a nation-state's polity, is a form of intrusive impertinence, *inseparable* from the intrusions we have made into nature when we systematically transformed it in our conception into natural resources. This penetrating *conceptual linking* of the metaphysical transformation of the concept of nature and the political transformation of the concept of humanity was vital to his understanding of the distinctiveness of modernity.[3] That is why the slogan 'Leaving the *world* alone' better captures the refusal of these transformations, and that is why Gandhi puts the genealogical question that interested him slightly differently and more ambitiously than I have when I ask the question: 'How did the concept of nature transform itself into the concept of natural resources?'

Gandhi would have liked my question; he even implicitly sought an answer to it. But he would have worried that talk of 'nature' would ghettoise the issues into merely ecological ones. The point here is not to fasten on 'nature' in some isolated, self-standing sense, but rather to speak with all the force of the repository that ordinary language provides about nature in a much broader sense that includes within its meaning something like: *nature in its whole range of relations with its inhabitants, and a tradition and history that grows out of these relations*. And to capture this much broader phenomenon of nature, Gandhi, like Heidegger, spoke of the 'world' and he wished for us to bring to the world, so conceived, an entire moral psychology that, I believe, Wittgenstein too gestures towards in that memorable phrase as something to be 'left alone'. His genealogical question, therefore, was not exactly the one I have posed, but rather the much larger question: When and by what conceptual transformation did the 'world' cease to be a place merely to live in and become instead a place to master and control?

Why, then, have I insisted on formulating the question in my narrower and less ambitious way? Because I want now to present the genealogy that answers this question more gradually and patiently than Gandhi did, by situating him in a very specific tradition that illuminates his thought and helps to expound it. In that tradition, a metaphysics about nature in the narrower sense *led up to*—via very deliberate integrations—the larger political intrusions of making us over that which made Gandhi anxious. I also want, however briefly, to display the details of the causeway by which this leading up was done in a way that Gandhi's more encapsulated treatment in his unsystematic, instinctive remarks never really did.

So, finally, what was Gandhi's answer to the question as *I* have posed it? In its most immediate rhetoric, the answer he gave put the blame on modern science. Some of the rhetoric by which he did so was crude and conflated, conflating in particular a very specific *metaphysics* that grew around modern science with *science itself*, which he claimed had desacralised the natural world and thereby made it prey to a technological control that was completely alien to his Vaishnavite and ultimately Bhakti ideals in which the human soul flourished only because the human body it suffused was quite continuous with the *spiritually suffused natural environment* it inhabited.

I want to now rotate the angle of this thought to a quite distant place and intellectual history of which Gandhi had no detailed knowledge, but with which he had extraordinarily detailed affinities. I want to seek a genealogical excavation at another site than India in the early twentieth century when (and where) Gandhi wrote. We need to turn to Early Modernity in Europe that Gandhi thought was in fundamentals not dissimilar in its mentality and its materiality to Indian life around him, providing its people with the same crucial choices for their future as the choices that confronted his own people in his own time.

For the sake of focus, I restrict myself to mid- and late seventeenth-century England.[4]

I repeat that on his lips and pen, the question and the anxiety about the transformation of the concept of nature into the concept of natural resources was an essentially religious person's question and anxiety. But my claims here aim for something more general in aspiration since I think it is a question that any of us might ask with no particular sympathy for the notion that religious people alone can feel a sense of anxious loss in that transformation. With this aim of generality in place, let me, then, turn to saying something to situate the *very issues* that Gandhi was raising in a more secular idiom and philosophy than his, stressing more the notion of *value* in nature than the notion of the *sacred* or the spiritual in nature, which was the dominant theme for Gandhi as well as his antecedents in seventeenth-century English dissent in which I situate him.

II

To motivate the more secular version of Gandhi's ideas about nature, I appeal to a more abstract form of philosophical argument than anything found in Gandhi.

There is an acute philosophical insight—to be found more or less explicitly in Spinoza—that one cannot both *intend* to do something and *predict* that one will do it at the same time.[5] This insight generates, in its turn, a very basic philosophical distinction between two points of view. When one predicts that one will do something, one steps outside of oneself and looks at oneself in a detached way as the object of causal and motivational histories, just as someone else might look at one, and so this might be called a 'third'-person point of view. But when one intends to do something, one is not a *detached observer* of oneself, one is asking and responding to the question 'What should I do?', one is an *agent*, in the 'first'-person point of view. If this is so, then it is an implication of Spinoza's point that one cannot both intend and predict at the same time, that one cannot both take the first-person point of view and the third-person point of view on oneself at the same time. We *can* occupy both points of view, but we *cannot* occupy both points of view at *once*.

Spinoza's interest in this distinction is in how it holds as two contrasting perspectives *on ourselves*. But I want to argue, by extension, that there is an *exactly similar distinction* that can be made, not on our perspective on our*selves*, but on our perspective on the *world*. We can have a detached perspective on it, a perspective of study as is found in natural science, and we can have a perspective of agency on the world, one of responding to it with practical engagement rather than with detached observation and explanatory purpose. (The point is not that we are not agents when we are studying the world in a detached way, but that we are taking a perspective of detachment on it rather than one of practical engagement.)

An absolutely crucial question arises, then: What would the world have to be like for it to not merely be the object of detached study but something that *prompts* our practical *engagement*? What must the world contain such that it moves us to such engagement? One obvious answer is that it contains *values* and, when we perceive them, we respond with our practical agency. Why should values prompt such a response rather than a response of detachment? Because values, by the sorts of things they are, make *normative* demands on our agency, demanding not explanation from us but action. So, this perceiving of evaluative properties in the world, given the sort of things they are, is always and *necessarily* perception from the first-person perspective, not just as in Spinoza, where that is a perspective on ourselves, but a first-person perspective on *the world*.

Thus, if we extend the implications of Spinoza's insight as I have, we get a picture of values in which values are not *merely* something *we* create and 'project' onto the world (a favourite metaphor of David Hume's, implied also by the views of Adam Smith on the subject of values) but they are (or at any rate, often are) things that are found *in the world*—as I said earlier, a world of nature, of others who inhabit nature with us, and of a history and tradition that accumulates in the relations among these, and within which value is understood as being 'in the world'.

Such an extension of Spinoza's view gives an argument for a somewhat sanitised Aristotelian ethical picture as it is read by interesting recent scholars such as John McDowell.[6] It also allows one to finesse the interminable dispute of the last few centuries between the followers of Kantian conceptions of morality on the one hand and those of Adam Smith and Hume on the other, taking a stand against the former by placing values and agency squarely in the ordinary perceptible world of 'phenomena' (rather than 'noumena') which we inhabit and perceive, and against the latter by insisting that values are not merely a matter of our desires and moral sentiments, but are part of the world around us to which our desires and moral sentiments are formed as responses. And, if values are part of the world, including nature, it follows that the world, including nature, contains things that are not countenanced and explained by natural science—a secular re-articulation of the sacralisation of nature that Gandhi thought essential to resisting the universal reach and sway of the outlook of science upon nature and the world.[7]

We can now raise our version of the genealogical question that so interested Gandhi: Why has this very natural way of thinking about values as being in the world, including nature, found so little place in the history of thought about value in the last few centuries of philosophy? The answer to this question, at its deepest, lies outside of philosophy itself, at least as it is understood narrowly and as I have done in the last few paragraphs; it is found in one central intellectual strand in our *cultural* history, in a phenomenon that can be traced, using a term that Weber put into currency, to describe it: 'disenchantment'. For many centuries, this natural way of thinking about values as being in the world that I have presented within the secular terms of my own atheistic intellectual orientation had its source in the presence of a divinity which was, in many a view, itself immanent in the world. And it is this source which was undermined in the modern period that Weber described (somewhat crudely and omnibusly) with that term and, as a result of its undermining, the very idea that value could be in the world was replaced by the idea *either* that values were grounded in and therefore, in the end, reducible to our desires and moral sentiments and could only by our projection be thought as being in the world (Hume and Adam Smith), *or* that they were not in the world at all but in a noumenal realm of pure will and practical reason (Kant).

There is a widespread tendency, which is understandable ever since Nietzsche's celebrated slogan, to put this point about disenchantment in terms that summon the image of the 'dead Father'. But there are pitfalls, if one does so without care. This carelessness is rampant in the current revival of tired Victorian debates about the irrationality of belief in a God and in his creation of the universe in six days a few thousand years ago. It is a common thread in the recent 400-page tree-killers[8] which pour scorn on such irrational beliefs that they view them in terms of one's continuing immaturity, one's persistence in an infantile reliance on a Father whose demise was registered by philosophers (Nietzsche, but Hegel before him) more than a century ago, and one's abdication of responsibility and free agency in the humbling of oneself to an authority that is not intelligible to human concepts and scientific explanations.

What goes entirely missing in this simplistic picture is the intellectual as well as cultural and political *prehistory* of the demise of such an authority figure.

Well before his demise, brought about I suppose by the scientific outlook that we all now admire and which is rightly recommended by the authors of these tedious tomes, it was science itself and nothing less than science which, far from registering his demise, proposed instead in the late seventeenth century a quite different kind of fate for the Father, a form of *migration*, an *exile* into inaccessibility from the visions of ordinary people to a place outside the universe, from where, in the now more familiar image of the clockwinder, he first set and then kept an inert universe in motion. And it is the theology and politics and political economy surrounding this deracination of God from the world of matter and nature and human community and perception that is worth expounding in some detail so as to understand its large and abiding effects.

There is no Latin expression such as *Deus deracinus* to express the thought I want to expound. The closest we have is *Deus absconditus* (hidden God) which, though it is meant to convey the inaccessibility of God, conveys to the English speaker a fugitive fleeing. Rather, I want to stress the idea that it is from the roots of nature and ordinary perceptible life that God was quite assiduously removed. 'Racine' or roots is the right description of his immanence in a conception of a sacralised universe from which he was torn away, exiled by the metaphysical outlook of early modern science (aligned with thoroughly mundane interests).

There is no understanding the infantilism of our current religious yearnings that does not acknowledge the significance of these intellectual developments of that earlier period.

The world from which he was exiled, no longer, as a result of that exile, an *anima mundi* (a vital force), was then assiduously argued to also be no longer something to which we were answerable in our moral agency. All value came instead from us; it owed to nothing but our utilities and gain, and even when there was an acknowledgement of our capacity for sympathy and moral sentiments, this was not seen as our responsiveness to the normative demands of a world suffused with value, but something that we (in Hume's and Adam Smith's metaphor) *projected* onto the world and which, as that idea was developed in the tradition that followed, we kept under the control of the demands of efficiency and consequence and utility.

Why, one might ask, should the fact of the Father's exile to an external place as a clockwinder have led to an understanding of the universe as wholly brute and altogether devoid of value? Why was it not possible to retain a world laden with values that were intelligible to all who inhabited it, despite the unintelligibility and inaccessibility of the figure of the Father? Why must value require a sacralised site for its station, without which it must be relegated to proxy, but hardly proximate, notions of desire and utility and gain?

It might seem that these questions are anachronistic, suited only to our own time when we might conceivably (though perhaps not with much optimism) seek *secular* forms of *re-enchanting* the world. One cannot put them, at least not without strain and artificiality, to a period in which value was so pervasively considered to have a sacred source. The removal of such a source in that period, to inaccessibility, was bound to leave the world configured in one's conception as merely brute, subject to nothing but causal laws, bereft of value, reducing value itself to either utility or to subjective psychological dispositions summarised in such terms as 'desire' or 'utility', or, when aspiring to the moral, as 'sympathy' and 'sentiment'. But even if we cannot put these questions to a worldview which was, by our thoroughly modern lights, restricted to fewer conceptual options, we can ask a diagnostic question: What forces prevented the *development* of, the coming to be of, the idea (which I have in my own brief sketch derived from Spinoza and extended onto the world) that the world is *enchanted* with evaluative properties whose normative demands on us, even if now thought of in purely secular terms, move our first-person point of view to a responsiveness into moral agency? The diagnosis has many elements and needs more patient elaboration than I can give in a short essay, but here are some of its elements.

I have said that my (somewhat grotesque) neologism 'Deus deracinus' would have served the thought I want to express best, but the word we have, 'Deus *absconditus*', in another respect suggests something of what I want to capture. The phrase, quite apart from standing for the inaccessibility of God that was insisted upon by the late seventeenth-century ideologues of the Royal Society, conveys a certain anxiety that lay behind their insistence. 'Conditus' means 'put away for *safeguarding*', with 'abs' reinforcing the 'awayness' and separateness or inaccessibility of where God is safely placed. So, we must ask why the authority figure should need safeguarding in an inaccessibility, what dangers lay in his immanence, in his availability to the visionary temperaments and capacities of all those who inhabit his world. And why should the scientific establishment of *Early* Modernity seek this safekeeping in exile for a Father, whom its successor in *late*, more mature, modernity would properly describe as 'dead'?

There are three things to observe at the very outset about this exile of the Father for some 200 years until Nietzsche announced his demise.

First, the intellectual history of the Early Modern period records that there was a remarkable amount of dissent and very explicit dissent against the notions that produced the exile, dissent by a remarkable group of intellectuals, who were most vocal first in England, which is my focus, and the Netherlands, and then elsewhere in Europe.[9] Second, there was absolutely nothing unscientific about these freethinkers or their dissent. They were themselves scientists, then, of course, called natural philosophers, fully on board with the new science and the Newtonian laws and all its basic notions, such as gravity, for instance. They (who did not make the conflation that Gandhi did) were only objecting to the *metaphysical* outlook generated by official ideologues around the new science, who began to dominate the Royal Society, in which the neo-platonist Isaac Newton of his private study was given a quite different official face by people such as Robert Boyle and Samuel Clarke, a public move in which Newton himself acquiesced. And, third, the metaphysical outlook of the dissenters was suppressed and the Royal Society ideologues won out and their metaphysics became the orthodoxy, not because of any superiority, either metaphysical or scientific, but because of carefully cultivated *social factors*, that is to say, because of the alliances they formed with different groups such as the Anglicans on the one hand and the commercial and mercantile interests of the time on the other.[10]

It is this exile of God, which had the effect of rendering the universe brute and inert, that implied the transformation of an ancient and spiritually informed conception of nature into the sort of thing that was available now for predatory extraction by commerce and the elites that grew around it. It is not that extraction (on a much smaller and less systematic scale and with a much lower profile) did not take place until then, but in a wide range of social worlds such extracting as occurred was accompanied by rituals of reciprocation intended to restore the balance as well as show respect towards nature, rituals undertaken after cycles of planting and even hunting. From Max Weber, we are familiar with the idea that capitalism was an outgrowth from certain attitudes towards work and economy, but of far greater transformational significance was the way in which a desacralised conception of the world made it prey to a scale of unthinkingly ruthless extraction in the form of mining, deforestation and the kind of plantation agriculture which we today call agribusiness. I have written of this elsewhere.[11] What I want to stress now is not merely the predatory commercial attitudes towards nature that surfaced with these metaphysical changes, but other sorts of consequences that the exile of the Father had on the scope for a *democratic* culture that developed in that period.

In the great revolutionary decade of the 1640s in England, almost half-a-century prior to our scientific dissenters, Gerrard Winstanley, the most well-known among the radicals, had declared that 'God is still in motion' and the 'truth is hid in every *body*'.[12] This way of thinking about the corporeal realm had for Winstanley, as he puts it, a great 'leveling purpose'. It allowed one to lay the ground, first of all, for a democratisation of religion. If God was everywhere, then anyone may perceive the divine or find the divine within themselves, and therefore may be just as able to preach as a university-trained divine. The significance of this is not to be run together with the cliché about the Protestant Reformation's sustained opposition to the priestcraft enshrined in popery. That opposition was chiefly generative of a pious and possessive individualism via its demand for an individualistic relation to God, finessing institutional demands of Catholic forms of piety, whereas the resistance of the radical sectaries was a resistance precisely to the orthodox Protestantism that had emerged out of that opposition to popery; and this radical resistance came from a desire not to join these orthodoxies in their individualism, but rather out of a desire to allow for the democratic availability of the knowledges of value by which *governance* could be as collective as possible so as to match their ideal of possessing and cultivating the common collectively. Winstanley's opposition to the monopoly of so-called experts was, therefore, by no means restricted to the religious sphere. Through their myriad polemical and instructional pamphlets, he and a host of other radicals had reached out and created a radical rank and file population which began to demand a variety of other things, including an elimination of tithes, a levelling of the legal sphere by a decentralising of the courts and the elimination of feed lawyers, as well as the democratisation of medicine by drastically reducing, if not eliminating, the costs of medicine, and disallowing canonical and monopoly status to the College of Physicians.

The later scientific dissenters were very clear too that these were the very monopolies and undemocratic practices and institutions which would get entrenched if science, conceived in terms of the metaphysics of the Newtonianism of the Royal Society, had its ideological victory.

Equally, that is to say, conversely, the Newtonian ideologues of the Royal Society around the Boyle Lectures administered by Samuel Clarke saw themselves, without remorse, in just these conservative terms that the dissenters portrayed them in. They explicitly called Toland (to name just one) and a range of other scientific dissenters 'enthusiasts', a term of opprobrium at the time, and feared that their alternative picture of nature and matter was an intellectual ground for the social unrest of the pre-Restoration period when the radical sectaries had such great, if brief and aborted, popular reach. They were effective in creating with the Anglican establishment a general conviction that the entire polity would require orderly rule by a state apparatus around a monarch serving the propertied classes, and that this was just a mundane reflection, indeed a mundane *version*, of an *externally* imposed divine authority which kept a universe of brute matter in orderly motion, rather than an *immanently* present God in all matter and in all persons, inspiring them with the 'enthusiasms' to turn the 'world upside down', in Christopher Hill's memorable, eponymous phrase. To see God in every body and piece of matter, they anxiously argued, was to lay oneself open to a polity and a set of civic and religious institutions that were beholden to popular rather than learned and scriptural judgement. So the frontal attack in the late seventeenth century on the scientific dissenters' metaphysics of a sacralised world was motivated not just out of the consideration I have already discussed in my work elsewhere on Gandhi—freeing nature for the extraction by newly emerging capital—but was motivated by an anxiety to prevent at all costs this epistemic or *cognitive* democratisation that had made the revolution of some decades earlier such a threat to this newly emerging alliance of interests between the scientific establishment, the Anglican church, the commercial interests and the oligarchies developing the statecraft needed to pursue these interests together.

It is these alliances brought together by these anxieties which ensured that the exile of the Father from his immanent presence strictly entailed that a desacralised world would contain no residual evaluative properties that might provide alternative, more secular sources of enchantment.

To repeat, it did so first with the argument that ideas of enchantment would prove an obstacle to taking what one could with impunity from nature's bounty. Not merely the seemingly ineradicable inequalities but the cultural detritus and psychological desolation of the economic culture that emerged from this over the centuries are with us everywhere, and I bring no news in saying so, except in having insisted that it had its metaphysical origins in an Early Modern exile of the Father, long prior to his death, a point which makes a great difference to how we should understand the charges of infantilism that are made against our current religiosity that still seeks reliance on the authority of the

Father. And, second, it melded this economic culture inseparably with a political outcome supported by the quite different argument that I am stressing in this chapter: the argument that the priestcraft emerging from scripturally trained and learned divines from the universities that were needed to comprehend an exiled deity, unavailable to the perception and comprehension of ordinary people, was to be integrated—by the very same alliances—with the elite possession of the *cognitive and informational* sources of power *quite generally*, whether in matters of law or medicine or the offices of government and administration. The idea that values to live by are available in the ordinary perceptions of a desacralised world we inhabit would demote these knowledges to something more arcane, by making the sources of political morality much more democratic, an anti-vanguardist conception of value that in a global tradition of radical dissent goes from Winstanley to Gandhi.

It was precisely the threat of the democratisation of value that was arrested in the Early Modern developments I have been stressing, and it was replaced instead by the ideals of civility generated by the courts of a monarch and the propertied classes, a phenomenon well studied by Norbert Elias, though I would add one crucial functional gloss—part Freudian and part Nietzschean—to his illuminating survey of their historical importance (Elias 1978, 1982, 1983). These courtly civilities did not merely contrast with the rude social turmoil of a brute populace. They formed themselves into a screen that had the function of hiding from the Early Modern European courts themselves the cruelties of their own perpetration, recognising cruelty as the sort of thing that can only really occur in the lifestyles and the behaviour of the rude populace. And, as I have argued elsewhere, this screening function morphed from its site in the ideals of civility in the Early Modern period into the site of the codifications of rights and constitutions in the orthodox liberal frameworks of late Western modernity, which, despite all the great good they have done and are deservedly admired for, similarly hide from the West the cruelties of its own perpetration on distant lands, allowing the West to recognise cruelties only in those distant societies (e.g., Saddam's Iraq, the Ayatollahs' Iran, Mugabe's Zimbabwe) where they are unaccompanied by the concealing formalities of such liberal codifications. This was partly at least the source of Gandhi's indifference to what is widely cherished in liberal doctrine.

III

If, as I have argued, the process of disenchantment that led to familiar forms of alienation began with the deracination of value from nature and the world, leaving the world brute and bereft of anything that would present us with normative constraints or that would make any normative calling upon us, then something, however brief and general, needs to be said, as I conclude this chapter, about what it is that makes the idea of values *in the world* a fundamental source of an unalienated life.

I have been at pains to say that there existed highly active dissenting voices that spoke with prescient alarm and protest in Early Modern Europe against the consequences they foresaw in the opportunistic tendencies developing around the metaphysics being forged around the new science. The orthodox liberal frameworks that theoretically consolidated these tendencies is what we have inherited from the defeat and silencing of the radical freethinking dissent of the late seventeenth century. These cramped frameworks have left little room for us to develop the potential in some of the most genuinely radical elements of the Enlightenment—often dismissed by the orthodoxy as 'irrationalist' criticisms emanating from a 'counter'-Enlightenment.[13] (The sleight of hand that exploits ambiguities in the terms 'rational' and 'irrational' in this context needs patient unravelling, which I have presented in the prequel to this chapter [Bilgrami 2006a] and will not rehearse here.)

The defeat of the dissenters in that earlier period pre-empted any meaningful construction of the Enlightenment's own most idealistic commitments and slogans over the next century or more. The familiar slogan of the ideals of liberty, equality and fraternity, in particular, was disallowed any significant *integrated* role in the polities that emerged in European nations; and, quite apart from the failure to apply those ideals in practice in some genuinely integrated way, we do not even have any serious *theoretical* understanding of their deep interrelations. The promise that was held out in Marx's work for such an understanding lies fractured partly as a result of the influential distinction between the early and late Marx, and what we have left of that trio of ideals in the orthodox liberal framework, as a result, is an interminable and seemingly irresolvable zero-sum tension between the values of liberty and equality, with an endless bickering about how much to stress the value of one over the other.[14]

The notions of alienation and disenchantment are—surprisingly, perhaps—key notions to invoke here because this tension can have no resolution and the bickering can have no end without the realisation that there is no justification for either equality or liberty that does not see them *both* as required for an *unalienated* life, for a life, that is, in which the value of *fraternity* informs the value of both equality and liberty, such that there is no equality nor liberty (autonomy) that is genuine which does not also show that the lack of liberty or equality is intolerable by *the lights of fraternity itself*. Fraternity is, in this sense, the cement for liberty and equality, and without some such cementing there is no scope for an unalienated life, no resolution of the zero-sum tension I mentioned that has dominated the political assumptions of the last two centuries. The slogan's trio of ideals has never been genuinely *triangulated* in this way in the liberal theorising that congealed around them in the high European Enlightenment. Admittedly, the idea of such a theorised triangulation is not an argument, only a sketch or schema of how an argument should proceed, but should one be able to construct such an argument, there would be very large theoretical possibilities to be plumbed. There is no space to do that here (although I say a word more about it in closing remarks in the last note to this chapter). But even without such an argument fully in place, we can at least lay the ground with the conceptual ingredients I *have* presented briefly here for the claim that no such ideal of an unalienated life, in which notions of liberty and equality are *not* at odds, can find its soil without some form of secular re-enchantment of a world lost to the social and cultural forces that exiled the Father, as I said, well before his death. This is because the ideal of a world enchanted with value is the basic condition for the very possibility of human agency, which, in turn, is the most elementary and fundamental element in the promise of an unalienated and fraternal social life.

In situating my claims in the Spinozist point I began with, I had already suggested that the idea of values being *in the world* is in some important sense *of a piece* with the fact that *we* possess freedom or agency. To put it flamboyantly, for subjects who do not possess agency (or abdicate it), there is darkness in the world, at just the points where agents can perceive values in it, and it is the darkness of something alien that makes one want to 'master' it and 'conquer' it, a rhetoric to which Freud too was often prone in describing our early psychic development. With this rhetoric, we lose sight of the more relaxed ideal of *merely* 'living' in the world (and we should note with some despondency how revealing it is that we are driven to use the qualifier 'merely' to describe something so basic as living), an ideal that reaches towards the kind of agency and engagement that make possible an unalienated life. And I want to claim that if you take the position that Hume and Adam Smith and their widespread intellectual legacies do, i.e., that values lie not in the world but in our desires and moral sentiments, you make it quite difficult to see how we can so much as possess the full-fledged form of agency they uncritically assume we do possess.

This may seem like a tall claim, since surely they can insist that acting on our desires and moral sentiments *is* an expression of our agency. But that is a superficial understanding of what it takes to be an agent. Let me show why this is so by giving a crucial and concluding argument that links the very possibility of our agency with the notion of enchantment that I have been trying to explore. The argument will build on the insight in Spinoza with which I began.

Before I do, some confusing ground needs to be cleared. I have said that to see the world as enchanted is a precondition for possessing agency and therefore for living an unalienated life. And to see the world as enchanted in a sense that we can accept in our own secular frameworks is to see it as suffused with values. Although such a notion of enchantment sits more comfortably with our more self-conscious secular commitments than previous more sacralised notions such as Gandhi's (or the seventeenth-century dissidents), it is still highly discomfiting to a familiar conviction of our time. It brazenly contradicts the widely held view that there is nothing in nature (and the world) that is not countenanced by natural science. So it is a notion that is bound to be dismissed as unscientific. I will not pause too long to confront this confused prejudice in detail except to say this. All that asserting the presence of value in nature (and the world) does is to imply that science does not have full coverage of nature (and the world). How on earth can this be unscientific? Something is only unscientific if it contradicts a proposition in some science. But *no science* contains the proposition that science has comprehensive coverage of nature. Only a philosopher (or scientists and journalists, like Dawkins [2006] and Hitchens [2007], playing at being philosophers) would assert such a proposition. And one can find the assertion to be bad philosophy, without being told, in turn, that one is doing bad science since it is not doing science at all. The point—surely a simple one—is that it is only unscientific to give unscientific responses to science's themes (as 'creationism' or 'intelligent design' do to the scientific theme of the origins of the universe); it is not unscientific to assert that not all themes regarding nature are scientific themes (and that is all that is asserted by asserting the presence of values in nature and the world).

Unlike this confused objection to enchantment, the picture of value found in Hume (1978) and Adam Smith (2002), which also opposes the idea that values are perceptible properties of the world, is not so easily dismissible. There is no simple confusion in their picture, and if it is wrong, it is wrong for very deep and significant reasons. On their picture of values, values are constructed out of our psychological states, such as our desires and sympathies, and so are ontologically reducible to them. By contrast, the picture of values that is being presented in this chapter claims that our *desires* are *responses* to *desirabilities* (or values) in the world (where 'world' is to be understood in the broad sense that I attributed to Gandhi at the very outset), a quite different ontology of value. This ontology may be resisted because of a fear that it aspires to some sort of implausible *objectification* of value. That is a fear that quite misses the point of this ontology. This chapter's interest in such an ontology and in finding the Humean picture wrong, its interest, that is, in seeking a secular enchantment of the world, is only to secure one of the most basic metaphysical sources of an unalienated life. Its interest is *not* to mount an objectivist resistance to ethical relativism by making values part of the external world, and therefore the same for all human beings capable of a clear and unmyopic perception of the world.

To say that something is part of the perceptible world cannot, in any case, be sufficient to repudiate relativism. Even natural science recognises that many of the objects and properties of the perceptible world that it studies are observed through the lens of theories. So, if observation of even physical properties is theory-laden, differing from theory to theory, it is hardly likely that the value properties in the world will not be differentially perceived by different cultures and even, often, by different individual subjects. Although I have general opinions on the subject of relativism, and am not a relativist in politics or morals (Bilgrami 2004), those opinions are of no relevance in the pursuit of my present preoccupations here. In opposing the Humean picture, I am far from denying that the human subject and human agency are an essential part of the idea that values are in the world. Indeed, I insist on their essential part and am about to give an argument for it. What I deny is that to say that values and human agency are of a piece with our agency in this way amounts to saying that values are in some sense created by us and projected onto the world rather than perceived by us as being in the world. That would be a confusion and philosophy is sometimes prone to it. To sum it up again in a sentence or two, the confusion is this. No one is tempted to say, on the basis of variable perception of physical properties in the world owing to the theory-ladenness of observation, that we create physical properties and project them on the world. Yet, we are constantly being told by the picture of value that I am opposing, that we must say this of value properties on the basis of variable perception of these value properties.

What, finally then, is my argument for the notion that we cannot understand the very idea of our agency without also seeing values as properties in the perceptible world around us? To answer this, we need to look a little harder at the relationship between desires and agency that I first presented in my earlier discussion of a distinction derived from Spinoza.

The philosopher Gareth Evans had once said illuminatingly that questions put to one about whether one believes something, say whether it is raining outside, do not prompt us to scan our mental interiority, they prompt us to look outside and see whether it is raining (Evans 1983: 225). That is to say, one not only looks outside when one is asked 'Is it raining?', but also when one is asked 'Do you *believe* it is raining?'.

Now, let us ask: Is this true of questions put to one about whether one *desires* something? When someone asks 'Do you desire x?', are we prompted to ponder our own minds or are we prompted to consider whether x is desirable? There may be special sorts of substitutions for x where we might ponder our own minds, but for most substitutions, I think, we would consider x's desirability. This suggests that our desires are presented to us as having desirabilities in the world as their objects.

Am I right to have extended the point that Evans makes about beliefs to desires as well, and to have argued on that basis that the world contains desirabilities or values? Suppose for a moment that I am wrong to have done so. What would that imply? That is, what would be implied if one thought that when asked 'Do you desire x', one did not look to the desirab*ility* of x itself, but instead scanned our own interiors to see if one possessed that desire of x. It would imply that our desires were presented to us in a way such that *what they were desires for* was available to us only as something that we could have access to when we stepped back and pondered our own minds in a detached way—in the *third* person. But now, if the presupposition of Spinoza's point is right and if agency is present in the possession and exercise of the *first*-person rather than the third-person point of view, that makes it a question as to how this conception of our desires could possibly square with the fact of our agency. By contrast, a conception of desires as reaching down all the way to desirabilities in the world *requires* us to be agents because *what* we desire is presented to us in the experiencing of the desiring itself, rather than presented to us when we stepped back to observe our desires, thereby abdicating our agency.

Compare two utterances I might make: 'This is desirable' and 'This is desired'. In the latter, I am *reporting* something about myself, reporting what I desire, having stepped outside of myself and perceived myself and my mind from the outside, as if a third person, scanning it for what I desire. It is precisely, in the Spinozist distinction I began with, a detached conception of oneself as an object rather than an agent. By contrast, in the former, I *express*, not report, what I desire. I make an utterance conceiving myself fully as an agent or subject rather than object. But notice that, in doing so, I necessarily see what I desire to be in the world, a desirability, a value property of something in the world. Thus, it makes all the difference to being an agent that we, in being so, possess states of mind such as desires that are responding to value properties in the world.

To experience ourselves as agents we must, *in the very experience itself*, also perceive the world as value-laden. The agent *within* cannot be what it is, it cannot have the experience of its agency and its states of mind such as its desires upon which it acts, without that experience itself also being the perceptible experience of values making demands on it from *without*. That *experiential identification* of agency within with value without is what—at the most general level—makes us (our inner world) unalienated in the (outer) world we inhabit. This equation or identification (*to experience yourself* as an agent is nothing other than to be *engaged with value in the world*) is due to a conception of desires that disallows us from being subjects who are merely the *passive* or detached receptacle of our desires and their fulfilments. And to disallow that, to see our desires and moral sentiments as *active* engagements with a world enchanted with values that normatively demand our desires and moral sentiments as responses, is the first and most abstract precondition for living an unalienated life.

One no doubt needs *other things* too in order to be unalienated, things about which Marx wrote with depth and insight, and which bear more directly on resolving the tension between liberty and equality in orthodox liberalism, but without this more fundamental and underlying condition that makes agency possible, one does not have, as it were, the *first thing*. In this sense, for all their differences, Gandhi's ideas were quite continuous with Marx, not something we should be surprised by, if we even so much as glance at his remarks on capitalism in *Hind Swaraj* or his account of the effects of the Lancashire cotton industry on India. 'Continuous' may be the wrong word, however. The idea of value and alienation he probed within a conception of 'the world', as I have been expounding it, did not develop as much as it underlay and provided the more basic backdrop for Marx's more detailed social and economic analysis of those ideas. Without such a conception of the world in which value *without* us is just the other side of agency *within* us, one would live in a quite real sense as aliens in the world; the world around us, in such a case, would be alien to our own sensibility and we could have no angle on it but one of *either* detached study on the one hand *or* conquest and control of something alien on the other—an impoverishing disjunction that pretty much describes the dominant tendencies of the modern period and the distinctive anxieties they have generated.

Gandhi, like Wittgenstein, saw that it is this alienation from the world, so conceived, that thwarts the 'natural' and the 'ordinary', both prompting us to construct a whole metaphysics around the detached outlook of science (a quite different thing from merely doing science) and prompting our practical agency to intrude into nature and into our own ordinariness, transforming each. No doubt, given their differences, each is transformed by different methods. The first is made over by systematically extractive forms of political economy, the latter by the politics of codes and principles that emerged in tandem with those economies. But the point is that both methods are a fallout of the same systematic attitude of alienated detachment generated by the Early Modern exile of the Father, which produces the wrong understanding of practical agency, one that undermines the practical temperament that 'leaves the world alone' and that allows 'us' (by which, as I said, he meant mere people, not citizens) to be *at home* in the 'world'.[15]

The phrase 'at home in the world' is a cliché that marks the most fundamental form of an unalienated life, which was, in Gandhi's understanding, the most cherished ideal that politics, in the end, must strive for. The effort of much of this chapter has been to integrate—through a somewhat non-standard genealogical reading of Gandhi, linking him to an early dissenting tradition of the Radical Enlightenment—a whole range of seemingly miscellaneous themes from metaphysics, science, politics and morals, so as to give some substance and point to that cliché.

Notes

1. I have used the phrase 'studied indifference' frequently to describe Gandhi's attitudes towards the political Enlightenment. However, as they have fetched some misleading responses, I should perhaps be clearer about what I mean. By 'studied', I mean a very *deliberate* position Gandhi took based on a quite *careful and diagnostic understanding* of the modernity that Enlightenment ideals ushered in. Not being a philosopher, he did not trace these ideas, as Nietzsche and Heidegger did, to their roots as early as the turn that is said to have taken place in the period after the pre-Socratics; nor did he explicitly situate them, as Michel Foucault did, in the specific institutions and discursive formations that were said to have formed after the collapse of Old Regime France. Still, his diagnosis understood very well the ideas and the institutions and the discourse around them that came with the modernity that the British introduced into Indian society; and, though it takes a lot of abstraction away from detail to see similarities between his critique of colonial modernity and the philosophical attack on the 'logocentrism' that was introduced by the Platonic Socrates or the Foucauldian critical scrutiny of the institutions and discourse of the French (and generally European) Enlightenment, the similarities are there and are not hard for the alert reader to unearth. 'Studied' is therefore a perfectly good word with which to describe the deliberately worked out nature of this critique.

The term 'indifference' is also apt because it should be emphasised that Gandhi was *not hostile* to the principles and codes and rights that define the political Enlightenment. He was too undogmatic and politically intelligent to fail to see their instrumental value in winning advantages for the disadvantaged in specific contexts of modern society. But, as I argue, he doubted that they had the power to make us better with respect to our humanity, and he refused to join the cheerleading he heard and read in the self-congratulatory rhetoric with which the Enlightenment was described, because he saw in that the source of a distinctive form of complacence, a complacence which, as I say ahead in the text, issued from an earlier development in the notion of 'civility' in Early Modern Europe. 'Indifference' seems to me a good term to describe this general scepticism on his part.

2. At the very end of my essay, 'Gandhi, The Philosopher' (2003), I had made the claim that Gandhi did not believe in politics. This claim was very cryptically made and much of the present chapter tries to spell out what I intended by it, something I am particularly keen to do since others who have since then been writing on Gandhi are now interpreting that cryptically made claim in ways that I think are quite misleading as an understanding of Gandhi.

3. It is worth noting a very interesting and, at least at first sight, a mildly paradoxical point here. I argue that Gandhi appealed in his own way and in his own words to the idea of 'leaving the world alone' rather than transforming it via capital (in its aspect of nature) and via the orthodoxies in political principles and codes that capital generated (in its aspect of humanity). But, for Gandhi, these rude *transformations* came as a result of an increasingly *detached* attitude towards the world, in its aspect of nature and of humanity. His view, as I expound further ahead, was that transformation (rather than leaving alone) of the wrong kind came from increasing intellectualisation and detachment. So the quick thought that 'surely leaving something alone requires detachment from it' is shown to be too quick. It is *engagement* with the world that allows one to leave it alone. That is the mild paradox, at first sight. But, as I argue (most explicitly in the last section, but really through this section and the next as well), there is no paradox here at all. For the explicit *semantic* disentangling with the term 'detachment' needed to remove this air of paradox, see the last note.

4. This chapter is a sequel to my essay, 'Occidentalism, the Very Idea: An Essay on the Enlightenment and Enchantment' (2006a), where I pledged to elaborate themes that I had only very briefly hinted at in its closing pages. In that prequel, I tried to demonstrate the detailed affinities between elements in Gandhi's thought and the thought of the radical sectaries in mid-seventeenth-century England as well as the somewhat later scientific dissenters such as John Toland and Anthony Collins in late seventeenth-century and early eighteenth-century England. See, also, my paper 'Gandhi, Newton, and the Enlightenment' (2006b) for an elaboration of these affinities. I repeat those points briefly here, but with a slightly different emphasis. In those essays, I had stressed the dissent against the links being forged between the metaphysics around the new science and the newly emerging commercial interests. In this chapter, given its eventual theme of what constitutes a democratic mentality, I

want to stress the links between that metaphysics and the emergence of an ideal of political governance. There is more of substance on these themes in my 'Reply to Bruce Robbins' (2007) and in a web symposium on my essay 'Occidentalism, The Very Idea' (2006a).

5. Spinoza, *Ethics* (1985). For a good exposition of this distinction, see Stuart Hampshire's *Freedom of the Individual* (1965). Hampshire's eventual understanding of Spinoza's insight is somewhat different from the use to which I will put it. He had in mind to ask the question: To what extent can one predict things about oneself without, in fact, implicitly at least, intending them? This Sartrian question may be a good one to eventually ask, but I will not ask it here. My interest is in the distinction between prediction and intention and the initial insightful instinct that to the extent that one can predict things about oneself, one cannot do so at the same time as intending to do them.

6. See McDowell's pioneering essay, 'Values and Secondary Qualities' (1985).

7. I should say immediately that to claim values are properties in the world (including nature) is not to populate the world and nature with extravagant forms of teleology (which is why I referred to the claim above as a *sanitised* Aristotelian view.) No vitalism, for instance, is implied by the claim. And though I use the metaphor of values in the world *making* normative *demands* on us and our agency, this is mere metaphor, and there is no implication that the value properties in the world external to human beings are intentional properties. The reason for this is simple. Where there are intentional properties, it makes sense to criticise them and those who possess them. Thus, human beings criticise each others' intentional states, i.e., each others' intentions, beliefs, desires, hopes. But it makes no sense to say that we criticise nature and the world, except in the quite irrelevant sense in which one might say, 'That was a lousy sunset this evening'. So, though it is controversial (because it denies that natural science has full coverage of nature) to claim that values are in the world, including nature, it is not controversial in the way that vitalism and other such extravagant ontological doctrines are.

8. To name just two, Richard Dawkins (2006) and Christopher Hitchens (2007).

9. The most vocal was perhaps John Toland, a mercurial and brilliant figure of his time. These issues of the metaphysics of nature and the new science can be found in a series of works, starting with *Christianity Not Mysterious* in 1696, more explicitly pantheistic in statement in the discussion of Spinoza in *Letters to Serena* (1704), and then in the late work *Pantheisticon* (1724). It is widely thought that he coined the term 'pantheism'.

10. The best book on these themes remains Margaret Jacob's *The Radical Enlightenment: Pantheists, Freemasons and Republicans* (1981).

11. See all the references in note 4.

12. Quoted in Christopher Hill's *The World Turned Upside Down: Radical Ideas during the English Revolution* (1972: 236), which remains the *locus classicus* as an account of the radical sectaries of England in this period.

13. As, for instance, in the writing of Isaiah Berlin, who first introduced to English-speaking philosophers and political theorists a range of Romantic thinkers whose ideas were quite continuous with some of the ideas of the early radical dissent I have focused on. Berlin, though he was clearly fascinated by these Romanticist ideas, was also made very nervous by them and, assuming an orthodox understanding of the Enlightenment, dubbed them the 'Counter'-Enlightenment. (The term may not have been his invention, but he made much of it.) See particularly his essay 'The Counter-Enlightenment', in *The Proper Study of Mankind* (2000).

14. As is well known, this famous (infamous) and influential distinction between the early and late Marx became central to Althusser's reading of Marx (see some of the essays in *For Marx*, first published in 1965 and republished in 1996). For Marx's most explicit and well-known discussion of issues of alienation, see his *Economics and Philosophic Manuscripts of 1844* (1964). Something of a proof that Marx's ideas on these subjects were not restricted to the early works is that Gyorgy Lukacs seems to have reconstructed them at a time when those works were not yet available, that is to say, he reconstructed them from a reading of his *late* works.

15. The word 'detachment' has been variously used by philosophers to mean different things. Gandhi too talked with admiration of detachment, but what he meant by that is quite significantly at odds with the detachment generated by a disenchanted conception of nature and the world. Indeed, leaving the world (of nature and of its inhabitants) alone rather than making it over requires a detachment from the drives to master and control it. Such detachment Gandhi urged on us and himself. But to achieve it meant eschewing the other kind of alienated detachment that follows upon disenchantment. So, there is much semantic disentangling that is necessary with that word.

References

Althusser, L. 1996. *For Marx*. trans. B. Brewster. London: Verso.

Bilgrami, A. 2003. 'Gandhi, The Philosopher'. *Economic and Political Weekly* 38 (39): 4159–65.

——. 2004. 'Secularism and Relativism'. *boundary2* 31 (2): 173–96.

——. 2006a. 'Occidentalism, the Very Idea: An Essay on the Enlightenment and Enchantment'. *Economic and Political Weekly* 41 (33): 3591–603.

Bilgrami, A. 2006b. 'Gandhi, Newton, and the Enlightenment'. *The Social Scientist* 34 (5/6): 17–35.

——. 2007. 'Reply to Bruce Robbins'. *Critical Inquiry*, Spring 33 (3): 641–49.

Berlin, I. 2000. *The Proper Study of Mankind: An Anthology of Essays*. Ed. H. Hardy and Roger Hausheer, with a foreword by N. Annan and introduction by R. Hausheer. New York: Farrar, Straus and Giroux.

Dawkins, R. 2006. *The God Delusion*. New York: Houghton Mifflin.

Elias, N. 1978. *The Civilizing Process: The History of Manners*. Vol. 1. Trans. E. Jephcott. Oxford: Basil Blackwell.

——. 1982. *The Civilizing Process: State Formation and Civilization*. Vol. 1. Trans. E. Jephcott. Oxford: Basil Blackwell.

——. 1983. *The Court Society*. Trans. E. Jephcott. Oxford: Basil Blackwell.

Evans, G. 1983. *Varieties of Reference*. Oxford: Oxford University Press.

Gandhi, M. K. 1997. *Hind Swaraj*. Ed. A. Parel. Cambridge: Cambridge University Press.

Hampshire, S. 1965. *Freedom of the Individual*. New York: Harper and Row.

Hill, C. 1972. *The World Turned Upside Down: Radical Ideas during the English Revolution*. London: Temple Smith.

Hitchens, C. 2007. *God is Not Great*. New York: Warner Books.

Hume, D. 1978. *A Treatise of Human Nature*. Ed. L. A. Selby-Bigge. Oxford: Oxford University Press.

Jacob, M. 1981. *The Radical Enlightenment: Pantheists, Freemasons and Republicans*. London: George Allen and Unwin.

Marx, K. 1964. *The Economic and Philosophic Manuscripts of 1844*. Ed. D. J. Struink and trans. M. Miligan. New York: International Publishers.

McDowell, J. 1985. 'Values and Secondary Qualities'. In *Morality and Objectivity: A Tribute to J. L. Mackie*, ed. T. Honderich, 110–29. Boston: Routledge and Kegan Paul.

Smith, A. 2002. *The Theory of Moral Sentiments*. Ed. K. Haakonssen. Cambridge: Cambridge University Press.

Spinoza, Benedictus de. 1985. *Ethics. The Collected Works of Spinoza*. Vol. 1. Ed. and trans. E. Curley. Princeton, NJ: Princeton University Press.

Toland, J. 1969. *Christianity Not Mysterious*. London: S. Buckley.

——. 1704. *Letters to Serena*. London: Bernard Lintot.

——. 1751. *Pantheisticon*. London: S. Paterson.

Two

Swaraj and Sovereignty

Anuradha Veeravalli*

It has been acknowledged that few in the history of civilisations have had the moral strength to stand up against and offer resistance to a so-called legally constituted yet unjust regime of the state. Those like M. K. Gandhi and Martin Luther King are seen as unique men of great moral, even spiritual, strength, and perhaps strategy and charisma, who managed to not only offer non-violent resistance, but also command mass support in their fight against the hegemony and unjust laws of a state. There is interest in the story of their resistance, and the particular methods of resistance, such as non-violence or *satyagraha* (literally, 'truth force', whose political form was non-violent civil disobedience). As in Gandhi's case, the story needs telling for its sheer intrinsic value, and for the light it throws upon the human condition and its possibilities. However, there has been hardly any appraisal of these leaders' contribution to political theory. In fact, it would not be far from the truth to say that most believe there is no such contribution or, at the very least, that there is no systematic contribution.

Systematic Intervention

The contribution of Gandhi's thought to the Hindu tradition and its reform (Parekh 1999), to a critique of modernity and modern civilisation (Parel 1992), to non-violent action/resistance (Dalton 1995) and to nationalist discourse (Chatterjee 1993) has been well and variously covered. However, it is an appraisal of the contribution made to the theory of a given discipline that allows one to judge the systematic nature of an intervention in the history of ideas. This chapter addresses itself to this question and argues that Gandhi's understanding of *swaraj* (or

*The author is grateful to Ashis Nandy for commenting on an earlier version of this chapter and sharpening the focus of some of the arguments.

Originally published in *Economic and Political Weekly* 46 (5): 65–69, 2011.

what he called self-rule) offers a systematic critique, an alternative to the theory of sovereignty in modern political thought, and in the context of the modern nation-state. For Gandhi, swaraj extended the question of independence from British rule to a question about the very understanding and definition of sovereignty. It was not, as is believed by many, a matter simply of spiritualising politics. He addressed not merely the question 'Who has the authority to rule?' but the question 'Who has the supreme authority to rule?'. Therefore, the answer for him was not a simple matter of self-rule versus foreign rule or state rule versus anarchy, nor was it a matter of renunciation of the world of politics for the moral. He was, in his response, presenting the possibility of a different theory of sovereignty with fundamentally different presuppositions about the relationship between civil society and the state.

A brief appraisal of the presuppositions and roots of sovereignty in the modern nation-state will serve to show the significance of Gandhi's intervention: how he targets crucial and constitutive presuppositions of the prevalent definition of sovereignty within the framework of the modern nation-state and how his understanding of swaraj strikes at the root of these presuppositions. Post-Enlightenment theories of sovereignty are more or less agreed on its definition as that which has 'supreme authority within a territory'. Thus supreme/exclusive authority and territory are the two constitutive principles of sovereignty in the modern nation-state.

The Social Contract

Theories of sovereignty in the liberal tradition, which have their basis in the social contract, are divided only in the emphasis they lay on civil society (in the lineage of Jean Jacques Rousseau's general will theory) as a source of this authority, or on the state (in the lineage of Thomas Hobbes' Leviathan) as its source. More recently, Giorgio Agamben (2005) argued that the use of the political and juridical impasse by states, which allows them to suspend the law and curtail the freedom of the individual/society in case of an emergency or security threat, are fast becoming the rule rather than the exception. Further, according to him, there is no theory of the state of exception and it is explained as founded in a state of necessity, i.e., expediencies of a state of siege or a political emergency. Agamben argues that the reason for the inability to constitute a theory that would explain the juridical status of the state of exception rests precisely in the fact that the state of necessity is itself presumed to be the origin or basis of the law. On the other hand, limits on the freedom and individual rights of persons are recognised as a necessity since stability is seen as a value in the liberal democratic framework. So, differences must cohere within a common system of values agreed upon by rational members entering into a social contract or under a given constitutional framework (Rawls 2005). Nozick (1974) goes further and argues that it would be well within reason to coerce the few who may not consent to the principles of the social contract to follow the will of the majority.

Concerns about the limits of sovereignty from the vantage point of society or the state is only a matter of emphasis, however, since their origin and underlying presuppositions are one and the same in modern political theory. Both ends of this spectrum presume: (i) that society is an artificial construct of individuals under the social contract; (ii) that the existence of the state is inevitable and necessary; and (iii) that civil society and the state come into being simultaneously and are in fact two faces of the same thing. This fact also becomes at once the rational basis for the sovereignty of the state being unquestionable, just as it becomes the basis of the need to limit the rights of individuals. In this way, the very constitution of sovereignty limits the possibility of the dialectic of state and society since they are at source one, and each is constitutive of the other. This is evident from the conclusions of both Rousseau and Hobbes who, along with John Locke, can be characterised as founders of the social contract theories in modern times. Although Rousseau emphasised the importance of the general will of the people, and therefore of civil society, he stated:

> Further, the Sovereign, being formed only of the individuals who compose it, neither has, nor can have, any interest contrary to theirs; consequently, the sovereign power need give no guarantee to its subjects, because it is impossible that the body should seek to injure all its members; and we shall see presently that it can do no injury to any individual in particular. The Sovereign, by its nature, is always everything it ought to be. (Rousseau 1947: 17)

Similarly, though Hobbes was in favour of the Leviathan, or powerful state, he said:

> But the rights, and consequences of Sovereignty, are the same in both. [Sovereignty by dominion, and by institution.] His power cannot, without his consent, be transferred to another: He cannot forfeit it: He cannot be accused by any of his subjects, of injury: He cannot be punished by them: He is judge of what is necessary for peace; and judge of doctrines: He is sole legislator; and supreme judge of controversies; and of the times, and occasions of war and peace. (Hobbes 1985: 252)

Here, Rousseau makes the point that there is no contradiction, or even possibility of contradiction, between the state and the people. The state can never injure its people. Hobbes makes the reciprocal point that the people cannot injure the state nor accuse the state of injuring them because it is the supreme judge of all that is good or bad for them. It is their conscience. In collapsing the distinction between society, the citizen and the state, only the private individual and everything that is private to them—religion, conscience, calling, all which by definition does not belong to the state or its society—can be in conflict with it. And within the framework of the modern nation-state—ideology, religion and conscience—this private individual necessarily represents the dark possibilities of the state of nature unless they cohere with, and are subject to, the common set of values that are agreed upon in the social contract. The individual cannot be sovereign, nor can they have a conscience except one that coincides with citizenship and the state. Therefore, only a citizen as subject of the state can have a conscience. In this, the state's definition of its sovereignty is the mirror image of the orthodoxy of established religion, and they are in crucial instances to be seen in complete conjunction in their disapproval of the voice of conscience, civil society and custom.[1]

Ironically, then, the individual is either the subject of the state as citizen, or its sovereign as member and official of the state. Thus sovereignty, within the framework of the social contract theories, presupposes not only a state of a person's alienation from themselves and their nature, but also that of the collective/civil society from its nature. Some have characterised this as a consequence of a contradiction in modern liberal states that separate the private sphere, where individual freedom is guaranteed, from the public sphere, where it is curtailed.

However, the real contradiction arises from the collapse of the distinction between civil society and the state in post-Enlightenment political theory, and not from the public-private dichotomy that rests on the dualism and conflict of the individual and the collective. There is room only for two players within modern political theory—the state and the individual. The proof of this lies, for instance, in statutory law, which recognises only criminal cases (state versus the individual) and civil cases (individual versus individual). Civil society is not in the picture either as the voice of the individual or of the collective. In addition, there is a persistent effort to bring civil law under the purview of criminal law, in consonance with the need to collapse the distinction between civil society and the state. Common law as a vestige of pre-Enlightenment systems of justice and governance is the last bastion of a civil society that is not identified with the state. The public interest litigation (PIL) can be seen as a new avatar of common law and modern India's unique contribution to the attempt to break the overlap of state and civil society in the modern nation-state. In 1980, after the Emergency, the Indian judiciary put this law in place, and it allowed the judiciary or any individual (not necessarily an affected party) to initiate litigation against the state/government in the public interest.

Sovereignty and Territoriality

This understanding of sovereignty in conjunction with the condition of territoriality then separates one nation-state from another. Each with its secure territorial boundaries is an independent sovereignty, with independent aspirations of freedom and defence mechanisms. Thus each state takes on the nature of an individual and the conditions of individuals in the state of nature are replayed with respect to the relations between nation-states until another contract comes into being in the creation of a system of sovereign states. The two World Wars of the twentieth century re-enacted the possibilities of the state of nature on the international stage. The United Nations (UN) and the UN General Assembly would have to follow the trajectory of the limits of sovereignty between state and society that we have discussed above: the state and its methods of law and order would prevail over that of civil society.

The territoriality condition of sovereignty theory presupposes that the jurisdiction of a state and nation overlap, just as it presupposes that the person and citizen and civil society and the state are coextensive. That this understanding has always been contested is seen from the fact that border disputes abound in the world, where ethnic communities contest both the existing territorial boundaries of the state and its sovereignty.

It is within this context of the ultimate collapse, in political theory and practice, of the distinction between state and civil society, both conceptually and territorially in the post-Enlightenment discourse on sovereignty, that Gandhi's discourse on swaraj intervenes. Some have argued, on the other hand, that it is in the dualism of individual and collective, private and public spheres,[2] and the secular and the religious that Gandhi mediates (Nandy 2000). However, the dualisms that constitute the modern nation-state are not the premise on which the vocabulary of Gandhi's satyagraha and swaraj stand. He systematically disbands the presuppositions of the modern state and its laws. First, non-violence is not a personal or private virtue but 'Non-violence is the Law of our Species, as Violence is the Law of the Brute' (Gandhi 1969: 156). It is not the religion of the recluse but of the common people. Thus Gandhi sets aside the dualism of human/individual and the collective/society in the state of nature of the social contract. For him, it is a matter of common people/civil society versus the state. Second, the *satyagrahi* is conceived as a foot soldier of non-violent opposition to all aggression or use of power, whether by oneself or the opponent, in the cause of the vindication of truth or justice. The satyagrahi shall neither be subject to the law of the state, nor be party to its execution as member of the state. On the other hand, Gandhi constitutes the personal (not 'private') and the political (not 'public') spheres as merely two types of reasons for which satyagraha may be offered:

> So the doctrine came to mean vindication of truth not by infliction of suffering on the opponent but on one's self.
>
> But on the political field the struggle on behalf of the people mostly consists in opposing error in the shape of unjust laws. When you have failed to bring the error home to the lawgiver by way of petitions and the like, the only remedy open to you, if you do not wish to submit to error, is to compel him by physical force or by suffering in your own person by inviting the penalty for the breach of the law. Hence *Satyagraha* largely appears to the public as Civil Disobedience or Civil Resistance. It is civil in the sense that it is not criminal. (ibid.: 179)

If one were to think that he said this only incidentally, he makes himself clear again when he says: 'Civil Disobedience is civil breach of unmoral statutory enactments' (ibid.: 181).

In the first instance, Gandhi rejects the dualism of the individual and the collective since, in civil society, the real issue is the negotiation of self and other, whether that other is god/truth, man or nature. In the second instance, he implicitly rejects the dualism of the private and the public and emphasises instead the personal and the political spheres, the first involving the vindication of truth or justice between individuals and the second between the people and the state. In the latter case, he clearly overturns the classification of law in the modern nation-state: a case of individual versus the state is necessarily representative of a case of civil society against the state and is a civil, not a criminal, case. By implication, a case is criminal only when there is a threat to civil society by the use of violence or divisive forces between individuals and between groups of individuals, but this is best negotiated by civil society itself, and with least state intervention. This will become clear from the examples discussed ahead in this chapter.

Gandhi's Theory of Sovereignty

The theory of sovereignty proposed by Gandhi is based on the clear separation of the origin, constitution and methods of the state from that of civil society. Thus, it is not surprising that Gandhi bases his understanding of swaraj or, as he translates it, self-rule, on three presuppositions that are fundamentally different from the accepted definitions of sovereignty in the modern nation-state: (i) it presupposed the necessary differentiation and separation of civil society from the state in their origin and constitution; (ii) the possibility of self-reform rather than control over, or freedom from the other, was seen as a necessary condition of sovereignty; (iii) it disposed of territory as a definitional condition of sovereignty; rather, sovereignty defined the relation/frontier (not boundaries) between territories of different nations and of self and other. Territory was neither an object of control, nor of acquisition or exploitation. The good of the self or one's country rested in the good of the neighbour.

This understanding of swaraj as presenting a theory of sovereignty allows us to see a unity of method and thought in Gandhi's approach to several issues that pertain to the political and the political economy. To begin with, one can understand why it was not imperative for Gandhi that the British leave India for the country to be free. It was only a matter of last resort, when the impossibility of any attempt at self-determination, not of the state but of civil society, vis-à-vis crucial issues concerning modernity/'civilisation', Hindu-Muslim relations and the problem of untouchability became evident that Gandhi called for *poorna* swaraj (complete self-rule). It was the impediment to self-reform that the British posed, the inability to set one's own house in order, that was crucial since without self-reform, independence would just be a matter of form and not substance. Their insistence on remaining within the framework of the modern nation-state, and therefore in the role of supreme arbiter of all social issues, did not permit them to join in the effort of civil society to reform itself.

The issues that Gandhi raised with respect to the political economy can be categorised as those relating to *swadeshi* (which one may translate as the territory of the self as well as that of one's nation). This he understood not in terms of the private space/freedom of individuals or private property or national territory, but as a question of the body, labour and mode of production, i.e., as that which related the self and the world. Thus national sanitation, involving the maintenance of clean roads and environment, was something that could not be postponed even for a day.[3] Similarly, work must involve labour that sustains the relationship between spirit and the body, the person and the body politic, and the body politic and the body-natural/cosmos in the act of production and reproduction; there cannot be freedom with respect to one at the expense of the other. It is only this understanding of swadeshi that allows it to be non-exclusivist. And it is this non-exclusive understanding that determines swadeshi as a sign of sovereignty.

Swaraj within this scheme is not a means of distancing self from other (body, body politic or cosmos) or of establishing jurisdiction or territory between nations.[4] It signifies a frontier of mutual respect, love/non-violence and service of the neighbour/opponent, located in the material and political culture of the people rather than in a relationship of power, mutual fear and exploitation. Thus the draft resolution on foreign policy discussing relations with the territories of other nations, circulated by Gandhi to members of the working committee of the Indian National Congress prior to India's independence, said:

> Indeed whilst we are maturing our plans for establishing *Swaraj*, we are bound to tell the world what relations we wish to cultivate with it. If we do not fear our neighbours, or if although feeling strong we have no designs upon them, we must say so. We are equally bound to tell the world whether we want to send our sepoys [soldiers] to the battle fields of France or Europe. (Gandhi 1967a: 161)

The principles of relations between nations become clear in the following passage that locates what exactly was wrong with the British presence in India:

> India's greatest moment of glory will consist not in regarding Englishmen as her implacable enemies fit only to be turned out of India at the first available opportunity but in turning them into friends and partners in a new commonwealth of nations in the place of an Empire based on exploitation of the weaker or underdeveloped nations and races of the earth and therefore finally upon force. (ibid.: 162)

Language as Ontological Reality

In the case of the Hindu-Muslim conflict, Gandhi's choice of Hindustani as the vernacular language of India is significant. It signified the dialectic of Urdu and Sanskrit (or Urduised Hindi and Sankritised Hindi) in the simple and spontaneous currency of spoken language and thus the unity of Hindus and Muslims. This he proposed not merely for north India but as the national language across the length and breadth of the country. For those in south India who protested, he was insistent in his persuasion that Hindustani was clearly the most suitable to be the common language of India. This was one thing he was willing to institutionalise with the setting up of the Hindustani Prachar Sabha (Association for the Dissemination of Hindustani).[5] This involved a conscious break with the Hindi Sahitya Sammelan (Hindi Literary Conference) that favoured Sanskritised Hindi, the language of brahminical Hinduism, as the national language. Gandhi, however, did persuade Purushottam Das Tandon and other members of the Hindi Sahitya Sammelan to pass a resolution stating that they held Urdu, which represented the Arabic-Persian-Islamic influence, to be a form of Hindi and that they were not against Urdu.

However, the significant point here was that the solution did not lie in constitutional changes to be enforced by the state, like a uniform civil code, or, on the other hand, of legislation on religious freedom. It lay in strengthening the actual and possible dialect of communication among the people of both communities. Besides, for those of us trained in the discipline of philosophy, the positivist tradition brings home to us the difficulties of representing the ontological reality of general or abstract terms such as 'society', and therefore of the truth of their existence. Gandhi, a natural with fundamental puzzles such as these, with brilliant simplicity and with clarity edging on clairvoyance, proposes language as the ontological reality and truth of society and the proof of its unity in a variety constituted by dialectics of difference, contradiction and complementarity. Hindi movies bear witness to the truth of Hindustani being this language that articulates this truth of the unity in the variety of India.

Gandhi described Partition, when first proposed by the Muslim League, as vivisection. For him, the Hindu and Muslim communities constituted one living body, a common civilisation, and both had worked for centuries to strengthen the bonds of unity between them, something that could not be defined by geographical boundaries. He made anguished and persistent pleas to the Muslim League and its leaders, as much as he pleaded with the leaders of the Indian National Congress, to consider whether they actually had the support of the Muslims of India in believing that the two communities had nothing in common—neither religion, nor language, nor customs. He was clear that the demand for Partition on religious grounds was an untruth. It went against the grain of any religion: 'Religion binds man to God and man to man. Does Islam bind Muslim only to a Muslim and antagonise the Hindu? Was the message of the Prophet peace only for and between Muslims and war against Hindus or non-Muslims?' (Gandhi 1963: 294).

In the event that the people actually felt the truth of the separate destinies of the nations, Gandhi was willing to go along with their wishes, but not with the British as arbiters. He felt that India must gain peace and freedom from British rule, as one nation, and only then must Hindus and Muslims decide to part. However, the irony of the demand on non-religious grounds, i.e., on the grounds of forming a nation-state on the presuppositions of post-Enlightenment conceptions of sovereignty, is brought home in this comment of Gandhi's on Jinnah's[6] demands:

> Pakistan, according to him [Jinnah] 'in a nutshell, is a demand for carving out of India a portion to be wholly treated as an independent and sovereign State.' This sovereign state can conceivably go to war against the one of which it was but yesterday a part. It can also equally conceivably make treaties with other States. All this can certainly be had, but surely not by the willing consent of the rest. (ibid.: 305)

Similarly, Gandhi was against a legal and constitutional enforcement of separate electorates and rights of the untouchables. It would divide Hindus into two communities; it would neither bring home to the Hindus the great shame of the practice of untouchability, nor remove the perpetuation of untouchables as a separate class. This was a matter internal to Hinduism. Unless it took account of untouchability and performed penance for the ills of untouchability, it would have no swaraj. This was a matter for self-reform, to be dealt with by a committee of Hindu reformers, and not a matter for the state. In fact, separate electorates would make the label and class of untouchables a permanent fixture:

> Let this Committee and let the whole world know that today there is a body of Hindu reformers who are pledged to remove this blot of untouchability. We do not want on our register and on our census untouchables classified as a separate class. Sikhs may remain as such in perpetuity, so may Muslims, so may Europeans. Will untouchables remain untouchables in perpetuity? I would prefer rather that Hinduism died than that untouchability lived.[7]

The distinction between sovereignty and power, a frontier or a medium of communication and a territorial boundary, whether national, religious or linguistic, is fundamental to Gandhi. Sovereignty is not power over another but being witness to the dialectic of self and other; a frontier is not a boundary between territories but a point of their meeting and a condition for possible dialogue.

The Rama (from the epic *Ramayana*) that Gandhi so revered symbolised the possibility of the rule of Rama ('Ram *rajya*'), even when in exile, without territory and out of power. It is not the appropriation or renunciation of territory, but sustaining the separation of and dialectic between the state and civil society even while remaining in exile from the seat of power that presents the true test of sovereignty. It becomes quite clear then why Gandhi was so adamant that the Congress must be dissolved on the eve of Independence. The logic of his understanding of sovereignty told him that the Congress' rightful role would be as the opposition rather than as ruling party—a party in exile from the seat of power. In fact, there would be no 'party' in opposition, but only independent community workers whom the people knew from their work in the community and who therefore truly represented them in Parliament.[8] Only then would the separation between civil society and the state, their method and goal be clear and distinct. Only then would there be an opportunity to govern without the power of the state.[9] Only then would the dialectic of state and society and self and other be kept alive in any real/true sense of the term.

The experiment of the Tibetan people and the Dalai Lama as sovereign in exile is not in vain, after all.

Notes

1. J. P. S. Uberoi noted the following as one of the factors affecting the possibility of national pluralism in his preface: 'The priest and the prince, whenever they rule together, either through a state-established religion or a religion-established state, are the enemies of civil society, its national autonomy, customs and morality' (1999: x). This explains Ashish Nandy's insightful comment, made in a different context, on Gandhi's method of reform and resistance: 'All his life, Gandhi sought to free the British rather than the Indians from the clutches of imperialism, and the Brahmins rather than the untouchables from the caste system' (1978: 172). I attribute this to Gandhi's recognition of the consonance of the presuppositions of the modern nation-state and its religious orthodoxy in their definitions of sovereignty and rejection of an independent ontological and political space for the will of civil society. Thus it was the state, in this case represented by the British, and the religious orthodoxy represented here by the Brahmins, who needed to be emancipated/rescued from their definitions of sovereignty.

2. Thomas Pantham (1983), in an illuminating essay on Gandhi's contribution to political theory, argues that his concept of satyagraha is a response to the

problematic of liberal democracy which presupposes a dualism of individual liberty and social harmony. He sees Gandhi's swaraj therefore as an experiment in participatory democracy and the mediation of the public and the private spheres.

3. 'I venture to submit that conservation of national sanitation is *Swaraj* work and may not be postponed for a single day on any consideration whatsoever. Indeed if *Swaraj* is to be had by peaceful methods it will only be attained by attention to every little detail of national life.' From 'A National Defect', *Young India*, 25 April 1929, cited in *Political and National Life and Affairs* (Gandhi 1967a: 95).

4. 'My patriotism is not an exclusive thing. It is all embracing and I should reject that patriotism which sought to mount upon the distress or the exploitation of other nationalities. The conception of my patriotism is nothing if it is not always in every case without exception consistent with the broadest good of humanity at large. Not only that but my religion and my patriotism derived from my religion embrace all life. I want to realise brotherhood or identity not merely with the beings called human but I want to realise identity with all life, even with such beings as crawl on earth' (Gandhi 1929: 107). 'Our nationalism can be no peril to other nations, inasmuch as we will exploit none just as we will allow none to exploit us. Through swaraj we would serve the whole world' (Gandhi 1931: 79).

5. In 1942, Gandhi, along with other members including Rajendra Prasad, drew up the draft constitution of the Hindustani Prachar Sabha. Gandhi did not see it as opposed to the Hindi Sahitya Sammelan, which he had been a member of since 1918, but as having a different focus and agenda: of disseminating the national language Hindustani 'as the medium of contact and intercourse between the various provinces with different provincial languages, which may come to be used throughout India for social, political, administrative and such other purposes of the nation' (Gandhi 1956: 112–13). It was not the Hindi versus Urdu debate that was crucial, but the Hindustani versus English opposition that was crucial in deciding what the national language of India should come to be.

6. Muhammad Ali Jinnah, originally a member of the Indian National Congress during the struggle for freedom from British rule, broke away from the party when he saw that freedom was in sight, to put forward the demand for a new and independent state for the Muslims of India. He succeeded in persuading the British to partition India and became the founding father and first president of Pakistan. Pakistan was established on the eve of India's freedom from British rule.

7. From Gandhi's speech at the last meeting of the Minorities Committee, at the Round Table Conference in London, 1931 (Gandhi 1967b: 315).

8. 'Power that comes from service faithfully rendered ennobles. Power that is sought in the name of service and can only be obtained by a majority of votes is

a delusion and a snare to be avoided.' From *Young India,* 1924, cited in *Political and National Life and Affairs* (Gandhi 1967b: 12).

9. 'Under a Free Government, the real power will be held by the people .... The mightiest Government will be rendered absolutely impotent if the people realising power use it in a disciplined manner and for the common good .... It must be remembered that only an infinitesimal proportion of the people can hold positions of responsibility and power in a country's government. Experience all the world over shows that the real power and wealth are possessed by people outside the group that holds the rein of Government.' From *Young India,* 1930, cited in *Voice of Truth* (Gandhi 1969: 366). 'By its very nature non-violence cannot "seize" power, nor can that be its goal. But non-violence can do more; it can effectively control and guide power without capturing the machinery of government. That is its beauty.' From *Towards New Horizons,* 1959, cited in *Voice of Truth* (Gandhi 1969: 357).

References

Agamben, G. 2005. *The State of Exception*. Chicago: University of Chicago Press.

Chatterjee, P. 1993. *Nationalist Thought and the Colonial World.* Minnesota: University of Minnesota Press.

Dalton, D. 1995. *Mahatma Gandhi: Non-violent Power in Action.* New York: Columbia University Press.

Gandhi, M. K. 1929. 'My Conception of Patriotism'. *Young India* IX (14): 107–08.

——. 1931. 'Question of Safeguards'. *Young India* XIII (16): 78–79.

——. 1956. *Thoughts on National Language*. Ahmedabad: Navajivan Publishing House.

——. 1963. *The Way to Communal Harmony,* comp. and ed. U. R. Rao. Ahmedabad: Navajivan Publishing House.

——. 1967a. *Political and National Life and Affairs*. Vol. I. Comp. and ed. V. B. Kher. Ahmedabad: Navajivan Publishing House.

——. 1967b. *Political and National Life and Affairs*. Vol. II. Comp. and ed. V. B. Kher. Ahmedabad: Navajivan Publishing House.

——. 1969. *The Voice of Truth*. Ed. Shriman Narayan. Ahmedabad: Navajivan Publishing House.

Hobbes, T. 1985. *Leviathan*. Ed. C. B. Macpherson. London: Penguin.

Nandy, A. 1978. 'Oppression and Human Liberation. Towards a Third World Utopia'. *Alternatives* IV: 165–88.

——. 2000. 'Gandhi after Gandhi after Gandhi....'. *The Little Magazine* 1 (1): 38–41.

Nozick, R. 1974. *Anarchy, State and Utopia*. New York: Basic Books.

Pantham, T. 1983. 'Thinking with Mahatma Gandhi: Beyond Liberal Democracy in Political Theory'. *Political Theory* 11 (2): 165–88.

Parekh, B. 1999. *Colonialism, Tradition and Reform: An Analysis of Gandhi's Political Discourse*. New Delhi: Sage Publications.

Parel, A. J. 1992. 'Mahatma Gandhi's Critique of Modernity'. In *Comparative Political Philosophy: Studies under the Upas Tree*, ed. A. J. Parel and R. C. Keith, 163–83. New Delhi: Sage Publications.

Rawls, J. 2005. *Political Liberalism*. New York: Columbia University Press.

Rousseau, J. J. 1947. *The Social Contract*. Ed. and revised by C. Frankel, trans. anon. New York: Hafner Publishing Co.

Uberoi, J. P. S. 1999. *Religion, Civil Society and the State: A Study of Sikhism*. New Delhi: Oxford India Paperbacks.

Three

GANDHI'S *SWARAJ**

A Revisit

SUDARSHAN IYENGAR

Mohandas Karamchand Gandhi returned to India from South Africa after a long stay of nearly 23 years. His going there was a chance occurrence. He had failed to set up a practice as an England-trained barrister in Mumbai or Rajkot. Divan Kaba Gandhi's scions' financial position had worsened over time, and young barrister Mohandas wanted to better the financial position of the family with his practice. While he was struggling, a proposal came up to provide legal assistance to a Muslim business house in South Africa that was entangled in litigations, and this gave Mohandas an opportunity to better his livelihood prospects. He notes the following in his autobiography:

> This was hardly going there as a barrister. It was going as a servant of the firm. But I wanted somehow to leave India. There was also the tempting opportunity of seeing a new country, and of having new experience. Also I could send £105 to my brother and help in the expenses of the household. I closed with the offer without any haggling, and got ready to go to South Africa. (Gandhi 1970: 86)

As is well known, the events in Mohandas's life in South Africa took different and dramatic turns. He was transformed from a householder seeking an honest but paying livelihood to a *mumukshu*,[1] and the path was of political and social service of the community. He was acutely

---

*This chapter is a revised version of a presentation made at the international seminar 'Debating Swaraj after One Hundred Years of Gandhi's Return from South Africa', 4–6 October 2015, Central University, Gandhinagar, and of an invited lecture at the 'Second International Conference on Diaspora', NIRMA University, 10–11 January 2015. I thank Professor Manas Chatterji and Dr Dhananjay Rai for the invitations. I also thank those who commented on the presentations and the anonymous reviewer for his incisive comments and suggestions.

conscious of his duty to his self and towards humanity. One of the key elements in the concept of *swaraj* or self-rule that he evolved later during his stay in South Africa was a sense of duty. On that cold winter night when he was pushed out from the train at Pietermaritzburg station, Gandhi did some hard thinking while sitting in the waiting room. In his autobiography, he writes:

> I began to think of my duty. Should I fight for my rights or go back to India .... It would be cowardice to run back to India without fulfilling my obligation. The hardship to which I was subjected was superficial—only a symptom of deep disease of colour prejudice. I should try, if possible, to root out the disease and suffer hardships in the process. Redress for wrongs I should seek only to the extent that would be necessary for the removal of the colour prejudice. (Gandhi 1970: 94)

Gandhi spent nearly two-and-a-half decades performing his duty and, in the process, walked his talk on the swaraj he had conceptualised in 1909 in *Hind Swaraj or Indian Home Rule*. For him, swaraj was the formation of a non-violent society. The unit was the individual. The effort to bring about swaraj meant the effort to achieve swaraj at the individual level and, simultaneously, to work towards political, social and economic swaraj in society. The concept of swaraj that Gandhi propounded was deeply embedded in Indian culture. Gandhi returned from South Africa essentially to work towards swaraj with the people in India. His personal journey towards achieving swaraj for the self had already begun. What was the idea of swaraj that Gandhi wanted to work for when he returned to India? Is the idea still relevant 77 years after his passing?

The first part of this chapter attempts to understand Gandhi's thoughts on swaraj soon after his return to India. The second part explains the differences in Gandhi's and Nehru's perceptions before India's independence. The third and last part of the chapter discusses the relevance of 'Gandhi's return' in terms of his thoughts and philosophy of swaraj.

I

On 9 January 1909, Gandhi and Kasturba alighted from a ship in Bombay (now Mumbai) to a grand civic reception. Kasturba and he wore traditional

Kathiavadi[2] attire to signify their homecoming with their culture intact. The trustee in Gandhi emerged in the response he gave at the reception.

> At a reception to Mr. and Mrs. M. K. Gandhi at Ghatkopar [Bombay] on Monday, Mr. Gandhi was presented with an address enclosed in a silver casket, with fetters made of gold .... Mr. Gandhi, in acknowledging the gifts, described the silver casket and the fetters as somewhat unsuitable to a person who had neither a roof over his head nor locked doors to his house .... A function like the one they held, he said, was most uncongenial to him, and the temptations it involved would tend to spoil a person like him whose only thought was to serve his Motherland, irrespective of praise or blame, with no expectation of any reward whatsoever. The only idea behind his work was duty .... He hoped for nothing and wished for nothing, beyond being able to fulfil the duty that lay before him. He entreated them all to accept whatever service he could give, and not to give him costly presents which he could not use, and which could be put to far better uses. He sincerely trusted that they would not misunderstand him; he was only expressing his innermost feelings. (Gandhi 1964: 3)

Gandhi was looking forward to an intimate and warm traditional reception. He expressed this at Shantiniketan on 17 February 1915, some five weeks after his arrival in India. He said:

> The delight I feel today I have never experienced before. Though Rabindranath, the Gurudev, is not present here, yet we feel his presence in our hearts. I am particularly happy to find that you have arranged for this reception in Indian style. We were received with much pomp in Bombay, but there was nothing in it to make us happy. For there, purely western ways were imitated. We shall proceed to our goal in our own eastern ways and not by imitating the West, for we are of the East. We shall grow up in the beautiful manners and customs of India, and true to her spirit, make friends with nations having different ideals. Indeed, through her oriental culture, India will establish friendly relations with the eastern and western worlds. (ibid.: 24)

In a literal sense, Gandhi returned to India with a well laid-out task. He wanted to work towards obtaining swaraj, as discussed in *Hind Swaraj*. Anthony Parel (1997) has noted that *Hind Swaraj* was a treatise with a strong critique of the modern civilisation that Gandhi witnessed during his stay in London as a student studying law, and later during his stay in South Africa where he was able to understand clearly the politico-economic strategy of a powerful industrialised England. The treatise also contains an analysis of India's situation. It also suggests the alternative path that the country should follow. *Hind Swaraj* is not a mere exercise in scholarship, criticising Western civilisation and providing an erudite vision for an alternative;[3] rather, it is a deeply and intensely realised discourse on the state of Western civilisation and the author's ideas about the desired direction of change. An unusual aspect of *Hind Swaraj* is the solemnity of the author's commitment to work towards this vision. At the end of the treatise, Gandhi wrote: 'In my opinion, we have used the term "Swaraj" without understanding its real significance. I have endeavoured to explain it as I understand it, and my conscience testifies that my life henceforth is dedicated to its attainment' (ibid.: 119).

On his return from South Africa in January 1915, Gandhi was determined to be a change-maker. Following the advice of his political guru Gopal Krishna Gokhale, he explored the country and understood its people before entering the public arena. In 1916, after joining full-fledged public life, he made three important speeches that explained his vision, mission and position: the much-discussed speech at the inauguration of Banaras Hindu University (BHU) on 4 February 1916; his discourse in Madras to the missionaries on *swadeshi* on 14 February 1916; and the Economic *v.* Moral Progress speech on 22 December 1916 in Muir Central College, Allahabad. The speeches contain the elements of swaraj which Gandhi had decided to work towards and mobilise the Indian people for.

Gandhi gave his first public speech at the inaugural ceremony of BHU. Pandit Madan Mohan Malaviya, who headed the BHU after Annie Besant, had perhaps thought that Gandhi would welcome the indigenous initiative. However, Gandhi used the inauguration to criticise the British system of education and warn the audience. Gopalkrishna Gandhi notes, 'The Gokhale-enjoined silence was broken by Gandhi .... He took on the British, he took on the Indians. He took on the Rajas, he took on the anarchists. He spared no one on the dais, nor most of those that comprised the audience' (Gandhi 2008: 178).

Gandhi's major point of criticism of the British education system was the medium of instruction in schools and colleges. He said,

> Our language is the reflection of ourselves, and if you tell me that our languages are too poor to express the best thought, then I say that the sooner we are wiped out of existence, the better for us .... Why this handicap on the nation? Just consider for one moment what an unequal race our lads have to run with every English lad ... that every Indian youth, because he reached his knowledge through the English language, lost at least six precious years of life .... The charge against us is that we have no initiative. How can we have any if we are to devote the precious years of our life to the mastery of a foreign tongue? ... But suppose that we had been receiving during the past fifty years education through our vernaculars, what should we have had today? We should have today a free India, we should have our educated men, not as if they were foreigners in their own land but speaking to the heart of the nation; they would be working amongst the poorest of the poor. (Gandhi 1964: 212)

To the Indians gathered on the occasion, he said,

> I visited the Viswanath Temple last evening and as I was walking through those lanes, these were the thoughts that touched me. If a stranger dropped from above on to this great temple and he had to consider what we as Hindus were, would he not be justified in condemning us? Is not this great temple a reflection of our own character? I speak feelingly as a Hindu. Is it right that the lanes of our sacred temple should be as dirty as they are? The houses round about are built anyhow. The lanes are tortuous and narrow. If even our temples are not models of roominess and cleanliness, what can our self-government be? (ibid.: 213)

To the rajas and the British, he said,

> His Highness the Maharajah, who presided yesterday over our deliberations, spoke about the poverty of India .... But what did we witness in the great *pandal* in which the foundation ceremony was performed by the Viceroy? Certainly a most gorgeous show, an exhibition of jewellery which made a splendid feast for the eyes of the greatest jeweller who chose to come from Paris. I compare with the richly bedecked noblemen the millions of the poor. And I feel like saying to these noblemen: 'There is no salvation for India unless you strip yourselves of this jewellery and hold it in trust for your countrymen in India.' (ibid.: 213–14)

To the anarchists, he said,

> But there is a class of anarchists amongst us, and if I was able to reach this class, I would say to them that their anarchism has no room in India if India is to conquer the conqueror. It is a sign of fear. If we trust and fear God, we shall have to fear no one, not the Maharajahs, not the Viceroys, not the detectives, not even King George. I honour the anarchist for his love of the country ... but I ask him: Is killing honourable? Is the dagger of an assassin a fit precursor of an honourable death? I deny it. There is no warrant for such methods in any scriptures. If I found it necessary for the salvation of India that the English should retire, that they should be driven out, I would not hesitate to declare that they would have to go, and I hope I would be prepared to die in defence of that belief. (ibid.: 214)

Gandhi had returned to India with a resolve. He conveyed his political understanding of the situation, his critique, and indicated what he thought was the way forward.

Gandhi was invited to a missionary conference at Madras (now Chennai) within one week of his BHU address. There, he told his audience he had chosen to speak on swadeshi, a very delicate and difficult subject. Defining swadeshi with religion as its base, he said,

> Swadeshi is that spirit in us which restricts us to the use and service of our immediate surroundings to the exclusion of the more remote. Thus, as for religion, in order to satisfy the requirements of the definition, I must restrict myself to my ancestral religion. That is the use of my immediate religious surroundings. If I find it defective, I should serve it by purging it of its defects. In the domain of politics, I should make use of the indigenous institutions and serve them by curing them of their proved defects. In that of economics, I should use only things that are produced by my immediate neighbours and serve those industries by making them efficient and complete where they might be found wanting. (ibid.: 219)

Elaborating on how swadeshi would look at the religion, he said,

> Hinduism has become a conservative religion and therefore a mighty force because of the Swadeshi spirit underlying it. It is the most tolerant because it is non-proselytising .... It has succeeded not in driving, as I think it has

> been erroneously held, but in absorbing Buddhism … a Hindu refuses to change his religion not necessarily because he considers it to be the best, but because he knows that he can complement it by introducing reforms …. If there is any substance in what I have said, will not the great missionary bodies of India, to whom she owes a deep debt of gratitude for what they have done and are doing, do still better and serve the spirit of Christianity better, by dropping the goal of proselytising but continuing their philanthropic work? (Gandhi 1964: 220)

The essence of Gandhi's elaborations on swadeshi for politics and economics was related to his understanding of the social system with the village panchayat as a unit. He emphasised the autonomy of the village panchayat and recommended organising economic activities around it. He shared his belief that if the centuries-old wisdom of India would have been propagated in vernaculars, India would have made its own mark. On economic activities, he said,

> Much of the deep poverty of the masses is due to the ruinous departure from swadeshi in the economic and industrial life … I think of swadeshi not as a boycott movement undertaken by way of revenge. I conceive it as a religious principle to be followed by all …. The handloom industry is in a dying condition. I took special care during my wanderings last year to see as many weavers as possible, and my heart ached to find how they had lost, how families had retired from this once-flourishing and honourable occupation. If we follow the swadeshi doctrine, it would be your duty and mine to find out neighbours who can supply our wants and to teach them to supply them where they do not know how to, assuming that there are neighbours who are in want of healthy occupation. Then every village of India will almost be a self-supporting and self-contained unit exchanging only such necessary commodities with other villages where they are not locally producible. (ibid.: 222–23)

The speech at Madras was carefully crafted and delivered with force. Gandhi wanted to convey to the Christian missionaries, who were mostly from England and perhaps from Europe, that they should restrict themselves to philanthropic work. The socio-economic and political structures and institutions of India were based on the values stated in the Hindu religion. Going back to the systems of village panchayat, functioning socially under occupation-based associations with commonly agreed upon sets of rules and regulations, decentralised production of goods and services and the consumption of local goods and services were the key features of swadeshi. Moral values were the foundation on which these systems were based. Gandhi communicated the universality of his concept. While commenting on the English system of production, he was basically criticising modernity and its fallout. He wanted the Christian missionaries to understand that by proving their religion superior to the native religions and praising the lifestyle of their people (obviously of the English back home), they also became salespersons for the goods produced in England. Gandhi did not argue about the superiority of the Hindu religion per se, but he explained the holistic approach of life in the Hindu religion and the way of life involving political, economic and social systems.

Gandhi's third notable speech was delivered on 22 December 1916, in front of an impressive gathering at Muir College Economic Society. Besides the English professors teaching economics, there were prominent Indians in the audience too. Pandit Madan Mohan Malaviya presided and introduced Gandhi. Speaking on 'Does Economic Progress Clash With Real Progress?', Gandhi said,

> By economic progress, I take it, we mean material advancement without limit and by real progress we mean moral progress, which again is the same thing as progress of the permanent element in us. The subject may therefore be stated thus: 'Does not moral progress increase in the same proportion as material progress?' (Gandhi 1964: 311–12)

Gandhi had a problem with the logic of the formulation of the thesis of economic progress by economists. He said,

> They say that before we can think or talk of their moral welfare, we must satisfy their daily wants. With these, they say, material progress spells moral progress. And then is taken a sudden jump: what is true of thirty millions is true of the universe. They forget that hard cases make bad law. I need hardly say to you how ludicrously absurd this deduction would be. No one has ever suggested that grinding pauperism can lead to anything else than moral degradation. (ibid.: 312)

For Gandhi, there were two moral issues in economics. One, economic progress should end starvation among the masses in any society, and hence should not be evaluated by the number of millionaires. Second, what had happened to the moral progress of the millionaires? On the second point, he said,

> The only statement that has to be examined is whether it can be laid down as a law of universal application that material advancement means moral progress. Now let us take a few illustrations. Rome suffered a moral fall when it attained high material affluence. So did Egypt and so perhaps most countries of which we have any historic record. The descendants, kinsmen of the royal and divine Krishna, too, fell when they were rolling in riches. We do not deny to the Rockefellers and the Carnegies possession of an ordinary measure of morality but we gladly judge them indulgently. I mean that we do not even expect them to satisfy the highest standard of morality. With them material gain has not necessarily meant moral gain ... I observed almost invariably that the greater the possession of riches, the greater was their moral turpitude. (Gandhi 1964: 312–13)

He went on to qualify,

> This does not put an end to all material ambition. We should still have, as we have always had, in our midst people who make the pursuit of wealth their aim in life .... It is a beautiful thing to know that the wealthiest among us have often felt that to have remained voluntarily poor would have been a higher state for them. That you cannot serve God and Mammon is an economic truth of the highest value .... Western nations today are groaning under the heel of the monster-god of materialism. Their moral growth has become stunted. They measure their progress in £. s. d. American wealth has become the standard. She [*sic*] is the envy of the other nations. (ibid.: 314–15)

Gandhi was not an environmentalist or an ecologist by profession or fashion. In fact, during his times, environmental concerns were hardly brought to attention. And yet he pointed out to the intensive resource use inherent in the Western model of development and civilisation. He quoted extensively from a scientist named Wallace,[4] who had surmised that the decline in ethical stands and morals was a result of material progress. Describing Wallace's view, Gandhi said,

> He [Wallace] then shows how factories have risen on the corpses of men, women and children, how as the country has rapidly advanced in riches,

> it has gone down in morality. He shows this by dealing with insanitation, life-destroying trades, adulteration, bribery and gambling. He shows how, with the advance of wealth, justice has become immoral, deaths from alcoholism and suicide have increased, the average of premature births and congenital defects has increased, and prostitution has become an institution. (Gandhi 1964: 315)

Gandhi wanted economics as a discipline to be deeply influenced by ethics and morals. He strongly believed that economic progress, as understood only as limitless material progress, could hardly lead to moral or real progress. He had insisted upon the moral man dominating the economic man. According to Ajit Dasgupta, it was Gandhi's conviction that'one's behaviour as an economic agent could not be isolated from one's behaviour as an autonomous moral agent' (1996: 13). It was on this basis that he rejected the maxim of rational human behaviour with regard to the satiation of unlimited human wants. For Gandhi, human wants had to have their limits. He knew that beyond a point material goods would no longer satisfy wants. He advocated self-restraint—those who have enough should not be aspiring for more. Economic swaraj to Gandhi meant every individual limiting the demand for material wants through self-regulating behaviour.

To conclude, the person who had left India for South Africa was an honest truth seeker, a staunch believer of non-violence and a God-fearing individual who was trying to help rebuild family fortunes by practising law: M. K. Gandhi, Bar-at-Law. The person who returned to India in January 1915 was a social activist who led a unique *satyagraha*[5] against the British rulers and was a transformed individual through a personal inward spiritual journey with very strict standards. Gandhi had returned with a continued firm commitment to one's self and to the nation that he thought had digressed onto the wrong path and should be brought back on course.

Gandhi practised swaraj or rule over self. According to Gandhi, regulating the self was a necessary condition for achieving 'home-rule', i.e., freedom from British rule. Gandhi suggested satyagraha as a method to force the British to leave the country. A true *satyagrahi* had to practice rule over self as well, which was also what swaraj meant. Gandhi, after his return to India, practised swaraj until his last breath. He created a community large enough to demonstrate and influence people in the country about the importance of the practice of self-rule and satyagraha in letter and spirit, which had an impact so powerful that it led the British to leave the country. After Independence, however, the direction changed. Gandhi had anticipated this in *Hind Swaraj*, and said,

> In effect it means this: that we want English rule without the Englishman. You want the tiger's nature, but not the tiger; that is to say, you would make India English. And when it becomes English, it will be called not Hindustan but *Englistan*. This is not the Swaraj that I want. (Gandhi 1963: 15)

Gandhi envisioned building a non-violent society through constructive programmes and achieving swaraj beginning with *gram swaraj* (village self-rule). The vision conflict began even before Independence. The next section offers a brief review of the differences between Gandhi and Jawaharlal Nehru, followed by a discussion on the course taken by a free India.

II

Gandhi returned to India from South Africa over a century ago. He wanted to take India towards his vision of *Hind Swaraj*. Although he led the struggle for political independence and parliamentary democracy, his ultimate goal was a society made up of hundreds of thousands of village panchayats and a decentralised production system. He wanted political and economic autonomy at the lowest possible unit: the village. Without denying the importance of organising economic and political activities at higher levels, Gandhi believed they had to evolve from the bottom up. He visualised society as an oceanic circle forming a learning community based on mutual respect and equality. He conceived the organisation of society as an oceanic circle, with societal structures as concentric circles, spreading outwards in an ever-widening and non-hierarchical fashion, from the individual at the centre, to family, school, town or city, state, country, continent and, ultimately, the world community. Unfortunately, his political heir Jawaharlal Nehru and his other followers in the freedom struggle did not share his vision of swaraj.

Nehru wanted a parliamentary democracy and socialistic state, modelled along the lines of some Western countries. His idea of India was that of a country which had a powerful state with a strong centre. The militarily powerful and industrially prosperous country of his dream was clearly in conflict with Gandhi's swaraj. Gandhi disapproved of the highly materialistic industrialisation of Western society.[6] It is nearly impossible to establish an industrial society without brute force. Hence, direct manifest violence and structural violence[7] become features of any such society. Gandhi was opposed to such a civilisation. His contemplation of a non-violent society was based on soul force, truth force and love force. Gandhi did not change his ideas even later in life. In a letter dated 5 October 1945, Gandhi wrote to Nehru about his vision and his response:

> The first thing I want to write about is the difference of outlook between us ... I have said that I still stand by the system of Government envisaged in *Hind Swaraj* ... I am convinced that if India is to attain true freedom and through India the world also, then sooner or later the fact must be recognized that people will have to live in villages, not in towns, in huts, not in palaces. Crores of people will never be able to live at peace with each other in towns and palaces. They will then have no recourse but to resort to both violence and untruth .... While I admire modern science, I find that it is the old looked at in the true light of modern science which should be re-clothed and refashioned aright .... My ideal village will contain intelligent human beings. They will not live in dirt and darkness as animals. Men and women will be free and able to hold their own against anyone in the world. There will be neither plague, nor smallpox; no one will be idle, no one will wallow in luxury. Everyone will have to contribute his quota of manual labour .... It is possible to envisage railways, post and telegraph offices etc. For me it is material to obtain the real article and the rest will fit into the picture afterwards. If I let go the real thing, all else goes. (Parel 1997: 150–51)

Let us remember that this was a time when India's destiny was being shaped. One does not know the extent to which Gandhi's ideas were understood by the masses, but he depended on Nehru to carry forward his ideas. Gandhi appealed to Nehru with reason. In the same letter, Gandhi wrote,

> I want our position vis-à-vis each other to be clearly understood by us for two reasons. Firstly, the bond that unites us is not only political work. It is

> immeasurably deeper and quite unbreakable. Therefore it is that I earnestly desire that in the political field also we should understand each other clearly. Secondly, neither of us thinks himself useless. We both live for the cause of India's freedom and we both would gladly die for it ... I want to live to 125 for the service of India but I must admit that I am now an old man. **You are much younger in comparison and I have therefore named you as my heir. I must, however, understand my heir and my heir should understand me.** (Parel 1997: 151; emphasis added)

Nehru responded hurriedly, promising to write or engage in discussion later. But what he wrote, even in a hurry, is sufficient to understand that on the vision of a new social order and ways and means of forming it, he differed with Gandhi in a fundamental sense. Nehru was in agreement with the basic values of truth and non-violence, but not on the content and the method of achieving it. On 9 October 1945, he wrote:

> I do not understand why a village should necessarily embody truth and non-violence. A village, normally speaking, is backward intellectually and culturally and no progress can be made from a backward environment. Narrow-minded people are much more likely to be untruthful and violent .... Then again we have to put down certain objectives like a sufficiency of food, clothing, housing, education, sanitation etc. which should be the minimum requirements for the country for everyone .... Again it seems inevitable that modern means of transport as well as many other modern developments must continue and be developed .... If that is so, inevitably a measure of heavy industry exists. How far will that fit in with a purely village society .... If two types of economy exist in the country there should be either conflict between the two or one will overwhelm the other. (ibid.: 152)

Nehru also categorically brought in the issue of foreign aggression as he wrote:

> The question of independence and protection from foreign aggression both political and economic has to be considered in this context. I do not think it is possible for India to be really independent unless she is a technically advanced country. I am not thinking for the moment in terms of just armies but rather of scientific growth. In the present context of the world we cannot even advance culturally without a strong background of scientific research in every department. (ibid.: 152–53)

Apart from the deeper difference on the method of formation of the society in free India, Nehru clearly admitted that as a treatise on the vision of free India, *Hind Swaraj* had never registered in his mind. He had in fact thought that even Gandhi had grown beyond it and hence a convinced reference to it again in Gandhi's letter dated 5 October 1945 surprised Nehru. In his response Nehru writes:

> It is many years ago since I read *Hind Swaraj* and I have only a vague picture in my mind. But even when I read it some 20 or more years ago it seemed to be completely unreal. In your writings and speeches since then I have found much that seemed to me an advance on that old position and an appreciation of modern trends .... As you know Congress has never considered that picture, much less adopted it .... You are right in saying that the world, or a large part of it, appears to be bent on committing suicide. That may be an inevitable development of an evil seed in civilization that has grown. I think it is so. How to get rid of this evil, and yet how to keep the good in the present as in the past is our problem. Obviously there is good too in the present. (ibid.: 153–54)

It can be clearly seen that Nehru, Gandhi's heir apparent, lacked conviction about the thoughts expressed in *Hind Swaraj*. How convinced important leaders like Sardar Patel and others were on the matter is not clearly known. Patel did not have a socialist orientation. He would have preferred a free enterprise-based economy with strong agriculture.[8] However, at the time when the socio-economic policies of independent India were being formed, hardly any leader swore by *Hind Swaraj*. Nehru in a sense was correct as almost no one in the Congress remembered *Hind Swaraj*. Gandhi firmly believed that unless his vision in *Hind Swaraj* became the vision of Indians and that of entire humanity, real democracy and real progress were not possible.

It appears that Gandhi did not reply to Nehru's letter, but he did write a letter on 13 November 1945 where a reference was made about a meeting between them. Gandhi wrote,

> It is necessary that we understand each other well and that others also should clearly understand where we stand. It would not matter if ultimately we might have to agree to differ so long as we remained one at heart as we are today. The impression I have gathered from our yesterday's

talk is that there is not much difference in our outlook. To test this I put down below the gist of what I have understood. Please correct me if there is any discrepancy.

1. The real question, according to you, is how to bring about man's highest intellectual, economic, political and moral development. I agree entirely.
1. In this there should be an equal right and opportunity for all.
2. In other words, there should be equality between the town-dwellers and the villagers in the standard of food and drink, clothing and other living conditions. In order to achieve this equality people should be able to produce for themselves the necessaries of life, i.e. clothing, foodstuffs, dwellings and lighting and water.
3. Man is not born to live in isolation but is essentially a social animal independent and interdependent. No one can or should ride on another's back. If we try to work out necessary conditions for such a life, we are forced to the conclusion that the unit of society should be a village, or call it a small and manageable group of people who would in the ideal, be self-sufficient (in matter of their vital requirements) as a unit and bound together in bonds of mutual cooperation and inter-dependence. (Nehru 1958: 359)

Gandhi wrote this letter about three years before his assassination.

The majority of leaders, including Nehru, perhaps failed to understand Gandhi's position. Nehru was for collective choices. India adopted a planned social and economic model and perhaps suffered a serious setback because of this. Gandhi would not have allowed this to happen had he lived longer. He would have offered satyagraha and organised constructive work in villages, taking them as a socio-economic unit. Nehru assumed a crucial and powerful role for the state to achieve the welfare of individuals. Gandhi did not and Nehru seems to have missed this completely. It appears that Nehru had little patience to deal with Gandhi's position. He did understand and support his values, though. Going back to the letter of 9 October 1945, he wrote,

> *There is today in the world a tremendous acquisitive tendency both in individuals and groups and nations, which leads to conflicts and wars. Our entire society is based on this more or less. That basis must go and be transformed into one of cooperation, not of isolation which is impossible.* (Parel 1997: 153; emphasis added)

But after this recognition, Nehru was perhaps compelled by circumstances as he read and understood them and embarked on a path that ended in an unequal society and a democracy that mainly serves the manipulators.

Gandhi had understood that an independent Indian government would not follow the *Hind Swaraj* vision of swaraj. He planned a meeting of all constructive workers in Sevagram, Wardha, to discuss the future course of action in the first week of February 1948. A day before he was assassinated, he had finalised the constitution of the Lok Sevak Sangh, which was to be the new *avatara* of the Congress. His assassination, however, created uncertainty. The meeting was eventually held on 11–15 March 1948 with Rajendra Prasad presiding (Gandhi 2007). The Lok Sevaks were to work for swaraj as envisioned by Gandhi.

The deliberations brought out two viewpoints. One group shared Gandhi's vision and was committed to carry forward his work in the manner outlined by him in the constitution of the Lok Sevak Sangh. The second group, representing various organisations, wanted to form an overarching federation and execute constructive programmes.[9] Two towering personalities—Acharya Vinoba Bhave and Jawaharlal Nehru—enjoyed the confidence of most senior Gandhians who had gathered.[10] Both had a significant following, albeit in different quarters. Nehru shared his concerns and ideas vis-à-vis running the government and the role of state in development. He categorically admitted his inability to implement Gandhi's swaraj and provided justifications for this. After intense discussions, the gathering left it to Vinoba Bhave to communicate which direction Nehru should take the nation and how the group would carry forward Gandhi's agenda of swaraj. At this critical juncture, Vinoba Bhave was in favour of Nehru and his policies for development. The gathering, now known as Sarvodaya Samaj, was to provide ground support to Nehru's state-led reconstruction of India.[11] Vinoba Bhave provided the leadership for Sarvodya Samaj. He, on his own initiative, led the 'Bhoodan movement', which drew international attention. His famous formulation was that, contrary to the way in which land was taken through *katla* or killing (the Telangana violent movement against zamindars [feudal landlords] in the early 1950s), by *kaanoon* or law (land reforms were being implemented and zamindari was abolished), he was instead applying *karuna* or compassion to get the land as gift from big landowners, to be distributed to the landless and the poor. There is no doubt it was a unique socio-political movement, but it could not transform into a major programme that would change landownership patterns in the country and bring about an egalitarian distribution of land.[12] By the time the Bhoodan movement was declared over in the late 1960s, India had already marched on to a mixed economy model with a socialist bent, and serious problems in the working of the economy had started becoming visible. The gross domestic product (GDP) could not grow beyond 3.5 to 4 per cent per annum, not enough to alleviate the poverty of a substantial proportion of the population.

Till 1985, India followed the Nehruvian path with some deviations. State-led economic development had a limited impact. Initially, for the first two decades, the slow rate of economic growth was ridiculed as the 'Hindu rate of growth'.[13] The process of liberalisation, privatisation and globalisation began in 1985 and the economy was opened completely in 1991. Since then, business has indeed expanded greatly across the country. In many states, economic growth has been phenomenal. Ravindra H. Dholakia[14] has shown that compared to the growth experience in the 1980s, the 1990s registered significantly higher growth in some states. The continuous compounded average growth rate (CAGR) of the GDP for the Indian economy from 1980–81 to 1991–92 was 5.3 per cent. It rose to 5.9 per cent in the periods 1991–92 and 2003–04. The annual GDP at factor cost at 2004–05 prices registered impressive growths, ranging between 6.8 per cent in 2008–09 and 9.6 per cent in 2007–08 (GoI 2011). The average for the period 2004–10 was around 8 per cent. The mood was generally positive and many economists and trade and business associations were pushing for further reforms. Market-led growth with globalisation improved economic growth significantly, touching a high of 9 per cent per annum. Material prosperity for some boomed. The middle class also swelled.

However, inequality increased and continues to do so, along with social ills and conflicts. Poverty in India has reduced in terms of proportion: from an all-time high of about 60 per cent of the population living below the poverty line in the early 1970s to 25 per cent in rural areas and about 13 per cent in urban areas in recent times. But the absolute numbers read differently with 20 crore (0.2 billion) in rural areas and about 6 crore (60 million) in urban areas still living below the poverty line. With health and education being privatised rapidly, the incidental poverty figures in both rural and urban areas would rise significantly. It does not take time to slip into structural poverty from incidental poverty because indebtedness becomes chronic. Hence, the relevant question in this context is: Has India gained Gandhi's 'swaraj'? The answer is no, mainly because the country did not take the path he suggested. There definitely was an attempt to decentralise political power structures with the constitutional amendments for local self-government, i.e., Panchayati Raj. But the effective devolution of political and economic power could hardly take place.[15] Could we build a liberal socialist democracy in the country as Nehru dreamt? The answer is no here too because liberty in its desired form was not granted by the state to the citizen; the economic model which ultimately unfolded was: 'there were some who were more equal than others', and democracy as a political system is practised top-down and not bottom-up.[16] The following section attempts to explain why we have failed to achieve Gandhi's swaraj and why it remains relevant even today.

III

Ajit Dasgupta begins his analysis of Gandhi's economic thought by saying, 'Gandhi's commitment to the proposition that "ultimately, it is the individual who is the unit" inevitably led him to an individualist, rather than a collectivist [position]' (Dasgupta 1996: 13). Western liberal thought also hailed the individual and individual liberty as supreme. Democracy and free market were the institutions through which individual liberty could be celebrated. Gandhi critiqued the civilisation that emerged in the West based on these principles. He presented an alternative of swaraj that meant both self-rule and rule over self. As mentioned earlier, the world and India after Independence disregarded Gandhi's foundational idea of swaraj. Instead, they chose the market and state and supreme institutions to negotiate liberty for the modern individual. Nehru was the main architect of this rebuilding of India. The previous section discussed how, prior to Independence, Nehru clearly rejected Gandhi's proposition of swaraj. Anthony Giddens, in his commentary, has exposed the limitations of both 'Right' and 'Left' philosophies. He discusses a 'Third Way' as a possible alternative and argues that some countries were already moving in that direction. At one end, it is conservatism which ideologically places a strong emphasis on 'the individual'. The facilitating agency is the free market, which will get the best out of individuals and is therefore the best for society. On the other end are communism and socialism that place 'a firm emphasis upon the role of the state in generating both solidarity and equality' (Giddens 2005: 34).

The debacle of the Marxist or socialist system has been very prominent. Marxian philosophy was based on the premise that the communist system had the capacity to form a social system that would create more wealth and distribute it more equitably. After World War II, the socialism bug bit most countries. In the West, socialism was adapted into moderate, parliamentary socialism. The welfare state, although a creation of both capitalist and communist thinkers, came to be owned ultimately by the socialists. Free market thinkers were relegated to the background soon after World War II, and most economies accepted the welfare state. After 1970, both communist and socialist systems started to fail. According to Giddens, 'Socialism also failed to grasp the significance of markets as informational devices, providing essential data for buyers and sellers. These inadequacies only became fully revealed with intensifying processes of globalisation and technological change from the early 1970s onwards' (ibid.: 5). By this time, another important problem had surfaced, and it was ecological. The communist and socialist systems, however, did not address the ecological question at all. Capitalistic societies with a welfare state also witnessed problems. Market failure was accepted in the case of public goods. The unemployment problem was to be solved with social security. It was expected that as the economies expanded and production boomed, the state would become more equipped to provide welfare. This does not happen consistently, though. Welfare states are sensitive to ecological concerns, but find it difficult to tackle them effectively. The state's presence becomes too prominent with weak delivery. Thus, the thesis of neoliberalism was born.

Let us now understand clearly that the dominant role of the state is questioned under both systems. The state, under both systems, has failed. Communism and socialism in their pristine form appear to have vanished forever, at least in the democratic societies.[17] Capitalistic systems with welfare states are trying to cope with the new situation with two different theses. The one that appears to be more popular is the neoliberal thesis, where the role of the government is minimal. The other is where the government is different. This is what Giddens calls the 'Third Way' and according to him, it holds better promise. Let us first review the neoliberal thesis.

The neoliberal thesis has a pathological aversion to the state. It also follows from the classical liberal thesis that believed in the superiority of the market over all other agencies for economic transactions. The rational economic individual is the kingpin in the system. Thus, much of the government's role is assumed by civil society. This means that some assumption is made about the individual and civil society. The values that were put forward and accepted during the economic transformation of Europe in the early stages of the Industrial Revolution were Protestant values. It was believed that honest and hardworking individuals trying to maximise their individual and family welfare would form a harmonious and prosperous society. And, obviously, the free market was the best agency to provide an equal opportunity to all to simultaneously determine individual and social welfare. A neoliberal thesis also assumes similar civil society features under changed circumstances in the present. Giddens has quoted David Green, who has listed some features thus, 'The virtue of civil society, if left to its own devices, are said to include "Good character, honesty, duty, self-sacrifice, honour, service, self-discipline, toleration, respect, justice, civility, fortitude, courage, integrity, diligence, patriotism, consideration for others, thrift and reverence"' (Giddens 2005: 12). Clearly it is the individual who, with such virtues, creates the civil society. Gandhi would have been very happy to read the list because it includes more virtues than he had prescribed for the ashram inmates under Ekadash Vrat or eleven vows.[18]

But neoliberalism is in trouble. Giddens draws attention to the paradox in neoliberal thesis. Traditionally, market fundamentalism has been most favoured by conservatism, which always meant a cautious and pragmatic approach to social and economic change. The continuity of this tradition is central to the idea of conservatism. Tradition contains the accumulated wisdom of the past, and therefore supplies a guide to the future. Free market philosophy under the neoliberal thesis is pinning its hopes for the future on unending economic growth produced by the liberation of market forces. Devotion to the free market on the one hand and to the traditional family and nation on the other is self-contradictory.

Individualism and choice are supposed to stop abruptly at the boundaries of the family and national identity, where tradition must stand intact. Although it might appear to be a remote connection, the repeated failures of negotiation meetings at the World Trade Organization (WTO) are indicative of this conflict between unfettered freedom, market fundamentalism and conservatism. The dynamism of market forces undermines traditional structures of authority and fractures local communities. Neoliberalism creates new risks and uncertainties, which it asks citizens to simply ignore.

Thus, under the neoliberal thesis it is the individual who has undergone a metamorphosis. The 'rational economic man' appearing in traditional economic theories has not always been so in practice. The basic value accepted is maximisation. Maximisation is a game of 'no limit' which gives rise to greed. It sacrifices rationality. Professor Stanislav Menshikov, co-chairman of the Russian section of the Economists Allied for Arms Reduction (ECAAR) says, 'All economies that are based on these principles (maximisation of utility and profits) tend to create and promote unequal conditions for the people'.[19] The other argument of the market fundamentalist, according to Menshikov, is that it is the natural order of things because it proceeds from human nature in which greed and the need to maximise material benefits prevail. If God has created human beings that way, how can one change? The evidence does not support this claim either. It appears that individual behaviour holds the key for the social order, rather than the other way round. Let us examine whether the 'Third Way' really shows the way for sustainable societies and what kind of individual appears in that scheme and how liberated and individualistic they are.

To begin with, the 'Third Way', or 'neo-socialism' as I would like to call it, accepts the failure of old-style social democracy with Keynesian policies. The assumptions the old system made were: a traditional family form where husbands worked and wives looked after the children and elders, a homogenous labour market, mass production in basic sectors, an elitist and patronising state, and largely domestic economies. These assumptions no longer hold true. Neo-socialism responds in two ways. One, it argues for compassion towards the weak. This has been there from the beginning and arises out of the reality that the market is unable to take care of those who do not fall in its sphere. Second, and as a consequence of the first, one cannot argue for minimum government, but one will have to have a government that works. As Giddens, chief promoter of the 'Third Way', argues, 'The restructuring of the government should follow the ecological principle of "getting more from less", understood not as downsizing, but as improving delivered value' (Giddens 2005: 74). 'Third Way' politics assumes that the basic changes, which are exogenous, are: globalisation, transformation in personal life and our relationship with nature. An examination of transformation in personal life would lead us to inspect carefully the emerging individual and their values.

New individualism is being explained variously. There appears to be a rise in the 'me' generation, which is proceeding fast towards a 'me first' generation. If personal liberty gains paramount importance, the problems between liberty and equality will have to be tackled *de novo*. A 'me first' society would harm the social solidarity which both the neoliberal and the neo-socialist have to achieve. The causes attributed to this 'me first' individualism are different. Neoliberals blame it on the new permissiveness of the 1960s and neo-socialists would blame it on the rise of market fundamentalism. However, we lack sufficient evidence to substantiate any of the reasons. The new individualism rejects traditions and traditional values. Neither the family nor the individual is the unit. This might not necessarily mean total moral decay, however. New postmodern values are prominently appearing in which the individual is keen to see basic human rights, ecological values and sexual freedom established. It is worth recalling here that despite deep concerns, the ecological problem cannot be addressed in either the market fundamental environment or in the communist or social democratic welfare state environment. Overall, the situation is complex indeed. Individualism with 'me first' characteristics and new moral concerns can turn in any direction. Neither the neoliberal nor the 'Third Way' seems sure about the future. Both systems fail to ask some fundamental questions that matter for societies to be sustainable. The issue of sustainability is raised only in the context of environment and ecology, and there too the debate does not take a clear stand: an environmental disaster, doomsday scenario, is not yet so near, but not so far either that it will never happen. Ecological issues are far more complex than what economists are trying to grapple with.

What, then, is the way out? Gandhi's core ideas of swadeshi, village republics, small businesses, self-employment, dignity of labour, and trusteeship of wealth are all dubbed as anachronistic in today's digital world (Jagannath 2016). Best-selling historian Yuval Noah Harari has this to say about Gandhi and his vision.

> Mahatma Gandhi's reading of the Vedas caused him to envision independent India as a collection of self-sufficient agrarian communities, each spinning its own Khadi cloths, exporting little and importing even less. The most famous photograph of him shows him spinning cotton with his own hands, and he made the humble spinning wheel the symbol of the Indian nationalist movement. Yet this Arcadian vision was simply incompatible with the realities of modern economics, and hence not much has remained of it save for Gandhi's radiant image on billions of rupee notes. (Harari 2018: 132)

It has been conveniently forgotten that it is Gandhi's core ideas that build a moral force in society. Although they do not exhibit this explicitly, neither technology, including artificial intelligence and machine learning, nor systems based on them are and would be value-neutral. When we see interest in Gandhi rekindled, it is a clear admission of gross neglect of the 'autonomous moral agent' and celebration of the 'economic agent' focussed mostly on body and material growth, which has deeply disturbed harmony with the self, among selves and with nature. This might appear rather naive and therefore unacceptable, but Gandhi had understood and explained this culprit. Focus on body alone makes an individual acquisitive and greedy. Such individuals in collectives would like to acquire control over nature in their own settlements and countries, as well as in other countries. The process of gaining economic power and control backed by political machinations has been explained by Takis Fotopoulos (1996). He examines the various approaches employed by economists and environmentalists to resolve economic and ecological crises. He does not see much hope in the Brundtland Commission Report on sustainable development or in the concept of deep ecology which blames anthropocentricity for ecological problems. He says that both the Left and the Right make similar assumptions. Specifically, 'the proposals made by both ends of the political spectrum, despite appearances, do not differ significantly between them, as both the Right and the Left take for granted the existing institutional framework of the market economy and liberal democracy' (ibid.: 173).

Fotopoulos criticises both solutions and comes up with a proposition which is unclear and does not touch the individual or their preferences. His recommendation for a way out is expressed thus:

> So, what is needed to open the way for new forms of social organization is the development of a similar mass consciousness about the failure of 'actually existing capitalism' to the one that led to the collapse of 'actually existing socialism'. Today, there is a pressing need to transcend both the neoliberal market economy and socialist statism in order to put an end to economic misery, which oppresses the majority of the world's population, and to arrest the ecological destruction which threatens us all. (ibid.: 181)

I have shown in sufficient detail that our views have to change and move closer to the Gandhian perspective. With the individual at the centre, rule of self or swaraj may hold the key for the human being of the future. Of the eleven vows, truth, non-violence, chastity (controlling the senses), non-stealing and non-acquisitive or non-possession are the most important. Fearlessness and control over the palate are two auxiliary vows essential to practising truth and non-violence. Swadeshi and bread labour would facilitate the formation of a non-violent polity and economy. In this sense, swadeshi and swaraj are *dharma*. For Gandhi, practising dharma as a sense of duty towards self and society is religion.

> Gandhi focussed on the individual and his responsibility to the self (*vyakti*), fellow humans (*samashti*) and nature (*srushti*). To put it in nuanced Indian culture, the order for Gandhi was *vyakti, samashti and srushti*. Both individual and societal efforts have to be mended and mentored in a way where vyakti's interface with samashti is harmonious; every vyakti is an essential part of the processes in samashti. However, a vyakti's mindset in interacting with *prakruti* or nature has to be as described in the following verse from the *Ishavasya Upanishad*: '*Ishavasyam idam sarvam Yatkinchit Jagatyam Jagat; Ten tyaktena bhunjitha maa grudha kasyas wid dhanam*' ('Whatever there is changeful in this ephemeral world, all that must be enveloped by the Lord. By this renunciation [of the World], support yourself. Do not covet the wealth of anyone').

With advancements in science and technology as well as human achievements, nature has to be treated with respect and humanity must not cancel tomorrow. Although individual freedom is the ultimate goal, humanity needs to move ahead in the Gandhian way of education for freedom. Gandhi himself was a learner till the last day of his life. His kind of education, which would inform/influence the preferences and choices of individuals, was not confined to Indians, but extended to world citizens too. The resultant position would not be of pursuing limitless wants. Interestingly, very recently a traditional economist, Pulin Nayak, has suggested that Gandhi's proposition of limiting wants will have to be adhered to if we need sustainability solutions (Nayak 2020). It is imperative that the desire to acquire more and more go down so that the era of equality of rights and opportunities can then be established and the relationship between humans and nature alters, averting the ecological crisis.

Much of humanity across the globe has embarked on the path of acquiring limitless material prosperity and is mired in a serious environmental and ecological crisis. The uncontrolled desire to acquire material prosperity has multiplied violent conflicts that are destroying peace. The world is tired, employing all techniques of war known to man to gain peace. Gandhi returns with his swaraj.

NOTES

1. A *mumukshu* is a seeker of spiritual knowledge for the liberation of the soul from the cycle of life and death.
2. Of the Kathiawar Peninsula in south-western Gujarat. Also known as Saurashtra Peninsula.
3. On the contrary, as Parel (1997) notes,'even Gokhale thought that Gandhi had written (*Hind Swaraj*) in haste and that, upon reflection, he would revise the book's philosophy' (p. lviii).
4. Most likely Gandhi was referring to Alfred Russel Wallace (8 January 1823–7 November 1913), a noted British naturalist, explorer, geographer, anthropologist and biologist. He was co-discoverer of the theory of natural selection along with Charles Darwin. He was a social activist who considered the social and economic system of the nineteenth century as unjust.
5. Truth force, and a form of non-violent action.
6. Most of the discussions that follow are taken copiously from my article 'Inclusive Democracy: A Gandhian Perspective' (Iyengar 2013).

7. The concept of structural violence was first given by Johan Galtung, a peace researcher and well-known peace activist.

8. There is some reference to his thoughts on the economics of the country in his biography. See Gandhi (1991).

9. The main organisations were Charkha Sangh (Spinning Union), Gramodyog Sangh (Cottage Industry Union), Talimi Sangh (Educational Trust), Goseva Sangh (Cow Protection Union), Harijan Sevak Sangh (Union for Harijan Welfare), Hindustani Prachar Sabha, Hindustan Mazdur Sevak Sangh (Indian Labourers' Union), Adivasi Seva Mandal, and Kasturba Trust.

10. According to the list provided in *Gandhi is Gone* (Gandhi 2007), 46 persons participated in the March 1948 meeting in Sevagram, Wardha. Among them were Jawaharlal Nehru, Rajendra Prasad, Maulana Abul Kalam Azad, Zakir Hussian, Vinoba Bhave, Kakasaheb Kalelkar, Acharya Kripalani, J. C. Kumarappa and K. G. Mashruwala. It should be mentioned that Sardar Vallabhbhai Patel could not attend the meeting as he was not well, leaving many to wonder whether his presence could have altered the outcome.

11. Vinoba's decision removed the political struggle or satyagraha for swaraj from the Sarvodaya movement (Iyengar 2014).

12. There is substantial literature on the Bhoodan movement. For a summary understanding, see Iyengar (2007).

13. In the first six Five-Year Plans, the Indian economy only grew at about 3 to 3.5 per cent per annum. The phrase 'Hindu rate of growth' was coined by Professor Raj Krishna, member of the Planning Commission in 1978.

14. See Ravindra H. Dholakia's keynote address, 'Regional Sources of Growth Acceleration in India', to the International Regional Science Symposium and 40th Annual Regional Science Conference held in January 2009 at Nirma University, Ahmedabad.

15. For a detailed review of democratic decentralisation and Panchayati Raj institutions in India, see Nadkarni, et al. (2018).

16. Those interested in reading the debate, see Iyengar (2013).

17. Communist China has emerged as a variant communist model with the state reigning supreme within the nation and allowing market forces to play out in the open with respect to international economic systems. China's highly manipulative policies in politics, the economy, and science and technology are emerging threats to the global solidarity of human society.

18. Ekadash Vrat or eleven vows were suggested by Gandhi for all those individuals who are to practice the rule of self swaraj, particularly the ashram inmates in Sabarmati in the early 1930s. The collection of letters in which he explained each of the vows was compiled from *From Yeravda Mandir* (Gandhi 1932).

19. See Stanislav Menshikov's talk, 'Compassionate Economy Has a Future', at the 14th Padmapani Lecture on Compassionate Economy organised by Tibet House, New Delhi. For details, see https://www.louwrienwijers.nl/2002_compassionateeconomy.html (last accessed 29 November 2024).

References

Dasgupta, A. K. 1996. *Gandhi's Economic Thought*. London, New York: Routledge.

Fotopoulos, T. 1996. *Towards an Inclusive Democracy: The Crisis of the Growth Economy and the Need for a New Liberatory Project*. London, New York: Cassell.

Gandhi, G, ed. 2007. *Gandhi is Gone. Who Will Guide Us Now?* Ranikhet: Permanent Black.

——. ed. 2008. *Gandhi: Essential Writings*. New Delhi: Oxford University Press.

Gandhi, M. K. 1932. *From Yeravda Mandir: Ashram Observances*. Translated from Gujarati by Valji Govindji Desai. Ahmedabad: Navajivan Publishing House.

——. 1963. *The Collected Works of Mahatma Gandhi*. Vol. 10. New Delhi: Publications Division, Ministry of Information and Broadcasting, Government of India.

——. 1964. *The Collected Works of Mahatma Gandhi*. Vol. 13. New Delhi: Publications Division, Ministry of Information and Broadcasting, Government of India.

——. 1970. 'Autobiography'. In *The Collected Works of Mahatma Gandhi*. Vol. 39. New Delhi: Publications Division, Ministry of Information and Broadcasting, Government of India.

Gandhi, R. 1991. *Patel: A Life*. Ahmedabad: Navajivan Publishing House.

Giddens, A. 2005. *The Third Way: The Renewal of Social Democracy*. Cambridge: Polity Press.

Government of India (GoI). 2011. *Economic Survey 2010–11*. New Delhi: Ministry of Finance, Government of India, and Oxford University Press.

Harari, Y. N. 2018. *21 Lessons for the 21st Century*. London: Jonathan Cape.

Iyengar, S. 2007. '*Bhoodan* Movement as a Gandhian Approach to Resource Distribution and Development'. *Gandhi Marg* 28 (4): 402–21.

——. 2013. 'Inclusive Democracy: A Gandhian Perspective'. *Yojana* 57 (August): 53–60.

——. 2014. 'What Ails Gandhian Institutions?' *Seminar* 662 (October). Available at https://www.india-seminar.com/2014/662/662_sudarshan_iyengar.htm (last accessed 3 June 2025).

Jagannath, R. 2016. 'Gandhi and his Economics'. *Swarajya*, 22 October. Available at https://swarajyamag.com/magazine/gandhi-and-his-economics-2 (last accessed 3 June 2025).

Nadkarni, M. V., N. Sivanna, and L. Suresh. 2018. *Decentralised Democracy in India: Gandhi's Vision and Reality*. Oxon: Routledge.

Nayak, P. B. 2020. 'Present Crisis of Capitalism and its Reforms'. *Economic and Political Weekly* 55 (17): 42–48.

Nehru, J. 1958. *A Bunch of Old Letters*. Bombay: Asia Publishing House.

Parel, A. J. ed. 1997. *Hind Swaraj and Other Writings*. New Delhi: Cambridge University Press.

Four

Hind Swaraj
Metaphors of Political Community

Dhananjay Rai

Hind Swaraj goes beyond the definitional purpose of *swaraj* (self-rule). It is an outline of the political community, presented in the form of 20 metaphors. In other words, *Hind Swaraj* is an embodiment of 20 metaphors of the political community, which needs to be understood in the context of Gandhi's comprehensive engagement with components of the political community. However, the construal of *Hind Swaraj* as a text of the political community calls for certain methodological requirements, i.e., reading Gandhi's three texts (*Hind Swaraj* [1910], *Satyagraha in South Africa* [1928] and *An Autobiography or the Story of My Experiments with Truth* [1927/29]) in a delinked manner while reversing the evolution of arguments. It is then that *Hind Swaraj* can be construed as the arrival of the political community.

Anatomy of Gandhian Scholarship

The political community is the assertion of an 'ontological reminder' and the negation of 'ontological indifference'.[1] The ontological reminders consist of associational norms. The associational norm functions by way of two interrelated axioms, i.e., 'Why to associate?' and 'How to associate?'. In 'Why to associate?', people's eagerness to live collectively and interdependently becomes crucial in the political community. 'How to associate?' takes the first question further, i.e., the inviolability of interdependence. This inviolability cannot be left as a voluntary activity. Ontological indifference is the importance given to governing norms over the associational norms of a political community. The political community is a living entity wherein 'ontological reminder' exists as a perennial pursuit. The construal of swaraj as a political community overcomes two features of liberal political theory: conservative adjustment (political equality) and welfare adjustment (people as receivers).

Does Gandhi offer any signposts to the political community? As discussed in the introduction to this volume, swaraj must be construed as political community in Gandhi's thought. The arrival of this political community is a complex and necessary process that needs attention at two levels. First, reading his three texts (*Hind Swaraj, Satyagraha in South Africa* and *An Autobiography*) in a non-inchoate manner is crucial to a full understanding of the political community. Second, reordering the texts becomes a critical methodological concern. Before reading the three texts, though, the rich tradition of Gandhian scholarship/studies must be revisited. I highlight below some significant epistemological interventions in this context. These are not exhaustive but offer crucial markers of Gandhian scholarship.

1. The 'Gandhi–Ambedkar' debate, an important contribution that could be broadly divided into essentialisation (Ambedkar 2014; Rao 2009), de-essentialisation (Rodrigues 2011) and synthesis debates (Nagaraj 2010; Palshikar 1996).
2. The science debate, divided into either absolute opposition to science (Sahasrabudhe 2006) or no opposition to science (Guha 1995; Vishwanath 1997).
3. The modernity and postmodernity debates that zero in on the modernisation of tradition, making for a more active and practical world. A postmodern Gandhi promises a newer world (Rudolph and Rudolph 1967, 2006) and recovers the core of Hinduism and humanism of Western thought (Dallmayr 2017).
4. The 'anti-modern', salvaging India from the modernity and de-*Brahmanisation* discussion in Gandhi (Nandy 1980; Raghuramaraju 2012), where synergism becomes important with regard to the deprived and vulnerable sections of society.
5. The 'thinking beyond liberalism' debate, crucial in Gandhi. He was the first non-Westerner to develop political theory in the indigenous philosophical vocabulary (Parekh 1989). His was a swarajist struggle for political freedom from the amoral state. *Satyagraha* (truth force) is a transformation from private to public (Pantham 1995).
6. Gandhi, an actor in the struggle for independence (Chandra 2008), is also linked with women's empowerment. Breaking the domesticated ambience of women was one of Gandhi's rare achievements (Kishwar 1985: 1753–58; Basham 1971: 19–42). Unfortunately, conformism

was adopted in place of women's empowerment, and a critical evaluation of conformism is required (Patel 1988: 377–87).

7. The crucial 'exemplary model' debate in Gandhi: it is not 'what is good for me, would be good for others' but rather what is good for me must become an example (Bilgrami 2003).
8. The uniqueness of Gandhi's complete understanding and unity debate, i.e., the *purushartha* debate. Purushartha (the aims of life) is the establishment of the perfect relationship amongst four components: *kama* (love), *artha* (wealth), *dharma* (morality) and *moksha* (liberation from the cycle of reincarnation) (Parel 2007).
9. The transformation of Gandhi into the Mahatma in the subaltern discourse (Amin 1995).
10. Gandhi as a factor in the passive revolution of the bourgeoise (Chatterjee 1986).
11. Gandhi's Indian ideology, which is almost representative of Hindu rashtra or the Hindu state (Anderson 2012), countered by the synergetic notion of collective welfare (important in Gandhi) in which interaction between the 'least off' and 'well off' does take place for the negation of prosperity (Iyer 1988). It has been argued that Gandhi remains unparalleled in undermining untouchability in Hinduism (Nanda 1998).
12. The neo-Gandhian approach that emphasises philosophy more than the everyday practice of Gandhian rituals (Paranjape 1993).
13. The ecology movement and eco-feminism, which make Gandhi an important vantage point in environmental studies (Gadgil and Guha 1993; Mies and Shiva 2010).
14. The 'autobiographical approach' which derives the meaning of thought and action from Gandhi (Fischer 1950; Keer 1973).
15. Peace and conflict studies, which give immense importance to satyagraha as a technique of conflict resolution (Bondurant 1965; Galtung 1992; Naess 1965; Sharp 1960).

Gandhi and Political Community

The aforesaid studies are crucial and invaluable advancements in Gandhian studies. Two important concerns need substantial attention. First, there is an absence of the political community in these studies (epistemological problem). Second, there is an inchoate reading of Gandhi's three texts (methodological problem). In other words, the arrival of the political community (epistemological) in Gandhi is a complex and necessary process that needs attention, methodologically, at two levels: (i) reading his three texts in a de-linked manner is crucial for a full understanding of the political community; (ii) reordering the texts becomes a crucial methodological concern. Reversing the order of Gandhi's *Hind Swaraj, Satyagraha in South Africa* and *An Autobiography* generates an effective method to understand the political community. *An Autobiography* narrates the human condition, *Satyagraha in South Africa* outlines the transformation of the human condition and *Hind Swaraj* outlines the foundational principles of the political community.

For Eric Erikson, *An Autobiography*[2] is 'early and painfully conscious of a special mission' (Erikson 1970: 100). Gandhi explains the human condition from his subjectivity, formed through moral aphorism in three consecutive stages: (i) the formation of subjectivity; (ii) the assertion of subjectivity; and (iii) the narration of the human condition. Formation, assertion and narration work in tandem. Moreover, moral aphorism includes both moral (personal and normative) and ethical (social setting or standard of good and bad) dimensions. In the realm of subjectivity, it is important to distinguish between the self and the soul. Gandhi may offer his narration as *atmakatha* or a story of the soul in some interpretations. The soul becomes essential for understanding. Atmakatha, as the story of the soul should be construed authentically in place of *An Autobiography*. However, *An Autobiography* as a narration of the self needs to be accepted due to Gandhi's approval of the translation from Gujarati to English. It means *An Autobiography* as a site of the self is important. Moreover, there can be formation and subjectivity of the self, but not of the 'soul'. Swaraj embodies rule of the self, not rule of the soul. The self is the core of Gandhi's formation of subjectivity through moral aphorism. The self is materialist, whereas the soul is a metaphysical entity. The self is formation, while the soul is eternal. The self is worldly and, in contrast, the soul has no birth or death. The self is a better category to quantify action and qualitative assertion, and is formed through the process of thinking and imitating.

Satyagraha in South Africa[3] outlines the ways in which the human condition transforms through satyagraha. Here, satyagraha is truth force/adherence to truth. The term 'passive resistance' is rejected since it embodies 'non-violence' as a weapon of the weak. Gandhi's satyagraha is a weapon of the strong *sans* violence under any circumstance whatsoever, along with an insistence on the truth. In most analyses, 'satyagraha' is regarded as a 'conflict-solving mechanism'. Conversely, I argue that Gandhi's satyagraha is the *transformation of the human condition*; it facilitates the construction of the technique that leads to transcendence. There are two tensions in satyagraha theorisation in the social sciences. First, satyagraha is not used as an 'organic' link between the human condition and political community. It has merely been used as a technique for conflict resolution. Second, this defeats the purpose of Gandhi's satyagraha, which he envisaged as the transformation of the self towards the political community. Gandhi's method is linked with the political community. However, in social science literature, Gandhi's satyagraha is used to locate the 'self' exclusively in the present political community. This defeats the purpose of Gandhi's technique. In the theorisation of satyagraha, this is called 'resistance'. It is transcendence.

At the outset, Gandhi's moralism appears to be conservatism. However, with the onset of satyagraha, or as it proceeds, transcendence begins. This changes subjectivity radically by 'revolutionising everydayness', 'rights-bearing collectives formed or based on rights' and 'transcendence'. Once the process of satyagraha starts, its progress cannot be controlled. Therefore, subjectivity withers away. There are two types of subjectivity: primitive subjectivity (rooted in socio-economic structures and backed by a long continuity) and autonomous subjectivity (self-determining will which is conscious of constraints and transcendences). In fact, it is 'the self-determining will that distinguishes the former from the latter'.[4] The primitive subjectivity starts shrinking, while the autonomous subjectivity starts expanding. The primitive subjectivity is closed, and the autonomous subjectivity is cosmopolitan.

Gandhi's subjectivity is unique. He was able to diminish his primitive subjectivity in order to strengthen autonomous subjectivity. This happened because of his direct participation in satyagraha. This, however, was not the case with Gandhi's followers or his inner circle. The latter was entrusted with various tasks like land distribution, opening ashrams in tribal areas and working for the upliftment of women and Dalits. Instead of invoking satyagraha, members of Gandhi's coterie invoked traditional Hindu sensibility. This greatly hurt the spread of Gandhi and his satyagraha and also diminished Gandhi's influence significantly in areas where transformation was needed.[5]

Hind Swaraj lays down the foundational principle of political community in the form of metaphors. Soon after its publication and arrival in 1910 in India, it was confiscated and banned by the British. The hermeneutics of confiscation offer an interesting summation. Neither *Satyagraha in South Africa* nor *An Autobiography*, which were produced inside the 'Empire', were ever confiscated. *Hind Swaraj*, the only book translated by Gandhi into English and produced outside the British Empire of India, was confiscated (the ban was lifted on 21 December 1938). The British thought the book would provoke an inexperienced mind to subvert British supremacy.[6] The use of the term 'supremacy' is distinct, and replaced the epithet 'British rule'. Rule signifies territorial control and is ephemeral, while supremacy is permanent. The confiscation is a moment when metaphors of the political community, seemingly challenging, are dismissed, and becomes the significant counter.

The moment of confiscation is also the culmination of the political community. By this time, Gandhi had narrated the human condition and invented satyagraha, both precursors to the political community (and written about decades later). In the text, the reader is an alter ego of the editor, from where the advancement of the latter takes place. Rejection by the editor is advancement; rejection by the reader is introspection. Metaphors of the political community are surrounded by both 'introspection and advancement'. Introspection rejects while advancement envisages. This thesis constitutes an important signature in the entire text. This political community is swaraj, arrived at after the discussion on subjectivity and satyagraha; it is formed through introspection–advancement. The complex structure is 'subjectivity–satyagraha–swaraj'.

'Metaphorical reading' has invited comprehensive academic attention. Gandhi's writings are filled with metaphors and used for comprehensive understanding. Against this backdrop, it is important to determine how Gandhi connected, through linguistic intimacy, with the past and the metaphors that have been made available to future generations by Gandhian studies.[7] The significance/non-significance of metaphors has been heavily debated. A metaphor '... raises deep epistemological and ontological issues' (Johnson 1981: 4). The modern notion of metaphor rejects the Aristotelian insistence on words rather than sentences and the distinction between figurative versus literal (ibid.: 5–6). Hobbesian and Lockean paradigms do dismiss the metaphor squarely. For Hobbes, metaphors are like *ignes fatui*.

> [T]he light of human minds is perspicuous words, but by exact definitions first snuffed, and purged from ambiguity; *reason* is the *pace*; increase of *science*, the *way*; and the benefit of mankind, the *end*. And on the contrary, metaphors, and senseless and ambiguous words, are like *ignes fatui*; and reasoning upon them, is wandering amongst innumerable absurdities. (Hobbes 1998: 32)

In the explanatory notes of *Leviathan*, *ignes fotui* entails useless fires (ibid.: 481). It has also been interpreted as 'stupid fires' or, more specifically in this context, 'as a metaphor for false enlightenment or illusion' (Newey 2014: 312). According to John Locke, 'figurative speech [is] also an abuse of language' (1997: 452).[8]

Donald Davidson revives the fierce criticism of the use of a metaphor beyond the literal meaning of the word. For him, 'metaphors mean what the words, in their most literal interpretation, mean, and nothing more'. '[A] metaphor doesn't say anything beyond its literal meaning (nor does its maker say anything, in using the metaphor, beyond the literal)' (1978: 32). Extended meanings cannot go beyond the original meanings of words (ibid.: 34). Davidson denies 'that metaphor does its work by having a special meaning, a specific cognitive content' (ibid.: 46). Therefore, the search for hidden meaning is not possible, given its absence (ibid.: 47).

The debate in defence of metaphors is furthered by, *inter alia*, Paul Ricoeur (1978, 2003), Mark Johnson (1981), and George Lakoff and Mark Johnson (2003). Ricoeur comprehends 'the metaphorical process as cognition, imagination, and feeling' (1978: 143–59). Therefore, he shifts, unlike Aristotle, from word to sentence: 'The bearer of the metaphorical meaning is no longer the word but the sentence as a whole' (ibid.: 145). The metaphor is the solution to the enigma. Metaphors force us to discern uncertain terrain between verbal and non-verbal (ibid.: 46–51). Feeling and imagination are important components of the metaphorical process. For Ricoeur, '[f]eeling is not contrary to thought' (ibid.: 156). With regard to 'the rule of metaphor', he is categorical that '[a]s figure, metaphor constitutes a displacement and an extension of the meaning of words; its explanation is grounded in a theory of substitution'. It is crucial to discern that language, by way of metaphors, envisages a new human world (Ricoeur 2003: 1). 'Ricoeur invests metaphors with meaning; Davidson denies that they mean anything besides what they mean literally. Each answer has as much to do with a conception of meaning and the theory of meaning as with an attitude toward metaphor' (Cohen 1978: 6).

Johnson (1981) and Lakoff and Johnson (2003) do mark a series of theorisations in defence of metaphors. Johnson rejects the 'literal truth paradigm', as espoused by Hobbes–Locke and the positivist tradition. There are three features of the 'literal truth paradigm':

> (1) The human conceptual system is essentially literal—literal language ('words proper') is the *only* adequate vehicle for (a) expressing one's meaning precisely, and (b) making truth claims, which together make possible correct reasoning by the philosopher. (2) Metaphor is a deviant use of words other than their proper senses, which accounts for its tendency to confuse and to deceive. (3) The meaning and truth claims of a metaphor (if there are any) are just those of its literal paraphrase. (Johnson 1981: 12)

According to Johnson, positivist criticism is based on the division between the cognitive and emotive function of language, and reduces scientific knowledge to literal and verifiable sentences. Metaphors depart from the cognitive function of knowledge (ibid.: 17). It is important to have extra-sentential and extra-linguistic knowledge to understand metaphors.

> We apprehend an utterance as metaphorical, not because of its literal falsity (though that may be a clue), but, more generally, because of a tension between the literal reading and its context (of which literal falsity is one instance). If there was not some tension, some 'contradiction', some 'clash', there would be nothing to suggest the metaphorical reading. (ibid.: 23)

Lakoff and Johnson's *Metaphors We Live By* was first published in 1980 and then in 2003 with an afterword. Consciously and unconsciously, metaphorical thought is very much a part of our mental life (2003: 244). Inference constitutes the centrality of metaphor. 'Conceptual metaphor allows inferences in sensory-motor domains (e.g., domains of space and objects) to be used to draw inferences about other domains (e.g., domains of subjective judgment, with concepts like intimacy, emotions, justice, and so on)' (ibid.). Lakoff and Johnson point out four 'persistent fallacies', i.e., false views of metaphors: 'metaphor (and its centrality) is to be located in concepts, not words'; 'by and large metaphors do not base on similarity but the cross-domain correlation of experiences'; 'the crucial concepts (time, events, causation, morality, and mind) are understood and reasoned by way of multiple metaphors'; 'metaphors are shaped by common nature of our bodies and shared ways of functioning in everyday world' (ibid.: 244–45). That metaphors are *only* linguistic expressions and devoid of conceptualisation and reasoning is fallacious (ibid.: 245). 'The nature of metaphor also is not a matter of definition; it is a question of the nature of cognition' (ibid.: 246).

They answer in the affirmative to the question: '*Do we systematically use inference patterns from one conceptual domain to reason about another conceptual domain?*' (ibid.). They reject the position that metaphorical mappings are *purely* abstract and arbitrary. In response to the question: '*Is all ordinary, conventionalized, everyday language literal, or can common everyday linguistic expressions be metaphorical?*', they say, '[a] great deal of everyday, conventional language is metaphorical, and the metaphorical meanings are given by conceptual metaphorical mappings that ultimately arise from correlations in our embodied experience'. 'In short, metaphor is a natural phenomenon' (ibid.: 247).

In the afterword to *Metaphors We Live By* (2003), Lakoff and Johnson correct their earlier position regarding the division of metaphors into 'orientational', 'ontological' and 'structural'. 'All metaphors are structural (in that they map structures to structures); all are ontological (in that they create target domain entities); and many are orientational (in that they map orientational image-schemas)' (ibid.: 264). Abstract concepts are accompanied by metaphors. Moreover, '[t]here appear to be both universal metaphors and cultural variation' (ibid.: 274).

Based on the aforesaid discussion, four aspects are crucial to metaphors. First, metaphors provide cognitive value. They cannot be reduced to only emotive concerns. Second, metaphors cannot be read literally. Meaning is extended beyond words. Metaphors are not ornamental expressions and do form concepts. Metaphors also have temporal locations. Acquaintance with temporal locations is crucial for the awareness and meaning of metaphors. Third, metaphors represent socio-economic reality. Reading metaphors *sans* socio-economic conditions is a misleading endeavour.

Metaphors of Political Community

Reading *Hind Swaraj* metaphorically does not discount its 'literal significance' or earlier scholarship on it. It unravels multiple dimensions and epistemic value combined with political action. *Hind Swaraj* offers a slew of metaphors. The 20 chapters are also metaphors that offer more than the literal meaning. There is the formation of concepts and they are not used ornamentally. Metaphors of *Hind Swaraj* provide cognitive and epistemic values. The text cannot be treated merely as an emotional outburst against British imperialism. *Hind Swaraj* (and its metaphors) has also a temporal location. Therefore, any reading of metaphors should be informed by the context. Metaphors do represent a social-economic outline. Reading *Hind Swaraj* in the outlines of the political community goes beyond the literal rigidities.

The metaphors in each chapter (chapter titles given in parentheses) in *Hind Swaraj* are outlined below.

1. **Seeking equivalence over benevolence** (The Congress and its Officials): In the first chapter, the metaphor of 'The Congress and its Officials' stands for 'seeking equivalence over benevolence'. In and around 1909, petitioning was a method used widely and frequently to request action or a decision. Gandhi appears to question the petitioning method by invoking home rule. Interestingly, he supported the 'greats', or the senior leaders of the Indian National Congress, but not their methods. 'Home rule' is invoked numerous times. It would be a mistake to ignore the reader completely since that is also a construction of Gandhi. For Gandhi, '[a] nation that is desirous of securing Home Rule cannot afford to despise its ancestors' (1997: 16). The tension in this sentence is apparent. 'Desirous of securing home rule' does come first without 'despising ancestors'. It exhibits a new churning. Rejecting the act of petitioning is a crucial component in Gandhi's schema of swaraj. In place of 'request for rights', there is an emphasis on 'equivalence by way of struggle'. Equivalence entails the unequivocal defence of an equal ontological being. The struggle for

rights avoids slipping into the territory of pity or becoming subject to passivity. The struggle for rights avoids two 'vital' mistakes: it rejects the discourse from above; in other words, 'benevolence' is not reliable. Human beings do require continuous autonomy in place of occasional or continuous benevolence. Second, a struggle charts its territory in terms of removing ambivalences, arriving at certitude and inclusivity. It also pushes people away from the realm of benevolence. Therefore, equivalence is prioritised over benevolence.

2. **Awakening a must for realising swaraj** (The Partition of Bengal). In the second chapter, the metaphor of 'The Partition of Bengal' stands for realising swaraj through awakening. Partition also does away with 'petition'. Gandhi makes this statement in the context of the partition of Bengal in 1905. He highlights both the irrelevancy of prattle and petitioning without force.

   > [R]eal awakening took place after the Partition of Bengal ... Lord Curzon ... took it for granted that Indians could only prattle, they could never take any effective steps. He used insulting language, and in the teeth of all opposition partitioned Bengal. That day may be considered to be the day of the partition of the British Empire'. (ibid.: 19)

   'After the Partition, people saw that petitions must be backed up by force and that they must be capable of suffering' (ibid.: 21). The idea of struggle/suffering becomes important in the context of partition and petition. The limitation of the petition is that it did not challenge any empire and regime. It delayed the process of assertion. Against the backdrop of 'objective conditions', petitioners, particularly in the British Empire, were destined to fail because of the unmitigated needs of colonialism and capitalism. Since the petition principle is also antithetical, it is bound to be broken. This gave birth to realisation or, in Gandhi's words, awakening.

3. **Discontent a must for awakening** (Discontent and Unrest): In the third chapter, the metaphor 'Discontent and Unrest' stands for the necessity of discontent for awakening. Discontent precedes awakening. Gandhi unequivocally underlines the significance of unrest to dispel the 'comatose state'. 'Radical Gandhi' could emerge from this postulation. For Gandhi, '[u]nrest is ... discontent' (1997:

24). For Gandhi, in 1906–09, 'so may the present unrest in India be considered a necessary and, therefore, a proper state. The knowledge that there is unrest will, it is highly probable, enable us to outgrow it. Rising from sleep, we do not continue in a comatose state' (ibid.). '[D]iscontent is a very useful thing. So long as a man is contented with his present lot, so long is it difficult to persuade him to come out of it. Therefore it is that every reform must be preceded by discontent' (ibid.: 24–25). In fact, in Gandhi's swaraj, discontent is not an erratum but an unavoidable necessity. For Gandhi, discontent leads to awakening from slumber and immense conditionalities. It forces us to comprehend the servitude which has been normalised. He cites an example from colonial India: the swadeshi movement helped people realise the normalisation of the condition of their exploitation, which was broken by the discontent against the British Empire.

4. **Swaraj as negation versus transformation** (What is Swaraj?). In the fourth chapter, the metaphor of 'What is Swaraj?' could be interpreted as 'structural transformation'. Gandhi adopts a unique method of describing categorically what 'Swaraj is not'. From this rejection emerges the idea of swaraj. Swaraj is not simply driving out 'English and retaining everything'. '[W]e want English rule without the Englishman' (ibid.: 28) is an untenable proposition and leads to a philosophical dystopia. In Gandhi, swaraj is not only negation, but also transformation. It rejects 'alien rule', which is not a biological premise, i.e., rule of the unrelated 'other'. Othering could come from within or outside. By and large, in discourses on political community, othering is generally 'outsideness' and the juxtaposition with 'our' is based on binaries. The negation of 'outsideness' is easy, quick and convenient. Since a superficial detachment from 'outsideness' is easy, its deployment becomes an easy decision. Complications arise when 'outsideness' comes in the form of a subsumption of 'insideness'. The former also shapes 'insideness'. Therefore, the removal of outsideness is not sufficient since it will be represented by insideness. The problem becomes further complicated since in many cases, insideness creates an infrastructure informed or developed in collusion with outsideness. Swaraj takes the question beyond negation and towards the transformation of structure which comprises both insideness and outsideness. Swaraj is structural transformation. Keeping the

exploitative structure while changing people is not fruitful, and merely changing people without changing the structure is not helpful either.[9]

5. **Abjuring delegation** (The Condition of England): The 'Condition of England' is essentially a metaphor for delegation. Delegation is abjuring the body and is a contested concept. It has invited serious attention and contestation even in Rousseau, for whom people are sovereign. Sovereignty cannot be represented. Rousseau rejects delegation, particularly by election:

> The English nation thinks that it is free, but is greatly mistaken, for it is so only during the election of members of Parliament; as soon as they are elected, it is enslaved and counts for nothing. The use it makes of the brief moments of freedom renders the loss of liberty well-deserved. (Rousseau 2002: 221)

Everyday participation becomes crucial in the decision-making process of the country. Gandhi underlines the problems with regard to delegation at two levels. First, representatives work for 'external influencers', who mediate between the electorate and the electors. 'The natural condition of that parliament is such that, without outside pressure, it can do nothing' (Gandhi 1997: 30). Delegation is bound to be mediated due to the ever-present external pressures, which are antithetical to the idea of people's sovereignty. Second, due to this mediation, the outcome is compromised. 'What is done today may be undone tomorrow. It is not possible to recall a single instance in which finality can be predicted for its work' (ibid.: 31). The problem is the absence of symmetry between the elected and the electorate by way of 'mediation' in the form of external influence. Since representatives, as Gandhi states, 'have neither real honesty nor a living conscience', because of mediation or the design of delegation, people are becoming external in terms of exclusion and external forces are becoming internal in terms of decision-making (ibid.: 32).

For Gandhi, the self-rule that is swaraj is the rule of the internal (self-control) and the external (self-rule). Defining swaraj as internal and external swaraj leaves little room for delegation. Delegation could be simplified as an externalisation of the self. Once the self becomes external, a desirous political self can no longer be formed. In other words, the abdication of the autonomous self, which is crucial for the thinking and acting self, takes place through delegation. The political self is formed in the absence of a thinking and acting self. This self becomes available for politics. Delegation thus compromises internal and external selves. Due to an emphasis on internal and external swaraj, the self retains the status of a thinking and acting being. This is translated into the political self, where being critical remains a high standard. The absence of delegation might herald the arrival of the political self in politics, but it is not political.

6. **Civilisation qua the rejection of modern civilisation (exclusivism)** (Civilisation). Civilisation is a metaphor for the rejection of exclusivism in the form of modern civilisation. For Gandhi, civilisation is prioritised over 'modern civilisation'. What constitutes this division between the two? He uses two imperative categories: *sudharo* (civilisation) and *kudharo* (modern civilisation). Civilisation or 'sudharo' is good conduct, which rejects exclusivism. A modern civilisation or 'kudharo' is not good conduct, and is therefore not true civilisation. Gandhi's immediate reference to modern civilisation pertains to the condition caused by 'industrialisation' and its outcome, 'imperialism'. Modern civilisation thrives solely on exclusivism through the conversion of everything into a commodity. Access to commodity signals the end of exclusivism in capitalism. There are two ways to interpret 'true civilisation' in Gandhi: as pre-modern days and as a rejection of 'modern civilisation', and proposing an alternative outside it. In the first interpretation, true civilisation cannot exist in modern civilisation. In several studies, a pre-capitalist communitarian *modus vivendi* is envisaged as an alternative to modern civilisation. Though Gandhi does not reject pre-modern civilisation, rejection of exclusivism remains an important concern.

This dilemma of choosing between pre-modern or modern civilisation is reflected in Gandhi. Three statements need careful analysis here. One, '[w]omen, who should be the queens of households, wander in the streets, or they slave away in factories'; second, '[f]or the sake of a pittance, half a million women in England alone are labouring under trying circumstances in factories or similar institutions'; third, '[t]his awful fact is one of the causes of the daily growing suffragette movement' (Gandhi 1997: 37). Gandhi seems comfortable with the first sentence but is critical of the second. He supports the third statement. The first statement seems comfortable with a 'communitarian' or pre-modern life. The second denotes modern civilisation. The third originates not from the first, but the second. The first statement does not produce the third condition; it is the second condition that does so. It would be erroneous to perceive the first condition as an emancipatory condition. The contradiction emerges in the second condition where the condition for the third is realised. Conformism, exclusivism and change become important categories. Since the rejection of exclusivism is a very important category, it leads to going forward (change), not backward (conformism). Rejection of exclusivism writ large in Gandhi by way of modern civilisation) becomes an important reference. Pre-modern civilisation has also been a terrain of severe exclusivism in the form of class, caste and gender. From the 'rejection of exclusivism' standpoint, it cannot be accepted. Therefore, both belong to 'kudharo', i.e., exclusivism. 'Sudharo' has to be fought for. It requires a transformation of the present and a rejection of the past.

7. **Responsibility** (Why was India Lost?): 'Why was India Lost' needs to be understood as a metaphor for responsibility: 'The English have not taken India; we have given it to them' (ibid.: 39); '[W]e gave India to the English than that India was lost'; 'The causes that gave them India enable them to retain it' (ibid.: 41). These statements are related to the idea of responsibility. Responsibility is 'activating the agency' and 'anti-passivity'. I/we share equal responsibility for changing contemporaneity and moulding the future. 'I as an eyewitness to the event' is rejected for I/we am/are 'becoming' a participant and shaper in the event. The activating agency is crucial for the realisation of being. This being is dynamic. This being is a material being by way of discarding extraterrestrial explanation. The otherworldly is non-significant. Anti-passivity avoids two crucial pitfalls: inertness and conformity, which together lead to *Brahmanism* and capitalism. Both are required for what Theodor Adorno calls 'negative integration'. A slew of measures like satyagraha becomes crucial for activating agency and working against anti-passivity.
8. **Ethical cosmopolitanism** (The Condition of India): 'The Condition of India' is a metaphor for 'ethical cosmopolitanism'.

> There is yet time to escape it [modern civilisation], but every day makes it more difficult. Religion is dear to me and my first complaint is that India is becoming irreligious. Here I am not thinking of the Hindu, the Mahomedan, or the Zoroastrian religion, but of that religion that underlies all religions. We are turning away from God. (ibid.: 42)

Although Gandhi uses religion and its vocabularies profusely, he redefines them as well. According to Anthony Parel, in *Hind Swaraj*, 'religion is understood in two different senses: as a sect or organised religion, and as an ethic, albeit one grounded in some metaphysic' (Parel 1997: 42). The second sense seems to be more plausible. Gandhi unsettles the megastructure of religion through the infusion of identity, which has been the cornerstone of religions. In place of religious identity, he construes religion as that 'which underlies all religions'. The singular identity collapses here. However, the tenacity of this proposal remains doubtful if the idea of god is still attached to each religion. This problem appears to be resolved when 'later' Gandhi redefines 'religion as self-realisation'. In this method, the realisation of the self becomes important, not the realisation of the self through god. Furthermore, self-realisation and self-recognition of each other are important, which is 'ethical cosmopolitanism'. This is crucial for many reasons, one of which is transgressing space. One belongs to all but not to anyone specifically.

The interesting twist in Gandhi is his further reduction of cosmopolitanism at the level of the 'self'. Cosmopolitanism is not only the external attire but also the integration of the self, while being consciously aware of it. The self-realisation of each other is an integrationist endeavour. Self-recognition of each other takes this further where assimilation is avoided by way of recognition. This can be called dialogical integration wherein the two are inseparable while identifying and respecting their distinctiveness as individuals. 'I' is not sufficient itself without 'you'. There is a real advancement in terms of 'I' and 'you' constituting 'we' without 'theirs'. Religious fundamentalism thrives on 'I' *sans* 'you'. 'We' is constituted without the dialectics of 'I' and 'you'. Absolutism thrives when the essentialisation of the self takes place through the absolute marginalisation of others.

9. **'Uncontrolled', a problematique** (The Condition of India (continued): 'Railway' is a metaphor for 'uncontrolled', which remains problematic

in the Gandhian lexicon. Gandhi's treatment of the railway must not be read as a celebration of inertness or anti-modernity or as being against motion itself. Railway *per se* was the subsumption of India in the form of imperialism (exploitation along with military mobility of the Empire). A caste-ridden Indian society required greater mobility. However, the railway came to India through the format of uncontrolled exploitation and uncontrolled political community. Railways, famines and irrigation need to be studied together. India faced several social famines and death because of the railways. Famines are natural phenomena, but what led to disaster was not having enough grains in storage. Colonial policies did not allow grain to be stored or hoarded, not even a meagre surplus. Grain was exported to metropolitan cities or other countries. The railways played a crucial, or perhaps singular, role in the export of grains, which led to severe grain scarcity, and death during famine. Gandhi points out that '[r]ailways have also increased the frequency of famines, because, owing to the facility of means of locomotion, people sell out their grain, and it is sent to the dearest markets' (Gandhi 1997: 47). Moreover, expenditure on or investment in irrigation was not prioritised and resources were spent on railways for export and strategic purposes. Guaranteed and recurring private benefits made it a lucrative investment. Gandhi, through his critique of the railways, critiqued the uncontrolled political economy.

His second critique is more philosophical and concerns the nature of the political community. The railway is a metaphor for uncontrolled polity in which the absence of aloofness is important. Earlier, people 'learned one another's languages, and there was no aloofness between them' (ibid.: 48). This statement may not be 'historical', but it underlines the normative necessities of what constitutes a relationship. 'Uncontrolled' entails the following condition in a political community: a train journey symbolises a journey that has a disconnect between the internal and external worlds, as well as one where the internal world has no control over the external. There is no way to control politics which is external to me, but should have been woven in dialectally, both internally and externally. Even the internal is clueless about the journey which is disjointed from the external world. In other words, it is a problematique to be a part of the political community in which destiny is intertwined with a clueless existence based on disempowering people.

10. **Alter ego** (The Condition of India (continued): The chapter 'The Hindus and the Mahomedans' can be read as a metaphor for 'alter ego'. This is a remarkable chapter for defining the nation, jolting majoritarianism and breaking constructed binaries between Hindus and Muslims, leading to the two communities becoming each other's alter ego. Unlike the classical definition of a nation that comprises religion, language and ethnicity, Gandhi underlines multiplicity in the nation. 'India cannot cease to be one nation because people belonging to different religions live in it' (ibid.: 52). 'In no part of the world are one nationality and one religion synonymous terms; nor has it ever been so in India' (ibid.: 53). Regarding majoritarianism, he states that '[i]f the Hindus believe that India should be peopled only by Hindus, they are living in dreamland' (ibid.: 52). Since the cow remains an important factor for 'binaries', his comments are important. In this context, his emphasis is more on 'usefulness' rather than 'religious'. 'The cow is the protector of India, because it, being an agricultural country, is dependent on the cow's progeny. She is a most useful animal in hundreds of ways' (Gandhi 1997: 54). This focus is not unproblematic. Why an ahistorical defence of the cow? Gandhi brings in the cow in the context of communalism and defends it through the economy. When the cow was becoming a central point of binaries, how was the economic aspect going to solve the communal problem? There are two subversions to Gandhi. The first shifts the focus from religion to the realm of the material. This method may not appear an effective way to counter communalism, but the cow question was put on the back burner. He also reminds us that 'cow-protection societies may be considered cow killing societies' (ibid.: 50).

A shift from religion to the material was needed for the second subversion concerning communalism. Gandhi omits the cow to bring parity between Hindus and Muslims. This compromise is a necessary step towards making both alter egos of each other. In other words, religions must enrich each other in terms of cementing diversity and developing a high level of tolerance. Interestingly, and particularly in Hindutva, the question of Hindu and Muslim is a binary question. In Hindutva, the dissolution of this binary takes place when assimilation is achieved socially and institutionally. Conversely, Gandhi 'proposes' the alter ego in place of 'binary'. The alter ego, while recognising different existences, rejects separate existence. Gandhi delineates 'different existence' and 'separate existence'. In a different existence, a community evolves, negotiates and makes spaces heterogeneous. Although community remains a problematique due to the focus on internal cohesiveness, Gandhi makes the alter ego an important category in the context of an inter-community relationship. In separate existence, the essence of community—used to show that some features attributed to a community are championed as supreme over others—acquires supremacy. This supremacy engulfs the existence of the 'other', particularly in majoritarianism. Theoretically, majoritarianism believes in 'separate existence', but in practice it is a celebration of the quintessential particular. Through an 'alter ego', Gandhi does not recognise 'separate existence', which avoids the supremacy of the quintessential particular (i.e., a certain community holds certain values, but this does not make it superior to others). Though the alter ego does not solve inner contradictions, it becomes useful in the context of secularism.

11. **Negation of arbitration** (The Condition of India (continued): Gandhi's rejection of lawyers must be understood as a metaphor for the negation of arbitration. Gandhi problematises lawyers as arbitrators, i.e., those profiting *sans* justice. This arbitration does not solve problems, but enriches the mediators/third party. 'Lawyers ... enrich themselves' (Gandhi 1997: 59). 'If people were to settle their own quarrels, a third party would not be able to exercise any authority over them.' 'The parties alone know who is right. We, in our simplicity and ignorance, imagine that a stranger, by taking our money, gives us justice' (ibid.: 61). In this way, Gandhi attacks liberalism/ liberal political theory to deliver justice through arbitration where deliverance is procedural rather than extending substantive justice. Arbitration is a relationship where there is blind acceptance of a decision but no real personal conviction of the outcome (i.e., that it has been fair or just). Even in moral decisions, arbitration remains an unethical intervention because of the cost involved. The moral purpose of the intervention is subsumed under the costs. The cost purpose of the intervention is amoral not only because it

converts the 'acceptance of a decision' into 'governmentality', but also because it does not offer a convincing outcome. Therefore, third-party intervention is untenable since it influences both the decision and the outcome and its acceptance through the cost factor, making it highly compromised.

12. **Appearance over essence** (The Condition of India (continued): Doctors are a metaphor for 'appearance'. Doctors restrict themselves to the body, with a bodily view of health that focuses on disease; however, the issue is to correct the deed or go to the essence. Gandhi highlights the dichotomy between mind and body: 'the business of a doctor is to take care of the body ... [After receiving medicines due to doctors' intervention] ... [m]y body thereby certainly felt more at ease, but my mind became weakened. A continuance of a course of medicine must, therefore, result in a loss of control over mind' (Gandhi 1997: 63). The difference between disease and deed is crucial in Gandhi. Gandhi's standpoint can be read as a summary rejection of the doctor by the patient. Treating the body without deeds is not only erroneous but also immoral, because it conceals the latter's impact on the former. This idea is also crucial in the work of Erich Fromm. Unlike Sigmund Freud, who related mental health to physiology, Fromm related it to human existence. It is through human existence that our mental health gets shaped (Fromm 1991). Gandhi's differentiation between disease and deed is important as it helps differentiate between appearance and essence. If the body is the only concern and treatment confined to it, then this is an engagement with 'appearance'. The treatment of appearance is not a diagnosis if linked with essence. Moreover, for Gandhi, a deed as an essence needs tangible attention. Gandhi, in his self-treatment, can also be accused of engaging with appearance or an overt reference to self-diagnosis of the body. If treated as a principle, the accusation is correct. However, if treated as 'protest' for delinking from deeds, it becomes a sublime standpoint. Overall, the human condition cannot be explained physiologically, but requires an explanation of socio-economic forces.
13. **Good conduct as inclusivism** (What is True Civilization?): A reading of this chapter must be preceded by two caveats. First, the reader needs to engage with other Gandhian philosophical tenets. Second, the tension between political philosophy and history is

evident. Gandhi locates his political philosophy in history. But this history is problematic due to violence that takes the form of class, caste and gender. Gandhi could have used *only* political philosophy to define true civilisation. However, in the anti-imperialist struggle, nationalist rhetoric was also used to exhibit historical superiority over the imperialists. The use of history in this way is momentary and short. Gandhi's political philosophy, on the other hand, remains important for a longer period. Therefore, between philosophy and history, the former becomes important. For Gandhi,

> [c]ivilisation is that mode of conduct which points out to man the path of duty. Performance of duty and observance of morality are convertible terms. To observe morality is to attain mastery over our mind and our passions. So doing, we know ourselves. The Gujarati equivalent for civilisation means 'good conduct'. (Gandhi 1997: 67)

Philosophically, with regard to true civilisation, 'Gandhi connects the notions of self-knowledge, duty (*farajj*), morality (*niti*), mastery over the mind (*man*) and the senses (*indriyo*)' (Parel 1997: 67). In the realm of political philosophy, if modern civilisation is 'kudharo', then true civilisation *ipso facto* becomes a site of inclusivism. Denoting it as 'good conduct' is not enough. Its components must be exhibited. In this regard, Gandhi highlights a synthesis between ethical means and ends. Ethical means decide true civilisation, i.e., swaraj. Components of 'sudharo' and inclusivism are intertwined. *Satya, ahimsa, apagariha, tapas* and satyagraha are a few components. Satya stands for unmediated truth. Directness is important to comprehend reality. Ahimsa is non-violation of the body—of self and others. It becomes crucial in the context of 'communal polarisation'. Absolute binaries are created in communalism, where the rigidity of the self and discarding of others are celebrated and endorsed. Apagariha is crucial for non-possession. Tapas or self-suffering is what we experience when we stand by our principles. Satyagraha is collective organisation for transcendence towards swaraj.

14. **Transcendence** (How Can India Become Free?): India's freedom is also a metaphor for transcendence. Gandhi resolves the dilemma

of liberal political theory through swaraj. Swaraj remains self-rule, internally and externally: '[W]e become free, India is free. And in this thought, you have a definition of Swaraj. It is Swaraj when we learn to rule ourselves'. Moreover, 'Swaraj has to be experienced by each one for himself' (Gandhi 1997: 73). These two constitute 'transcendence' from liberal political theory. Transcendence as a metaphor depicts the end of the dilemma, which is a crucial part of liberal political theory: that this theory focuses on the liberty of individuals and laws of the state. Both are quintessential parts of the theorisation and adaptation of liberal political theory. As compulsory components, they produce undesirable consequences in the form of perpetual tension between individual and state. In a liberal democracy, individual liberty is guarded while empowering the state: from an implementer of the law in *normal* times and non-implementer in *abnormal* times, which is also known as *state of exception*.

Two dichotomies emerge here. The exercise of liberty remains with the individual and guardianship rests with the state. In other words, it is the individual's wish to exercise liberty with further approval of the state. Liberal democracy seeks to protect individual liberty and is often marred by the almighty state. The problem lies elsewhere. Gandhi uses freedom in place of liberty. Freedom is more encompassing, and is an almost outward concern in place of inward concern in the case of liberty. The outward concern is expressed through the transcendence of an individual's freedom into collective freedom. Here, individual and structure both ensure freedom. In the case of individual and liberal discourse leading to the liberty principle, the individual attempts to ensure liberty while the structure remains antithetical to it. This is precisely because of the absence of a collective that ensures each other's freedom. Capitalism hinders the forming of such a collective due to the accrual of perennial benefits from free individuals and unfree states. This ensures a high degree of inequality.

15. **Rejection of teleology** (Italy and India): This chapter must be read beyond the 'immanent context' of the text to realise the futility of teleology. By way of metaphor, Gandhi rejects teleology. He problematises the 'own' in teleology and asks, 'how can the millions obtain self-rule?' (ibid.: 76).

> [Gandhi underlines] ... that people under several Indian princes are being ground down. The latter mercilessly crush them. Their tyranny is greater than that of the English; and, if you want such tyranny in India, then we shall never agree. My patriotism does not teach me that I am to allow people to be crushed under the heel of Indian princes if only the English retire. If I have the power, I should resist the tyranny of Indian princes just as much as that of the English. By patriotism, I mean the welfare of the whole people. (Gandhi 1997: 76–77)

After questioning the 'own', which is a dominant category in teleology, in terms of 'others are bad and ours are good', Gandhi questions the marginalisation of means in teleology. Compromised means produce compromised outcomes. The latter's sustainability is tentative. For him, 'what is granted under fear can be retained only so long as the fear lasts' (ibid.: 78). The rejection of teleology is a rejection of the teleological order as brute force. 'Sudharo' or good conduct is used against 'kudharo' or bad conduct, which is also teleological order. The premise of the destined end causes serious damage in the form of structural brutality. The 'self' is violently predestined. Such a self is different from the Kantian self—the noumenal self which is *a priori* and undetermined. It has a worth of its own. That the self can be *a priori* and yet undetermined is an important intervention. Gandhi's rejection of structural brutality takes place while adding another dimension to the self. If the self is violently predestined, it is for a teleological purpose that it lives under the dictum of others. It has no worth of its own. It works for others while deciding the existence of the self for others. In Gandhian normativity, it becomes a brute force that needs to be discarded.

16. **Deontological** (Brute Force): This chapter highlights the metaphor of deontological. Gandhi suggests that the 'belief that there is no connection between the means and the end is a great mistake' (ibid.: 81). He further points out 'that only fair means can produce fair results' (ibid.: 84). 'Deontological' is the Gandhian moment in political theory. So why does 'means' become a shaper of corresponding 'ends'? Is the excessive focus on 'means' not ethical romanticism? In normal circumstances, when exploitative structures violate all ethical considerations, why should the exploited follow the ethical desideratum, when following it becomes a defeatist strategy? This

argument is not without merit. However, Gandhi argues from a different entry point. 'Ethical means' is not a vulnerable category. Rather than treating 'means' as *mere* means, which ideally should lead to an 'end' in a corresponding and unilinear manner, it can itself be treated as a mediating zone in which several possibilities emerge. Ethical means is itself both the principle (normativity of values) and political act (assertion of values), both of which define the outcome. Since ethical means entail a fight against an unjust order, it cannot compromise either the principle or the political act, otherwise the result (end) cannot be just. In other words, to achieve a just outcome, it becomes imperative to have both the principle and the political act of egalitarian values. Against the prevalent utilitarian current, where the end is justifiable as per the majoritarian wish, there cannot be a just end if there are no ethical means. Expecting a just outcome without ethical means is an erroneous judgment. Therefore, deontology becomes important.

17. **Truth force to negate brute force** (Passive Resistance): Passive resistance is a metaphor of truth force. Gandhi uses truth force and soul force interchangeably for passive resistance to negate laws that are not ethical or are anti-human. In this way, passive resistance and disobedience become important canons in the political realm. He complains that history becomes only a record of war and kings, but not of passive resisters and soul forces. It is misconstrued that Gandhi rejects history but appeals for the inclusion of the teeming millions. History as mere records of wars is rejected in favour of history as a repository of passive resisters. 'Passive resistance is a method of securing rights by personal suffering .... When I refuse to do a thing that is repugnant to my conscience, I use soul-force ... [which] ... involves the sacrifice of self' (Gandhi 1997: 90). This sacrifice is superior to the sacrifice of others. Gandhi further suggests that following a law that is repugnant to our conscience is anti-human and anti-ethical. Moreover, the majority decision is not binding on the minority since it is not a guarantee of the ethical act. 'All reforms owe their origin to the initiation of minorities in opposition to majorities'. He links unjust laws to slavery. 'So long as the superstition that men should obey unjust laws exists, so long will their slavery exist. And a passive resister alone can remove such a

superstition' (ibid.: 92). To become a passive resister, one must 'observe perfect chastity, adopt poverty, follow truth and cultivate fearlessness' (ibid.: 96). Though ambiguities do exist while interpreting the terms, when understanding these as a political philosophy, they deliver non-religious meanings. In Gandhi, chastity is a discipline. It can also be construed as firmness. Likewise, poverty is not a celebration of nothingness, but is a rejection of 'pecuniary ambition' since 'pecuniary ambition and passive resistance cannot well go together' (ibid.: 97). Truth is the true position. Fearlessness is 'free from fear, whether as to their possessions, false honour, their relatives, the government, bodily injuries, death' (ibid.: 98).

Moreover, Gandhi rejects the charge that passive resistance is a weapon of the weak. Later, he called passive resistance satyagraha after he rejected a resistance that is passive and submissive. Satyagraha is the truth force. Why is it important in Gandhi and his political community, i.e., swaraj? Among numerous attributions, two are vital in the context of swaraj. One is a negation of conformism. Adherence to ethical means avoids the possibility of becoming an unthinking being. The autonomy of self and the absence of binaries negate the possibility of conformism. The second is a constant activation of agency, which is crucial for change. Truth force remains one of the core political projects of Gandhian political philosophy. Obedience is negated not due to metaphysical consideration, but as a part of the conscious political decision that is 'obeying to the unethical state', which amounts to a violation of self, truth and non-violence.

18. **Communicative action** (Education): Gandhi highlights education in the form of communicative action. In this way, education becomes a metaphor for communicative action.[10]

> Every cultured Indian will know in addition to his provincial language, if a Hindu, Sanskrit; if a Mahomedan, Arabic; if a Parsee, Persian; and all Hindi. Some Hindus should know Arabic and Persian; some Mahomedans and Parsees, Sanskrit. Several Northerners and Westerners should learn Tamil. (Gandhi 1997: 105)

Education as a 'communicative action' metaphor entails a slew of premises. Gandhi's schema of education, *nayi talim* (new education), combines education and craft. The idea is not the delinking of 'mind' and 'manual' (also called manual work). This is also reiterated in Marx (Fromm 1991). In Gandhi, as in Marx, this is important for an integrated human being. An excessive tilt towards the fetishisation of intellectual work is controlled by creating an equilibrium between mind and work. 'All I have shown is that we must not make of it [knowledge] a fetish' (Gandhi 1997: 102). This is the first step. The second step is undiluted learning, for which Gandhi advocates imparting education in the mother tongue. This ensures not only learning ability but also an understanding of one's surroundings: knowledge through learning and work along with an understanding of ecology through a language that is innately linked with people. This backdrop of education creates communicative action. How is education the communicative action in Gandhi? A self shaped by knowledge which has sources in learning and work, and language which has a direct origin in people and is understood and practised without dilution and in a decentralised manner paves the way for substantive deliberations. Delinking the relationship between intellect and craft creates a non-hierarchical order. An understanding of one's surroundings pre-empts any manipulation through an arcane language. These are important components for communicative action through a just conclusion and no violence. This communication becomes important for political action towards a decentralised democracy.

19. **Exploitation** (Machinery): For Gandhi, machinery appears to be a metaphor for exploitation. He reminds us that 'the workers in the mills of Bombay have become slaves' (ibid.: 108). Gandhi's idea of exploitation is a complex one. It needs elaboration on two accounts: 'technology' and 'political'. Technology is linked with exploitation. Instead of exploring a potential aspect of liberation in technology, Gandhi found technology restrictive, a theme that was explored in the works of Herbert Marcuse, who finds 'automation' to be the creation of 'one-dimensional man'. Capitalism needs profound production. It requires a massive use of technology for commodity production. In this entire process, a worker is alienated since they become a part of the extended machine. 'Dead labour' (machines) engulfs 'living labour' (worker) (Marcuse 2002). Gandhi locates the

problem in this engulfment, which limits the scope of the political. In the case of automation, the agency of the worker is negated due to the extended scope of the machine, which goes beyond production. It cripples *thinking* politically. Thinking politically entails being aware of the contradiction. The enslavement of technology mars any such awareness. Most Gandhian studies no longer locate exploitation between machine and human and rely on trusteeship to solve this contradiction. Gandhi himself provides an idea of trusteeship. Since trusteeship is antithetical to possession, following the principle of apagariha, it solves the problem of the machine by avoiding its overuse in production. The worker is liberated at both levels: alienation and de-possession.

Gandhi's first principle (engulfment) is limited by the second principle (trusteeship). Trusteeship is guided or mentored by capitalists or possessors of wealth in a 'caretaker' capacity. In the case of the first principle, capitalist accumulation will not take place. Therefore, there is no need for trusteeship due to the *im*-materialisation of accumulation. Therefore, trusteeship is infructuous, theoretically and functionally. Retaining the idea of trusteeship is the weakening of the first principle. The primary contradiction is located in capitalism. Gandhi's critique of technology is the rejection of possession and alienation, and thus of capitalism. But focusing and endorsing the caretaker model, i.e., the presence of the 'apagariha class', is accepting the presence of accumulation, which defies the logic of the first principle. Therefore, Gandhian studies need to prioritise the first over the second since the latter is a mere footnote and not the main text of Gandhi's work. After all, Gandhi said that '[i]t would be folly to assume that an Indian Rockefeller would be better than the American Rockefeller' (Gandhi 1997: 108).

20. **Future without violence and petition** (Conclusion): Gandhi interprets the future as swaraj or swaraj as the future. In his conclusion to *Hind Swaraj*, the future must be without violence and petition. Is it possible to envisage the future without ruling classes? Is it also possible to envisage participatory or deliberative democracy? Put differently, is swaraj defined in terms of the absence of ruling classes and the presence of deliberative democracy? For this, violence and

petition need further decoding metaphorically. Violence has always been an instrument of the ruling classes through class violence and ascriptive violence. Violence cements classes, caste, gender and race structurally. Violence violates the self with or without the consent of people. It seeks consent in exploitation and humiliation. Violence forces the reproduction of violence against selves, i.e., people reproduce violence against themselves by *accepting* exploitation or humiliation. Therefore, rejection of violence is a rejection of both the rule of ruling classes and reproduction of violence against itself. Gandhi emphasises that 'deportation for life to the Andamans is not enough expiation for the sin of encouraging European civilisation' (ibid.: 118). For swaraj to be a true democracy, it cannot be based on petition. Petition and deliberation are antithetical. A petition is hierarchical and obligatory. 'Mere petitioning is derogatory; we thereby confess inferiority' (ibid.: 113). Deliberation is participatory. The former is *for* consideration, whereas the latter is mutuality *sans* exclusivity. It is important to note that for ordinary people, deliberative democracy without the ruling class becomes a real axiom for swaraj. 'Real home-rule is self-rule or self-control' (ibid.: 118).

Some Unanswered Concerns

The crucial questions remain unanswered. Gandhi's political community omits numerous critical questions of our time relating to caste/untouchability, women, tribals and race, among others. The caste/untouchability omission invited serious attention. There are three plausible explanations for these crucial omissions in the political community. First, Gandhi deals with these crucial questions during the formation of his subjectivity through moral aphorism (*An Autobiography* covers significant chapters on the allusion to caste.[11]) Even in his narration of the human condition, both constitute important aspects. Before arriving at the political community stage, the problem is supposed to be resolved at the *satyagraha stage*. Second, like most of his contemporaries who focus on or search for a particular form of exploitation/humiliation, Gandhi searches for a vantage point. People primarily remain the colonial subject.

For the colonial subject, decolonisation becomes crucial. Third, the *varna*[12] question remains vital in Gandhi, who distinguishes between varna, caste and untouchability.

His unqualified rejection of untouchability and caste tells us that birth-based discrimination or ascriptive discrimination is not allowed. The problem is compounded when he supports varna. This support of varna cannot be birth-based due to his opposition to untouchability and caste. Why, then, does he support varna? The answer lies in his era. In Gandhi's era, the idea of differentiation was in full swing. The differentiation is not related to discrimination, but to work efficiency. The Weberian notion of bureaucracy thrives on differentiation. On this account, Gandhi's defence of varna and Weber's defence of bureaucracy are flawed propositions. Even the liberal constitutions are also faulted, which thrive on the specialised division of the judiciary, legislative and executive at the macro level and bureaucracy at the micro level. This produces nothing but technocrats. Though Gandhi offers a serious critique of technology vis-à-vis accumulation and capitalism, the efficiency argument through varna becomes problematic because efficiency is always construed as an intrinsic part of capitalist production. The original Gandhian critique of technology *essentially* rejects production *en masse* as a commodity which also, in turn, rejects the *efficiency* argument of varna. Varna, which also produces social rigidities, cannot be a tenable proposition even from an *efficiency* argument. Moreover, Gandhi's critique of caste and untouchability does not sync with his efficiency defence of varna. Therefore, after the rejection of varna as *efficiency*, Gandhi offers a far better world than what has been claimed on his part.

Notes

1. Ontological reminder and ontological indifference are explained in detail in the introduction to this volume.

2. Originally written in Gujarati as *Satya Na Prayogo* and published in *Navajivan* from 25 November 1925 to 3 February 1929. Later, a serialised translation by Mahadev Desai was published in *Young India* from 3 December 1925 to 3 February 1929. *Satya Na Prayogo Athava Atmakatha* was published in 1927 and 1929 in English in two volumes titled *The Story of My Experiments*

With Truth. The second volume mentioned Mahadev Haribhai Desai and Pyarelal Nair as translators. The second edition of *An Autobiography or The Story of My Experiments With Truth* was published in 1940. Pyarelal's name was deleted as translator in this edition (Suhrud 2010: 1–7).

3. The book unravels the history of satyagraha in South Africa in historical form. I argue that the book has a different and a distinct purpose. History has been dealt with in *An Autobiography* in narrative form. Though the book encompasses 20 years of Gandhi's stay (1893–1914) in South Africa, by Gandhi's own admission, 'The Satyagraha struggle of the Indians in South Africa lasted eight years', which are crucial to satyagraha (Gandhi 1927: xi). The book becomes important because satyagraha 'was the first attempt to apply the principle of Satyagraha to politics on a large scale' (Gandhi 1968: viii). The backdrop of satygaraha becomes crucial for eventual struggles like the Viramgam Satyagraha (1915), Indian Emigration Act (1917), Champaran Satyagraha (1917), Ahmedabad Mill Strike (1918), Kheda Satyagraha (1918), the Rowlatt Act (1919), Khilafat movement (1919), non-cooperation movement (1920), Dandi march (1930), and Quit India Movement (1941). The chapter's titles are also suggestive of *his* satyagraha: 'Grievances', 'Struggles', 'Satyagraha', 'Crooked policy', 'Arrest', 'Opposition and assault', 'Breach of faith', 'A bonfire of certificates', 'Farm', 'Breach of pledge', 'Women in jail', 'Great march', and 'All in prison'. These words are not words *sans* substantive meanings in 50 chapters.

Besides this text, Gandhi needs to be understood in context of his *ashrams* and the satyagraha he led therefrom. Gandhi established Tolstoy Farm (Johannesburg, 1910–13, named by Herman Kallenbach) and Phoenix Settlement (1904–14, near Durban). Gandhi shifted to Sabarmati Ashram in 1917, also known as Satyagraha Ashram, from Kocharab in Ahmedabad. The famous salt satyagraha or Dandi march started here on 12 March 1930. Sevagram (1936–48, village of service) was his last ashram.

4. I am thankful to the anonymous reviewer who asked for clarity on the two subjectivities. This sentence is borrowed from the reviewer's remarks.

5. For an extensive critique of *sewa* (selfless service), please read Srivatsan (2014).

6. See the 21-page resume of the book by Sir H. A. Stuart, Secretary of Home Department (Parel 1993: 240–54).

7. Ted Cohen points out the linkages between metaphors and linguist intimacy through two questions: 'what is the character of this linguistic intimacy, and how, in general and in detail, is it attained? And then what good is it—what is it for?' (1978: 12).

8. Johnson (1981) cites these analyses of Hobbes and Locke in his introduction to *Philosophical Perspectives on Metaphor* for a categorical refutation of the irrelevance of metaphors while further highlighting their significance.

9. The debate between Ralph Miliband (1969) and Nicos Poulantzas (1969) is important here.

10. Thomas Pantham compares 'Habermas' Practical Discourse' and 'Gandhi's Satyagraha' and finds the crucial difference between them: 'The main difference between Habermas and Gandhi is that while the former's practico-political discourse centres around communicative rationality and the force of better arguments, the latter's satyagraha is based not only on reason but also on love and self-suffering' (Pantham 1986: 190). Using Gandhi's education for communicative action is a sign of actual departure from a merely epistemology-based educational realm to a knowledge-action-oriented realm.

11. Even in the post-subjectivity formation phase, *Constructive Programme* (Gandhi 1941), which contains 19 items, remains important. Crucial concerns like 'removal of untouchability' (second point), women (ninth point), *kisans* (peasants) (fourteenth point), labour (fifteenth point), *adivasis* (sixteenth point) and lepers (seventeenth point) are discussed in the text.

12. Any of the four traditional social classes of India: *Brahman, Kshatriya, Vaishya, Shudra.*

References

Ambedkar, B. R. 2014. *Annihilation of Caste: The Annotated Critical Edition.* With an introduction, 'The Doctor and the Saint', by A. Roy. New Delhi: Navayana.

Amin, S. 1995. *Event, Metaphor, Memory: Chauri Chaura 1922–1992.* California: University of California Press.

Anderson, P. 2012. *Indian Ideology.* Gurgaon: Three Essays Collective.

Basham, A. L. 1971. 'Traditional Influences on the Thought of Mahatma Gandhi'. In *Essays on Gandhian Politics of Rowlett Satyagraha*, ed. R. Kumar, 17–42. Oxford: Clarendon Press.

Bilgrami, A. 2003. 'Gandhi, the Philosopher'. *Economic and Political Weekly* 38 (39): 4159–65.

Bondurant, J. V. 1965. *Conquest of Violence: The Gandhian Philosophy of Conflict.* Berkeley, CA: University of California Press.

Chandra, B. 2008. *Indian National Movement: The Long-term Dynamics.* New Delhi: Har-Anand.

Chatterjee, P. 1986. *Nationalist Thought and the Colonial World: A Derivative Discourse.* London: Zed Books.

Cohen, T. 1978. 'Metaphor and the Cultivation of Intimacy'. *Critical Inquiry* 5 (1): 3–12.

Dallmayr, F. R. 2017. *Democracy to Come: Politics as Relational Praxis*. New York: Oxford University Press.

Davidson, D. 1978. 'What Metaphors Mean'. *Critical Inquiry* 5 (1): 31–47.

Erikson, E. 1970. *Gandhi's Truth*. London: Faber & Faber.

Fischer, L. 1950. *The Life of Mahatma Gandhi*. London: Jonathan Cape, Thirty Bedford Square.

Fromm, E. 1991. *The Sane Society*. London: Routledge.

Gadgil, M., and R. Guha. 1993. *This Fissured Land: An Ecological History of India*. California: University of California Press.

Galtung, J. 1992. *The Way is the Goal: Gandhi Today*. Ahmedabad: Gujarat Vidyapith.

Gandhi, M. K. 1910. *Hind Swaraj*. Phoenix: International Printing Press.

——. 1927. *The Story of My Experiments with Truth*. Vol. 1. Trans. Mahadev Desai. Ahmedabad: Navajivan Press.

——. 1929. *The Story of My Experiments with Truth*. Vol. 2. Trans. Mahadev Desai and Pyarelal Nair. Ahmedabad: Navajivan Press.

——. 1941. *Constructive Programme: Its Meaning and Place*. Ahmedabad: Navajivan Publishing House.

——. 1968. *Satyagraha in South Africa*. Ahmedabad: Navajivan Publishing House.

——. 1997. *Hind Swaraj and Other Writings*. Ed. A. J. Parel. Cambridge: Cambridge University Press.

Guha, R. 1995. 'Mahatma Gandhi and the Environmental Movement'. *Capitalism Nature Socialism* 6 (3): 47–61.

Hobbes, T. 1998. *Leviathan*. Edited and with an introduction and notes by J. C. A. Gaskin. New York: Oxford University Press.

Iyer, R. 1988. *Non-violent Resistance and Social Transformation: Swaraj and Sarvodaya*. Oxford: Clarendon Press.

Johnson, M., ed. 1981. *Philosophical Perspectives on Metaphor*. Minneapolis: University of Minnesota Press.

Keer, D. 1973. *Mahatma Gandhi, Political Saint and Unarmed Prophet*. Bombay: Popular Prakashan.

Kishwar, M. 1985. 'Gandhi on Women'. *Economic and Political Weekly* 20 (41): 1753–58.

Lakoff, G., and M. Johnson. 2003. *Metaphors We Live By*. London: The University of Chicago Press.

Locke, J. 1997. *An Essay Concerning Human Understanding*. Ed. R. Woolhouse. London: Penguin Books.

Marcuse, H. 2002. *One Dimensional-man: Studies in the Ideology of Advanced Industrial Society*. London: Routledge.

Mies, M., and V. Shiva. 2010. *Ecofeminism*. Jaipur: Rawat Publication.

Miliband, R. 1969. *The State in Capitalist Society*. London: Weidenfeld & Nicolson.

Naess, A. 1965. *Gandhi and the Nuclear Age*. New Jersey: The Bedminster Press.

Nagaraj, D. 2010. *The Flaming Feet and Other Essays: The Dalit Movement in India*. Ranikhet: Permanent Black.

Nanda, B. R. 1998. *Gandhi and His Critics*. New Delhi: Oxford University Press.

Nandy, A. 1980. *At the Edge of Psychology: Essays in Politics and Culture*. New Delhi: Oxford University Press.

Newey, G. 2014. *The Routledge Guidebook to Hobbes' Leviathan*. London: Routledge.

Palshikar, S. 1996. 'Gandhi-Ambedkar Interface: When Shall the Twain Meet'. *Economic and Political Weekly* 31 (31): 2070–72.

Pantham, T. 1986. 'Habermas's Practical Discourse and Gandhi's Satyagraha'. *PRAXIS International* 6 (2): 190–205.

——. 1995. *Political Theories and Social Reconstruction: A Critical Survey of the Literature on India*. New Delhi: Sage Publications.

Paranjape, M. R. 1993. *Decolonization and Development: Hind Svaraj Revisioned*. New Delhi: Sage Publications.

Parekh, B. 1989. *Colonialism, Traditionalism, and Reform: An Analysis of Gandhi's Political Discourse*. New Delhi: Sage Publications.

Parel, A. J. 1993. 'Documentation'. *Gandhi Marg* 15: 240–54.

——. ed. 1997. *Hind Swaraj and Other Writings*.Cambridge: Cambridge University Press.

——. 2007. *Gandhi's Philosophy and the Quest for Harmony*. New Delhi: Cambridge University Press.

Patel, S. 1988. 'Construction and Reconstruction of Woman in Gandhi'. *Economic and Political Weekly* 23 (8): 377–87.

Poulantzas, N. 1969. 'The Problem of the Capitalist State'. *New Left Review* 1 (58): 67–78.

Raghuramaraju, A., ed. 2012. *Debating Gandhi: A Reader*. New Delhi: Oxford University Press.

Rao, A. 2009. *The Caste Question: Dalits and the Politics of Modern India*. Berkeley: University of California Press.

Ricoeur, P. 1978. 'The Metaphorical Process as Cognition, Imagination, and Feeling'. *Critical Inquiry* 5 (1): 143–59.

——. 2003. *The Rule of Metaphor: The Creation of Meaning in Language*. London: Routledge.

Rodrigues, V. 2011. 'Reading Texts and Traditions: The Ambedkar-Gandhi Debate'. *Economic and Political Weekly* 46 (2): 56–66.

Rousseau, J. J. 2002. *The Social Contract and the First and Second Discourses*. Edited and with an introduction by S. Dunn. New Haven: Yale University Press.

Rudolph, L. I., and S. H. Rudolph. 1967. *The Modernity of Tradition: Political Development in India*. Chicago: University of Chicago Press.

———. 2006. *Postmodern Gandhi and Other Essays: Gandhi in the World and at Home*. Chicago: University of Chicago Press.

Sahasrabudhe, S. 2006. *Gandhi's Challenge to Modern Science*. Goa: Other India Press.

Sharp, G. 1960. *Gandhi Wields the Weapon of Moral Power: Three Case Histories*. Ahmedabad: Navajivan Publishing House.

Srivatsan, R. 2014. *Seva, Saviour and State: Caste Politics, Tribal Welfare, and Capitalist Development*. New Delhi: Routledge.

Suhrud, T., ed. 2010. *An Autobiography or The Story of My Experiments with Truth: A Table of Concordance*. New Delhi: Routledge.

Vishwanath, S. 1997. *A Carnival for Science: Essays on Science, Technology and Development*. New Delhi: Oxford University Press.

Five

Gandhi, Economics and Welfare

Prabhat Patnaik

The purpose of this chapter is to argue, first, that the concept of the self-seeking 'economic agent', which is central to mainstream economics and is usually viewed as a 'natural' category, was rejected by Gandhi who saw it as being integrally linked to a particular production system; second, his advocacy of an alternative economic trajectory was related to the overcoming of the self-seeking 'economic agent'; and, third, there is in this context a strong overlap between the Marxist problematique and the Gandhian problematique (to use an Althusserian term), notwithstanding their well-known differences. This chapter, however, should be seen only as a particular reading of Gandhi, and not as an attempt at interpreting 'what Gandhi really meant'.

I

The whole of economics, leaving out the Marxist tradition, is based on two fundamental premises: (i) an individual is interested in increasing their own welfare; (ii) this welfare depends exclusively on the magnitude of the goods and services that they command.[1] The goods and services commanded by other individuals do not enter, either positively or negatively, into this function; and the person is presumed never to be 'unconcerned' about the value of this function, but always to prefer a higher value of it to a lower value.

This, however, leaves open the issue of how different *social states*, each defined by a vector of individual welfare values, or, more concretely, a vector of bundles of goods and services, each bundle in the possession of one particular individual in society, are to be compared. This question has occupied economics for long and has thrown up a variety of answers, of which the following one has enjoyed a fair amount of currency: *social state A is better than social state B if A has altogether a larger total bundle of goods and services (in a vector-wise sense) than B, and if the distribution of this bundle in A is* 'better' than in B.[2]

Clearly, this criterion cannot provide a complete ordering of all social states, and the question of what constitutes 'better' distribution remains to be specified. Nonetheless, if there can be some degree of agreement over what constitutes 'better distribution', which in certain contexts is quite possible, then it does provide a meaningful and useful criterion for comparing social states.

The issue that concerns us here, however, is a different one: a comparison of state A with state B is of relevance if we are discussing policy measures to take society from B to A, i.e., a comparison of social states acquires meaning in the context of intervention by the State. The State, however, is not a mystical 'outside' entity superimposed upon society: in a democratic polity, the State intervenes to give expression ideally to the will of the community of citizens. This, in turn, raises a number of issues, such as: How is this will formed? How is this will assessed?

This question of how this will is assessed has attracted much discussion. To what extent, for instance, can the method of majority rule be reasonably applied to determine the will of the community of citizens, each of whom has their own ordering of social states? This has been discussed by a host of writers, from Kenneth Arrow to Amartya Sen. But it does not concern us here. Likewise, the process by which individuals as citizens come to make an ordering of social states, how their views and opinions are shaped, is a matter that need not detain us here.

What is relevant for us here is the implicit dichotomy of perception of the individual that underlies this entire discussion, and hence, by implication, the entire non-Marxist strand of economics as a discipline. Individuals *in the realm of the economy* are supposed to be acting as entirely self-centred entities, concerned exclusively with the bundle of goods and services they can possess, and engaged incessantly in enlarging this bundle; but the same individuals *in the realm of the polity* are supposed to be concerned with improving the distribution of the total bundle of goods and services produced in the aggregate among *all* individuals. Mainstream economics, in short, postulates a split personality within each member of society: *they are both an entirely self-absorbed being and a being that transcends self-absorption at the same time; totally unconcerned with others and totally concerned with others at the same time; a thorough self-seeker as an 'economic agent' and thoroughly imbued with compassion as a 'political citizen' at the same time.*

To be sure, a democratic polity as we know it today did not exist, say, in Adam Smith's time; so it may appear invidious to accuse Adam Smith of seeing such a split personality in every individual. But the same dichotomy appears in a different form in writers from Smith onwards even when they are not cognisant of the 'citizen' role of the individual. The dichotomy appears in their writings as one between a civil society characterised by self-seeking individuals, and a State that rectifies whatever ills such self-seeking behaviour causes in civil society. This dichotomy runs, for instance, through the Cambridge School (of Alfred Marshall and Arthur C. Pigou), right down to J. M. Keynes, in whose work it is particularly pronounced, because the State intervention he visualised was massive, entailing nothing less than the socialisation of investment.

Keynes (1951) was of the view that 'individuals acting separately to promote their own ends were too ignorant or too weak to attain even these'. He also believed that the outcome of individual behaviour, even if not characterised by 'ignorance' or 'weakness', gave rise in the aggregate to social outcomes like mass unemployment, which could only be removed by State intervention. The irrational outcome in the aggregate of supposedly 'rational' self-seeking action on the part of individuals could be rectified only through the intervention of a 'rational' State. We are back therefore to the same dichotomy: the State as an embodiment of 'rationality' is as mystical as the transformation of the self-seeking economic agent into an enlightened political citizen (a transformation that is supposed to occur not over time, but merely through the act of putting on a different hat).

II

This dichotomy between a self-seeking 'economic agent' and an enlightened political citizen, which exists within the self-same individual, is how mainstream economics resolves a basic theoretical problem: How can a society remain viable where each person is exclusively for themselves? It is, in other words, an artificial construct to find a way out of this problem.[3]

But, it may well be asked: How real is this problem itself? Do people really act in a manner that exclusively promotes their self-interest? One answer to this question, which I find quite persuasive, is that capitalist commodity production compels them to act in such a manner, i.e., they act in a self-seeking manner not out of volition, not because they are vile or vicious, but because capitalist commodity production pushes them into a Darwinian struggle for existence where acting in any other manner threatens their economic existence. (Satyajit Ray's film *Mahanagar* depicts this conflict between economic coercion and human concern for a colleague facing victimisation with insight, but it ends on a note of false optimism, where human sympathy *at the individual level*, i.e., not taking the form of any collective struggle in defence of the colleague's rights, triumphs over economic compulsion.)

The fact of each 'economic agent' being concerned exclusively with self-interest therefore is not an unreal situation in bourgeois society, but represents, if not the exact empirical reality at any particular moment in time, the ideal, the pure distilled form of economic existence of the individual towards which bourgeois society in its 'spontaneity' advances. But the reason for this lies neither in some peculiarities of the superstructure of bourgeois society, nor in the mere fact of the use of money (which, after all, has been there for millennia), but in the fact of capitalist commodity production, which acts as a coercive force upon 'all "economic agents"', shaping their behaviour in a manner that has little to do with individual volition (Marx, it may be recalled, had called the capitalist 'capital personified').

The fact of individual behaviour being dictated by the coercion of the system of capitalist commodity production expresses the alienation introduced by such production, where the individual is the mere medium through whom the immanent tendencies of the system get realised, and any individual who refuses to play this role loses their position in the economic system. Individuals, in short, are coerced into playing their role on pain of ruin or starvation.

The overcoming of such alienation requires the overcoming of the system, but mainstream economic theory, whose horizon remains confined within the system and which cannot 'afford' to recognise the necessity of transcending the system, cannot also therefore 'afford' to recognise the fact of this alienation. It sees the self-seeking behaviour of economic 'agents' as 'rational' behaviour that comes 'naturally' to them, i.e., that comes when 'rationality' has been liberated from the shackles of custom and tradition, rather than as a result of coercion imposed upon them by the system of capitalist commodity production.

The other side of not recognising the alienation of individual 'economic agents' is to simultaneously endow them with the humanity and wisdom of political citizens. If the coercion of commodity production upon the individual is not recognised, then its coercion upon the State too is not recognised. The non-recognition of the 'spontaneity' of the system, and hence of individual alienation within it, has, as its counterpart, a recognition of the possibility of humane State intervention: the State can be brought in as a *deus ex machina* to cure the ills of the system because the system is malleable enough to allow scope for its humane intervention instead of being a 'spontaneous' one that compels the State to intervene only in specific ways, and that becomes dysfunctional, forcing a roll-back of such intervention, should it be of a kind that goes against the immanent logic of the system.

The dichotomy noted above, with its corollary of attributing a split personality to individual 'economic agents' in the context of a democratic polity, therefore, is only a logical extension of the denial of alienation under capitalist commodity production.

III

What is noteworthy about Gandhi is that he recognised this alienation, not necessarily in the way discussed above, but in his own way. In his famous article 'The Great Sentinel' (13 October 1921), he wrote: 'Our Non-cooperation is neither with the English nor with the West. Our Non-cooperation is with the system that the English have established, *with the material civilization and its attendant greed and exploitation of the weak*' (Bhattacharya 2005: 91; emphasis added).[4]

He clearly locates the origin of 'greed' and 'exploitation' in the material civilisation established by the English. The fact that the 'system that the English have established' did not in his mind refer merely to the system of using machinery, but rather to the entire gamut of social relations within which machinery was used and which determined the consequences of its use, was expressed by Gandhi in his rejoinder to Tagore's essay 'The Cult of the Charkha', which was published in *Young India* on 5 November 1925:

> Machinery has its place; it has come to stay. But it must not be allowed to displace the necessary human labour. An improved plough is a good thing. But if by some chance one man could plough up by some mechanical invention of his the whole of the land of India and control all the agricultural produce, and if the millions had no other occupation, they would starve, and being idle, they would become dunces, as many have already become. There is hourly danger of many more being reduced to that unenviable state. I would welcome every improvement in the cottage machine but I know that it is criminal to displace the hand labour by the introduction of power-driven spindles unless one is at the same time ready to give millions of farmers some other occupation in their homes. (ibid.: 125)

There is not a single point here on which a Marxist would disagree. Indeed, the Marxist argument would be that precisely because 'some other occupation' would not come to the millions displaced by machinery, the system that did such displacing needed to be overthrown, the system that Gandhi calls 'the English system' but which the Marxist would call 'capitalism'. Not surprisingly, the above-quoted views of Gandhi find a strong echo in Marx's remark in 'Wage Labour and Capital' that the more productive capital develops, 'the forest of uplifted arms demanding work becomes ever thicker, while the arms themselves become ever thinner' (Marx and Engels 1980: 94).

The fact that capitalism in the West did historically succeed in overcoming the mass unemployment initially generated, despite the massive technological progress it introduced, is not because of some intrinsic trait in capitalism to do so, as is often claimed, but because of two other factors (Patnaik 2013): one, mass emigration from Europe to the temperate lands of white settlement, where these émigrés drove the 'native' population off the land and gained employment as agriculturists (and in other occupations catering to the needs of these agriculturists); and, two, the export of unemployment to the colonies and semi-colonies where 'deindustrialization' was increasingly located. Gandhi saw the devastating effects of this deindustrialisation, and referred to Europe having made 'the exploitation of non-European races a religion. But it is a false religion bound to perish in the near future' (Bhattacharya 2005: 125).

A good deal of the discussion between Gandhi and Tagore was over the effect of this 'deindustrialization', with Tagore, both in his correspondence and in his novel *Ghare Baire*, referring to the improvement in the living standards of the peasantry that the substitution of cheap imported cloth for locally-manufactured cloth had brought about. There are two quite distinct issues here, one not touched upon in the correspondence between Gandhi and Tagore and the other that is touched upon.

The first issue, not touched upon in the correspondence, concerns the 'second-order effects' of deindustrialisation (Patnaik 2003). The argument that cheap imported cloth, even if it causes domestic deindustrialisation, improves the living conditions of the peasants presupposes that their incomes remain unchanged by deindustrialisation, i.e., that such deindustrialisation, while not having any adverse effects on their incomes immediately, a fact that can scarcely be doubted, *also has no adverse effects on their incomes over a period of time*. It presupposes, in other words, that deindustrialisation has no adverse 'second-order effects' on peasant incomes.

But since the displaced handloom weavers and other craft producers are thrown on to the land in the absence of any other livelihood, land rents go up and agricultural wages go down as a consequence of deindustrialisation, which is what happened in India in the nineteenth century. And this lowers the incomes of the peasants, the overwhelming majority of whom are tenants; it especially affects the poor peasants, who, in addition to not having any ownership rights (and hence being squeezed through higher rent), also work as agricultural labourers to supplement their income from cultivation and therefore get additionally squeezed through lower wages. Tagore's argument about peasants being better off because of cheap imported cloth ignores these second-order effects. Once they are taken into account, the argument becomes more difficult to sustain.

The second issue, which was touched upon in the correspondence between Gandhi and Tagore, and which is directly germane to the present chapter, is that the argument that peasants become better off presupposes a notion of well-being similar to that of mainstream economics, i.e., where well-being is defined exclusively with respect to the bundle of goods and services a person commands. *Gandhi rejected this notion entirely and herein lies the specificity of his argument.* It is worth quoting him at some length here:

> It is sinful to buy and use articles made by sweated labour. It is sinful to eat American wheat and let my neighbour the grain dealer starve for want of custom. Similarly it is sinful for me to wear the latest finery of Regent Street, when I know that if I had but worn the things woven by the neighbouring spinners and weavers, that would have clothed me, and fed and clothed them. On the knowledge of my sin bursting upon me, I must consign the foreign garments to the flames and thus purify myself, and thenceforth rest content with the rough *khadi* made by my neighbours. (Bhattacharya 2005: 90)

There are two alternative ways of interpreting these remarks. The first is that a person's well-being depends not just upon the magnitude of the goods and services at their command but also on their conformity to the notion of an 'ethical life'; the second interpretation is that my well-being depends not just on the amount of goods and services at my command but also upon the well-being of others, i.e., 'my neighbours', and the amount of goods and services at their disposal.

Gandhi would probably not have bothered to distinguish between these two alternative interpretations, and in fact it makes little difference to his argument. No matter which interpretation we take, it amounts not only to a rejection of the notion of 'well-being' or 'welfare' that lies at the core of mainstream economics, but also to an overcoming of the dichotomy between the self-seeking 'economic agent' and the humane and caring 'political citizen' of the split personality attributed to the individual in a bourgeois society.

If ethical considerations enter into the notion of 'welfare', then the pure 'economic agent' interested in increasing the goods and services at their command disappears; and with it also disappears its 'other', the so-called 'political citizen'. Likewise, if the welfare of my neighbour enters as an argument into my welfare function, even if attention is always confined exclusively to amounts of goods and services, then again the self-seeking 'economic agent' disappears, and so does the distinction between the uncaring 'economic agent' and the caring 'political citizen'. We therefore have, on either interpretation, an overcoming of the split personality of the 'individual'.

IV

Gandhi's suggestion that an individual's welfare must depend upon the welfare of their neighbours was not just an abstract ethical suggestion. He was aware of the association between individual behaviour and the trajectory of social development, and hence suggested an alternative trajectory of development for the realisation of this concept of individual welfare. If 'greed and exploitation' had been attendant upon the 'English system', then the realisation of a situation where my welfare depends upon that of my neighbour must require a rejection of the 'English system' and the pursuit of an alternative trajectory of development. The *charkha* or spinning wheel became the symbol of this alternative system, a metaphor, as it were, for what one might call 'non-capitalist development', and hence a condition for overcoming this split personality and alienation.

Gandhi's support for the charkha did not mean that every *individual* had to produce for their own needs. His exhortation to everyone to take up the charkha was just a transient measure which he justified in the following words: 'On knowing that my neighbours [the spinners] may not, having given up the occupation, take kindly to the spinning wheel, I must take it up myself and thus make it popular' (Bhattacharya 2005: 90). The economic arrangement that Gandhi had in mind for society at large, in short, was not individual self-sufficiency, but, in light of the earlier discussion, the organisation of the economy in units where it would be feasible for demand and technological change to be so adjusted that no unemployment resulted, that everyone could always remain gainfully employed.

Put differently, if Gandhi saw an individual's welfare as being dependent upon the welfare of their neighbour, then the concept of the neighbourhood that emerged from this, i.e., of the geographical area that could constitute an economic unit, was one where this was feasible. In fact, having shown why imported cloth should be boycotted since it took food away from the neighbouring weaver, Gandhi wrote:

> I do not hesitate to carry the doctrine to its logical limit and say that Bengal dare not import her cloth even from Bombay or from Banga Lakshmi. If Bengal will live her natural and free life without exploiting the rest of India or the world outside, she must manufacture her cloth in her own villages as she grows her corn there. (ibid.: 125)

Another way of understanding Gandhi's concept of the economic unit therefore is that the unit must cover a region in which self-sufficiency, without any exploitation of what lies outside the region, can become a reality. This concept no doubt requires further discussion, but its point of departure to my mind consists of two elements: first, all must be gainfully employed within it; and, second, it must impose no exploitation upon other outside units.

Gandhi rests his advocacy of the charkha, as the symbol of a non-exploitative development paradigm (which in effect means a non-capitalist development), on a particular premise: since there is no way out for humankind from its current predicament, characterised by exploitation by Europe of non-European societies, other than through the charkha, the only two courses open to it are (a) either to recognise its importance immediately, or (b) to recognise it after an intervening period of conflict. He sees his advocacy of charkha as a means of avoiding such conflict and hence as a means of showing humankind a peaceful way out of its current predicament. As he puts it:

> The non-European races will not forever allow themselves to be exploited. I have endeavoured to show a way out that is peaceful, human and therefore noble. It may be rejected. If it is, the alternative is a tug-of-war in which each will try to pull down the other. Then, when non-Europeans will seek to exploit the Europeans, the truth of the charkha will have to be realized. (Bhattacharya 2005: 125)

It is interesting, however, that Gandhi sought to bring the truth of the charkha to the exploited non-European society, i.e., to India, first. The reason he gave for it was a pragmatic one, namely that 'a drowning man cannot save others', that 'in order to be fit to save others we must try to save ourselves', which means that before the message of the charkha can be spread to the rest of the world, it must first be realised within India itself.

But, in addition, implicit in this apparent pragmatism was perhaps an understanding that an exploited society could more easily take to the charkha. This would be somewhat analogous to the understanding that had characterised the Russian *narodniki*,[5] who had believed that not having gone down the path of capitalism, Russia could perhaps bypass it altogether and make a direct transition to socialism. Likewise, Gandhi might have felt that not having developed capitalism (though this, needless to say, was not Gandhi's way of putting it), India could bypass it altogether, and take to the charkha (which was his equivalent of socialism) more easily because its people were exploited rather than being the exploiters.

Vera Zasulich, it may be recalled, had written to Marx asking him for his views on the possibility of Russia bypassing capitalism altogether and moving directly from the system of communal property of the *mir*[6] to socialism. Gandhi did not talk of socialism, but used the metaphor of the charkha to denote an alternative path of development to capitalism (or the 'English system', as he put it). A similar thought of an easier transition to the charkha in such a society could have been in his mind. And the theatre where such transition could occur, according to him, was the Indian village, since 'the city people are the brokers and commission agents for the big houses of Europe, America and Japan' (Bhattacharya 2005: 88).

Lenin's argument against the narodniki in *The Development of Capitalism in Russia* (1899) was that the old communal property system no longer existed and that Russia was already developing capitalism rapidly, so that the only revolution that could be visualised was not one that bypassed capitalism, but one that overthrew capitalism. In India, too, the fact that the way of the charkha was shunned when the country got its independence was symptomatic of Gandhi underestimating the power of what he had called the 'brokers and commission agents', i.e., of the Indian bourgeoisie in the broader sense. Bypassing capitalism was no longer historically possible; it had to be overthrown, a task that still awaits completion, but in circumstances far more formidable than when Gandhi had written.

V

Apart from this difference, however, which related to the 'moment' at which capitalist development had arrived in a country like India, there was the difference between the Gandhian problematique and the Marxist problematique with regard to the conception of the individual's 'welfare function'; a few words on this may not be amiss, though since this subject is less discussed, one could be clutching at straws.

The Marxist position also rejects the portrayal of the self-seeking 'economic man' as a 'natural' category, and posits as an end the individual who seeks self-fulfillment in and through the 'community' and whose notion of welfare therefore includes the preservation and the advance of the community. The coming into being of such an individual and of the community in which they are placed is visualised as the outcome of a historical process of struggle against capitalism.

Marx had expressed both the process and the end result, if only implicitly, in the following words:

> Large-scale industry concentrates in one place a crowd of people unknown to one another. Competition divides their interests. But the maintenance of wages, this common interest which they have against their boss unites them in a common thought of resistance-*combination*. Thus combination always has a double aim, that of stopping competition among workers, so that they can carry on general competition with the capitalists. If the first aim of resistance was merely the maintenance of wages, combinations, at first isolated, constitute themselves into groups as the capitalists in their turn unite for the purpose of repression, and in the face of always united capital, *the maintenance of the association becomes more necessary to them than that of wages .... Once it has reached this point, association takes on a political character*. (Marx and Engels 1976: 210–11; emphasis added)

Using the mundane language of mainstream economics, what this means is that the individual's welfare function now begins to have, as an argument, not just the bundle of goods and services that they happen to possess, but the defence and the preservation of the community.

There is a difference between having as an argument of the individual's welfare function the welfare of the 'neighbours' and having as an argument the defence of the 'community', a difference that corresponds perhaps to the distinction between humane altruism and collectivism. And there is a difference between a particular *denouement* coming into being through persuasion, which is possible for the formation of a humane altruism and its coming into being through a historical process of struggle which is necessary for the formation of the collective. This is the basic difference between the Marxian problematique and the Gandhian problematique, whence also follow other, more specific, differences with regard to the attitude towards the State, the size of the economic unit over which self-sufficiency should be attempted, and the nature and quality of the required decentralisation.

Notes

1. Strictly speaking, we should take into account the individual's access to 'leisure' in their utility function, but this is not done in the present discussion for the sake of simplicity, although our argument is unaffected by this simplification.

2. I should add that this criterion in this form has not been advanced by anyone; it is my way of interpreting the criterion provided by I. M. D. Little (1951) in light of Dobb's (1969) discussion and Samuelson's (1950) theorem.

3. The answer that Marxism gives to this problem, as we see later, is that the universe of self-seeking 'economic agents' is disrupted through the formation of 'combinations' among workers who thereby overcome their state of being isolated self-seeking atoms. Entering into 'combinations' therefore is the workers' way of disrupting the spontaneity of the system of capitalist commodity production, of which alienation is a necessary result.

4. All references to Gandhi's statements in this chapter, unless otherwise specified, are to Bhattacharya (2005).

5. Russian revolutionaries of the 1860s and 1870s were known as Narodniks. Nardoniki means 'going to the people'. For them, the road to socialism could be direct while bypassing capitalism.

6. Mir was a self-sustaining village community based on collective landownership in Russia.

References

Bhattacharya, S., ed. 2005. *The Mahatma and the Poet: Letter and Debates between Gandhi and Tagore 1915–1941*. New Delhi: National Book Trust.

Dobb, M. H. 1969. *Welfare Economics and the Economics of Socialism: Towards a Commonsense Critique*. Cambridge: Cambridge University Press.

Keynes, J. M. 1951. *Essays in Persuasion*. London: Macmillan.

Little, I. M. D. 1951. *A Critique of Welfare Economics*. Oxford: Oxford University Press.

Marx, K., and F. Engels. 1976. 'The Poverty of Philosophy'. In *Collected Works*. Vol. 6. Moscow: Progress Publishers.

——. 1980. 'Wage Labour and Capital'. In *Selected Works*. Vol. 1. New York: International Publishers.

Patnaik, P. 2003. 'On the Economics of Open Economy Deindustrialization'. V. V. Giri Memorial Lecture, 46th Annual Conference of the Indian Society of Labour Economics.

Patnaik, P. 2013. 'Capitalist Development and the Indian Society'. *The Marxist* 29 (1). Available at https://cpim.org/wp-content/uploads/old/marxist/201301-prabhat-capitalist-dev.pdf (last accessed 5 June 2025).

Samuelson, P. A. 1950. 'Evaluation of Real National Income'. *Oxford Economic Papers* 2 (1): 1–29.

Six

Spinning the *Swaraj*

Technology, Science and Experience in the History of the Spinning Wheel

Sadan Jha

Sakhi sab mili charkha chalabahu, jug paltabahu he
(Dear friends, ply the spinning wheel, turn the world upside down)
—Bhojpuri village song

Unless our hands go hand in hand with our heads, we would be able to do nothing whatsoever.
—Mahatma Gandhi

The possibility of all productive manufacturing lies in revealing. Technology is therefore no mere means. Technology is a way of revealing … techne is the name not only for the activities and skill of the craftsman, but also for the arts of the mind and fine arts. Techne belongs to bringing-forth, to poiesis; it is something poetic.
—Martin Heidegger

Introduction

Mahatma Gandhi once said, 'For me, nothing in the political world is more important than the spinning wheel' (Gandhi 1966a: 454–56). The charkha or spinning wheel, for Gandhi, was not just a tool for political emancipation, it was a metaphor of ancient work ethics and a symbol of economic and social reaction to British rule. The Gandhian charkha has been perceived by common folk in their own image and likeness, and became a part of the day-to-day life of the nation and its people. While the pre-colonial lives of this symbol were reworked by Mahatma Gandhi for his *swaraj* or self-rule, the postcolonial regimes of this symbol come to us in the forms of laughter, satire and a lost alternative space for modernity.

However, oscillating between its pre- and postcolonial lives, what matters crucially for me is the body of this symbol. History, if located at the sites occupied by the folk and if interrogated through folk registers such as folk songs, rumours and sayings, tells us that the imageries associated with the charkha are multiple and often appear to have contradictory meanings. For example, in one of the proscribed pamphlets, the charkha functions as a tool to make claim over the body of prostitutes (Amin 1995: 225, note 87); at another level, this symbol of non-violent Gandhian economy has been mobilised as a weapon (*sudarshan chakra*) of Lord Krishna; and, further, we find this charkha as 'a forgotten friend of Indian widows' (Jha 2004: 3113). This shows that the charkha was perceived by common folk in markedly different ways and generated imageries as violent as that of the machine gun. A proscribed pamphlet, 'Hamara Charkha' (date unknown), loudly claims: *Is charkhe main aisa fun hai/Jo aaj kal ki machine gun hai* ('This spinning wheel has such qualities, this is today's machine gun').

In this chapter, through the various 'communities of responses', I look at the intersection of three core rubrics in the history of the spinning wheel: science, technology and experience. While I reassert Gandhi's deep engagement with science and technology, his deployment of experience provides us with resources to critique modern science and technology rooted in the project of Western Enlightenment and closely entangled with colonial modernity. Experience lies at the core of both Gandhi's model and in the making of a modern scientific temper. Yet, the two differ sharply. Looking at this category of experience in Gandhi's engagement, this chapter brings together the Mahatma's emphasis on experience and philosopher Martin Heidegger's critique of modern science and technology when the latter goes into the core concerns of what the word *techne* (a form of knowledge) may inherit and offer to us.

Imagined Spinning Wheel

Those not familiar with the history of the spinning wheel may find it surprising that Mahatma Gandhi, at the time of writing his most famous treatise, *Hind Swaraj*, had neither seen the spinning wheel nor had any understanding of the difference between the loom and the spinning wheel. Yet he was quite convinced about the sacred nature of the exercise of weaving and hence when looms were written about, they were prefixed with 'ancient' and 'sacred' in *Hind Swaraj* (Parel 1997: 109). It was in London in 1909 that Gandhi 'saw' in 'a flash that without the spinning wheel there was no Swaraj'. This flash vision convinced him immediately that 'everyone had to spin'. He later wrote, 'I did not know the difference between a loom and a spinning wheel in 1908, though I had written about the latter in *Hind Swaraj* then' (Gandhi 1967a: 600, 1967b: 458).[1] This phase continued even after Gandhi's return to India from South Africa—he had actually not seen a spinning wheel. With the establishment of Satyagraha Ashram in May 1915 at Kocharab, Ahmedabad, Gandhi focused solely on cultivating a culture of hand-weaving.[2] In one of his earliest formulations of disciplining the ashram people to attain the larger objective, Gandhi prescribed a set of observances for the controllers of Satyagraha Ashram. This included vows of truth, non-violence, celibacy, control of the palate, non-stealing, non-possession, *swadeshi*, fearlessness and against untouchability. Here, the vow of swadeshi was directly linked with the vow of truth. It proclaimed that the votary of swadeshi 'will never use articles which conceivably involve violation of truth in their manufacture or on part of their manufacturers', forbidding the use of articles manufactured in the mills of Manchester, Germany or India. This norm was based on the premise of uncertainty of information about the manufacturing process in the mills (the premise being that the person taking the vow of truth 'cannot be sure that they'—the mills—'involve no such violation of truth'). Thus, the mills emerged as sites violating truthfulness.

Second, the premise was based also on the suffering of the workforce in the mills (explained in terms of workers' exposure to 'tremendous heat' that was 'something impossible to describe'). Along with this vow of truth, foreign and mill-made cloth was forbidden on the grounds of non-violence, non-stealing and non-possession. Artificial beautification, a marker attached with machine-made cloth, was another reason for rejecting such articles. Therefore, the vow of swadeshi required that the 'use of simple clothing made on simple handlooms and stitched in simple style, foreign buttons, cuts etc.' was to be avoided. The point worth paying attention to is the emphasis on handloom and the absence of concern for spinning. Further, this distinction is not clear in the section on weaving.[3]

However, this experiment with the loom made Gandhi aware of the significance of the spinning wheel on two major counts. The ashram had to depend on the supply of mill-produced yarn. He wrote that 'it was clear, that until we could do this (spinning) ourselves, dependence on the mills would remain. We did not feel that we could render any service to the country by continuing as agents of [the] Indian spinning wheel'.[4] He also came to understand that weaving was a caste-specific occupation and had limited appeal outside the weaving communities as a potential political symbol. This made him eager to know more about spinning and the charkha.

Colonialism, Ruptures and the Charkha

The history of the spinning wheel is also about those ruptures which were outcomes of colonialism and its various agencies. For a political symbol rooted strongly in the weaving cultures of the land, this history then inherits a possibility of revealing layers of displacement and dislocations of the traditional weaving culture in the wake of colonialism. Many a time the spinning wheel acted as an extension of the weaver's loom, which was more than merely the means of livelihood for a major chunk of Indian society. Historian Gyanendra Pandey writes, 'Even during severely straitened circumstances, many handloom weavers carried on, looms were sometimes "kept up merely in order that the children may not forget how to weave". In 1942, the magistrate of Azamgarh district wrote that the Julahas of Mau could still think of nothing but their looms and their religion' (Pandey 1983a: 110).

In India, weaving and spinning were much more than simply an indigenous way of producing textile goods. Spinning was very much a part of the daily lives and activities of women of almost all sections of society. William Crooke notes that spinning was the only industry in India performed by persons of all castes and concerning which there seemed to be no caste prejudice (1972: 509). Historians like C. A. Bayly (1998), B. S. Cohn (1996), Emma Tarlo (1995), Susan Bean (1980), and others have contextualised the mass appeal of Gandhian swadeshi and anti-foreign cloth campaign in the social history of cloth, cloth production and in the power of semiotics. Bayly writes that, in India, 'society spoke partly in "the idiom of cloth", though idiom is really too weak a word since cloth could actually transform power and transform relationships'. In his view, the disruption of the Indian economic fabric was 'a crisis of legitimacy for the new colonial rulers' (Bayly 1998: 190). Can we then argue that Gandhi's astuteness helped him in understanding this legitimacy crisis and developing a strategy by placing the spinning wheel at its centre and framing it as a symbol for the 'regeneration of a glorious past'? Thus, the economics of Gandhian symbols must be analysed by situating them in the context of the Gandhian notion of Indian life and his vision of India's well-being. Along with this, any reading of this Gandhian symbol of 'regeneration of a glorious past' must incorporate the various ways in which this symbol was accepted in the commoners' notion of defiance and in their strategies of resistance to colonial economy.

Locating the Charkha in Economics

'I must confess that I have read only one book on Economics', said Gandhi before an intellectual gathering of the Economics Society of Allahabad University in 1916. That only book of economics was the Bible (Pande 1994: 4). The audience was quite surprised, for what of economics could there be in the Bible? In fact, the answer lies not in the Bible itself but in the manner in which Gandhi experienced the tenets of the Bible. In Gandhi's approach, issues and doctrines were woven together and acted as a single undiversified whole with a heavy tilt towards moral progress over material development. For him, 'true economics stands for social justice and moral values'. He once said, 'Let us seek first the kingdom of God and his righteousness and the irrevocable promise is that everything will be added to us' (Gandhi 1922: 293). By refusing the rigid disciplinary boundaries of economics, Gandhi not only brought together economics, ethics, customs and beliefs, with special emphasis on the specificity of Indianness, but he also gave a new dimension and new meanings to each of these discursive categories. Gandhi once said, 'I must confess that I do not draw a sharp line or any distinction between economics and ethics. Economics that hurt the moral well-being of an individual or a nation are immoral and therefore sinful' (Huq 1985: 159).

This approach, which rejected discursive boundaries in favour of ethical human progress, can be accepted as one of the fundamental differences between the Gandhian notion of economic well-being and Rabindranath Tagore's conception of economics as a rational science, which formed one of the most provocative and philosophically enriched exchanges centred on the spinning wheel. Tagore's opposition to the Gandhian strategy of boycott of foreign cloth or his criticism of the Gandhian constructive programmes based on the charkha, as a whole, was centred more on the 'terms of discourse' and 'the use of moral language in place of the economics' (Bhattacharya 1997: 1–37). But the difference was certainly a more rooted one than being purely discursive. It could be located fundamentally as different ways of perceiving the Indian problem and its solution in the minds of these two intellectual giants. Tagore wrote to Gandhi in 1921: 'The question of using or refusing cloth of a particular manufacture belongs mainly to economic science'. He criticised the use of the 'magical formula that foreign cloth is impure', and thus argued that 'economics is bundled out and a fictious moral dictum dragged in its place'. Gandhi replied by rejecting any distinction between economics and ethics. He further added that all that Tagore knew about the khadi movement with the charkha at its centre was based on 'what he has picked up from table talk'.[5]

In fact, these exchanges with Tagore present some of the most powerful philosophical justifications of charkha ideology. Though not directly addressing the issue of the spinning wheel, both of them developed their arguments and counter-arguments by putting the charkha at the centre. For both these messiahs, the spinning wheel was the carrier of some abstract politico-philosophical positions.

Even for Gandhi, the charkha's significance lay only when taken along with a chain of other activities promoting rural cooperation; the only difference between Gandhi and Tagore was that the charkha was absent in the case of Tagore, while in the Gandhian framework the charkha occupied central position. Tagore seems to have retained a qualified scepticism and nationalist public opinion at that time was vociferously against him (Bhattacharya 1997: 17). Tagore's position on the issue of science and technology was that of an inheritor of the faith of the post-Renaissance era of Enlightenment (ibid.: 32). 'Some have protested that they never preached that only the turning of the Charkha should be engaged in. But they have not spoken of any other necessary work. Only one means of attaining Swaraj has been definitely ordered and the rest is a vast silence', said Tagore.[6]

For a proper appreciation of Tagore's criticism of the charkha programme, this debate needs to be placed in the context of: (i) different perceptions and approaches to universalism and human progress; (ii) the historical context of Tagore's responses when Bengal experienced communal violence following the abrupt end of the Non-Cooperation and Khilafat movements;(iii) Gandhi's deep faith in the value of experience, not merely as a valuable yet passive repository of knowledge, but as a constant and ever-changing presence guiding, shaping and remoulding his activities and value systems. We return to these three threads in one form or another while remaining focused on the spinning wheel rather than expanding into the vast field of Gandhian ideology.

In the darkness of the 'vast silence' that Tagore referred to, Gandhi comes before us not as a calculating political leader who pre-decides his activities, but as a person who was not merely ready to experiment and mould his course of action and who at times actually lacked a systematic well-formed knowledge base to back his interventions and ideology. Gandhi's strength, however, was not this lack of knowledge or his vulnerability when venturing into darkness or doing things enveloped in 'vast silences', but his faith in his innate values, in his grasp over the experiences of common people and his deep optimism, along with an obsessive self-belief to gradually transform vast silences into arenas of buzzing sounds. Tagore was right when he pointed out the lack of a clearly defined and coherent set of ideas and future course of action to attain swaraj at that historical juncture (Gandhi's concerns over caste and various other social evils acquired sharpness and systematic articulation in the late 1920s or the 1930s). We also find Gandhi lacking crucial information on the charkha or the charkha programme itself. As we noted earlier, he advocated the spinning wheel when he had not even seen one. However, this lack of information was never an obstacle for him. This should not be read as Gandhi's disinterestedness (he wanted to garner as much information as possible, reflected in his passion to locate a piece of spinning wheel and any information relating to it). There is no shortage of examples showing us Gandhi's zest for information. The point to emphasise here is Gandhi's privileging of experiences, personal or collective, over information.

Finding a Charkha

Till 1917, no one in Gandhi's ashram had any knowledge of spinning. Some working wheels in the ashram were used to fill pearns and bobbins for weaving, but no one knew that these could also be used as spinning wheels. Gandhi grew so impatient that he left no stone unturned to get information on the subject. This difficulty in procuring information on spinning also reflects the social composition of visitors to his ashram at this juncture. He later reflected: 'But the art being confined to women and having been all but exterminated, if there was some stray spinner still surviving in some obscure corner, only a member of that sex was likely to find out her whereabouts' (Gandhi 1970: 391). As we see later, Gandhi's conviction about the gendered nature of spinning only grew stronger, and shaped the imageries of the spinning wheel and the act of spinning in major ways in later decades.

Gandhi's search came to an end when he met a widow named Gangabehn Majumdar, first at the Broach Educational Conference in 1917 and later at the Gujarat Political Conference in Godhra the same year. Her qualities (fearless, independent and bold; Gandhi mentioned that she was someone who 'felt home on horseback'), simplicity and services to the suppressed section of society immediately attracted Gandhi's attention (ibid.). It was she who, through her wanderings in the Gujarat countryside, found the spinning wheel in Vijapur in Baroda state. The people of Vijapur were willing to resume spinning if provided with a regular supply of slivers and a buyer for the yarn spun by them. The news was communicated to Gandhi. Umar Sobhani, a mill owner from Bombay (now Mumbai), agreed to send a sufficient supply of slivers from his mill. However, Gandhi soon felt ill at ease to be at the receiving end of Sobhani's generosity. To resolve this dependence on the mills, the search moved towards finding carders who could supply the slivers. Once again, Gangabehn helped find one prepared to card the cotton at a monthly salary of Rs 35. A few youngsters were also trained in making slivers out of carded cotton. The cotton was procured from Bombay with the help of Yshvantprasad Desai. Weavers were located and contacted and they agreed to weave the yarn spun in Vijapur. In the ashram, too, the spinning wheel quickly gained a foothold and with Maganlal Gandhi's several improvements to it, the ashram began manufacturing wheels and spindles. The first piece of khadi manufactured in the ashram cost 17 annas per yard (ibid.).[7] Gandhi appealed to every *satyagrahi*—male, female and child—to propagate hand-spinning. He wrote that the mechanism (of the spinning wheel) was simple, the cost of a spinning outfit less ('only about Rs 3-8-0 to Rs 4'), learning how to spin fast and easy (in a couple of days), but the reward handsome (Gandhi 1965b: 4).[8]

By the middle of 1919, however, we find Gandhi and his colleagues faced with a challenging and pragmatic issue: finding a market for the khadi cloth they produced. In June 1919, in his 'Letter to Chhaganlal Gandhi', Gandhi wrote, 'I have heard that, in the old Swadeshi Store, no one looks at our Khadi' (Gandhi 1965a: 350–51, 1965c: 341). The difficulty was economic as well as in terms of the wider agenda—using khadi and spinning as a way to reach out to the people of the country and propagate the message of *satyagraha* and swadeshi. At both these levels it became crucial to cater to the demand of the vast geographic regions of the country. Unlike Gujarat, where Gandhi found it difficult to find spinning wheels and a community of weavers and spinners, other parts of the country (Punjab being the most reported in Gandhian speeches and correspondences) were still manufacturing hand-spun and hand-woven cloth (no matter how reduced the scale of this production). In this context, Gandhi wrote, 'In my view no one from Calcutta or elsewhere on that side is likely to order Khadi from us' (Gandhi 1965a: 350–51).[9]

Maganlal played a crucial role in developing the khadi programme and the spinning wheel in Satyagraha Ashram. He was the manager and in-charge of the ashram and the most trusted by Gandhi.[10] Gandhi wrote that 'without Maganlal, the Ashram would never have come to be founded. His shortcomings bespeak mine. When I said that I, too, was a novice, I meant it' (ibid.: 10–11).

I shall neither elaborate on the history of these ashrams nor on the manner in which ashram activities gradually expanded, giving rise to institutional structures in the 1920s that were networked primarily because of their association with the Indian National Congress. The history of the spinning wheel can be approached through the rise, decline and functioning of these organisations and establishments in both colonial and postcolonial periods. However, I choose to move frequently in and out of the history of the Gandhian movement in order to capture the multilayered discourse around the spinning wheel as I wish to locate the spinning wheel in the experiential domain of colonial as well as postcolonial society. It is less about the institutional discourse of this Gandhian symbol and more about the manner in which the spinning wheel represented the hopes and aspirations of a ruptured society and its common people.

A Symbol of Hopes and Aspirations

Historians have thrown light on the generations who lived through the alleged period of transition and the particularities of the colonial experience. In this period of transition, the most severe impact of British rule fell on small-scale and traditional industries for two primary reasons: technological obsolescence (hand tools competing with modern machinery and losing) and closer economic integration between India and Britain. Colonialism affected, quite severely, the yarn sector in the production of both cotton and silk threads, a factor explored by historians as part of an intense and prolonged debate broadly classified under an equally debated term, de-industrialisation, in Indian historiography. Historians are divided on the use of this term, its historical status as well as its geographic and sectorial impact. I shall not go into the details of this debate as there is no dearth of scholarship on this subject (Pandey 1983a). Here, I briefly touch upon the decline of cotton spinning that set the stage for the spinning wheel to reappear as the Gandhian machine gun later.

Studies by Amiya Kumar Bagchi and Tirthankar Roy, among others, have engaged with the question of the decline of the cotton textile industry in the nineteenth century; the scale of this decline, however, was open to debate (Bagchi 1976; Vicziany 1986). Bagchi, using the statistics of Francis Buchanan-Hamilton and comparing them with figures from later decades, attested to a general decline in the cotton textile industry and various other small-scale and traditional industries in the nineteenth century. His use of statistics has, however, been questioned. Acording to Tirthankar Roy, hand-spinning was 'more or less the only example of a major traditional industry that became extinct due to competition from imported British goods'. He suggests that the use of handlooms had declined in the nineteenth century and in 1833, India imported about 46 million yards of British cloth. In 1887, this figure went up to 2,100 million yards and the size of the market was possibly 3,300 million yards. Thus, imported cloth made up 65 per cent of the total market in 1887 while in 1833 it was no more than 5 per cent, pointing to a decline in the market share of handlooms in domestic cloth consumption, from 9 to 35 per cent in 50 years (Roy 2000: 126). In this period of decline, Roy has shown that, surprisingly, since the 1880s, handloom cloth production and labour productivity rose continuously for the next 50 years. One of the reasons for this growth is attributed to a number of improved technological tools. Another reason is the expansion of the total cloth market in nineteenth-century India. A recent explanation for the rise is market segmentation catering to two different types of consumers. All these trends suggest two different strands in the case of textile production in nineteenth- and twentieth-century colonial India: competition with large-scale industry in spinning and segmented markets between small-scale and large-scale industry in handloom weaving (ibid.: 127).

Away from statistical figures and the contested numbers debate, the story of the decline had a powerful presence among both nationalists and the administrator intellectuals writing and recording in the late nineteenth and early twentieth century. William Crooke writes that weaving, 'one of the earlier and upto modern times the most widely spread rural industry is now in a state of decline' (Crooke 1972: 508). George Grierson, in his *Bihar Peasant Life*, indicates an indirect marker of this decline when he writes that the Musalman weaver or *jolha* is the proverbial fool of Hindu stories and proverbs (Grierson 1885: 69). In the examples of the proverbs that Grierson cites, a jolha is a figure of caricature in a dislocated situation, away from his loom, doing some other task: *karigah char tamaasa jay, Nahak chot jolaaha khaay* ('He left his loom to see the fun, and for no reason got a bruising'). Another proverb says: *kaua chalal baas ken, jolha chalal ghaas ken* ('the weaver went out to cut grass [at sunset], when even the crows were going home') (ibid.: 70). Historians like Gyan Pandey, Sandria Freitag and Anand Yang have exposed the communal character of these proverbs, yet the decline and dislocations of weaving and weavers' lives remained a powerful metaphor both at the popular level and in the moderate nationalist's critique of colonial rule (Freitag 1980; Pandey 1983a, 1983b; Yang 1980).

The power of Gandhian discourse lay in the power of Gandhi's reading of this displacement of Indian traditions by colonialism. Gandhi hardly invented any idea or any symbols. All he did was carefully select and rework old symbols. This process transformed the nature of even ordinary everyday objects. Objects and metaphors that were closely related to a wide cross-section of Indian people and were part of the day-to-day life of the nation very soon acquired different connotations. Gandhi invested them with new meanings and gave them new vitality and life. By injecting political meanings into these symbols, Gandhi not only expanded the domain of the play of power, but by investing politics where it did not exist in conscious ways, he in fact also politicised the whole way of Indian life. In Geertzian terms, this was the politicisation of Indian culture. The charkha is one such case. The folklore of the Bhojpuri region captures some of the hopes when, in a Bhojpuri *gramgeet* (village song), womenfolk sing: *Ab ham katabi charakhaba piya mati jahu bideshwa. Ham katabi charkha sajan tuhu jaab mili ahi se surajabaa, piya mati* ('Now I shall ply charkha, Oh dear, please don't go to alien lands. Oh dear, I shall ply charkha and we shall attain Swaraj ... Oh dear, don't go') (Mishra 1998: 248; translation is mine).

Spinning the Technology

From the perspective of organised politics, the khadi movement (which was central to the propagation of the Gandhian ideology of the spinning wheel) had clear organisational motives. It formed the core of Gandhian followers. The extension of the spinning wheel ideology obviously meant the broadening of Gandhi's mass political base and strengthening his cadre organisation (Kripalani 1946). Along with organisational politics, one of the clear messages the spinning wheel conveyed was the removal of unemployment among Indians in a seemingly innocent approach to a very complex and integrated economic planning with immense faith in human potential. C. Shambu Prasad has analysed colonial strategies for replacing the Indian cotton culture with the import of American cotton seeds (Prasad 1999). He writes that the Gandhian khadi movement responded to the colonial challenge by providing alternatives to colonial science and knowledge systems at each and every level. The khadi movement pushed this claim by propagating an indigenous methodology of research. The response of the khadi movement was thus not only cultural but also very much cultural-technological, where visual technology played a crucial role in the dissemination of the message (Trivedi 2003). Maganlal and, later, Richard Gregg, were quite concerned about research and other aspects of resistance to Western science and knowledge in this field. Maganlal, who was responsible for organising ashram activities in general and spinning and weaving in particular, had himself introduced a lot of change and modifications in the design of the spinning wheel since its arrival in the ashram in 1917. He had devised the Magan charkha. In a letter to Prabhudas, dated 28 August 1932, Mahatma Gandhi wrote about the Magan charkha:

> I have been able to go upto 30 counts on the Magan charkha up to now. I shall be satisfied if I go upto 40 counts. The speed is very slow. It does not go beyond a hundred rounds an hour. It may go beyond that if I draw thick yarn. But I do not wish to do so. The cause of the noise that the wheel was making was discovered. Mahadev guessed it. The rod under the plate was broken and the plate stopped functioning altogether the defect was discovered. On the rod being replaced the noise stopped and the plate also started functioning perfectly. I, too, believe with you that there is much room for improvement. None has occurred to me yet. (Gandhi 1991: 340–41)

In another letter to Prabhudas, dated 21 October 1932, Gandhi announced his success in making one improvement in the Magan charkha. He changed the spindle frame and fixed that of the Gandiv charkha in its place, thereby introducing a spring. He wrote,

> The result was that yarn was easily drawn fine. I used to spin yarn of twenty counts with great difficulty and then had made some progress. Now I can easily spin yarn of thirty counts. The speed is still the same, that is, a hundred rounds per hour. Even a little more at times. I may be able to increase the speed as also the count. The spindle-frame needs some changes. But I have now no carpenter. The carpenter prisoners have been released on the completion of their terms. (ibid.: 358)

There is an abundance of such detailed descriptions on the performance of the spinning wheel in Gandhi's writings. The reason for these two extended quotations is to draw attention to a simple yet often ignored dimension in the history of images and symbols. The spinning wheel has often been reduced to being a mere symbol representing Gandhian swaraj, which leads to a fundamental anomaly as this perspective would deny the spinning wheel the characteristics of an object, a tool, a machine, a thing. Gandhi was obsessively concerned with technical details and finding ways to improve this thing called the spinning wheel. Since the initial discovery of the spinning wheel, Gandhi was determined to improve its performance as well as its design.

A prize of Rs 5,000 was offered to the person who could invent a portable spinning wheel using indigenous components, as far as possible, which could take on 10 spindles at a time.[11] A gentleman, Kale, was awarded the prize and for some time we find Gandhi in a state of immense joy over Kale's experiment. In one such letter to Maganlal, Gandhi asked 'if the spinning wheel designed by Kale can be kept working for eight hours at a stretch' (Gandhi 1966a: 129–30). In another letter, we find him instructing Maganlal to send a block of the spinning wheel and Kale's photograph to Anandanand, to get to know him personally, to collect some facts about Kale's life and education, and to take out the patent of the spinning wheel in Maganlal's name. He wrote: 'If Kale agrees, name the spinning-wheel "Gangabai Spinning-wheel". He wants it to be named after himself. If that is still his wish, name it accordingly. Inscribe the name and other particulars on the spinning-wheel in Devnagari and Urdu scripts' (Gandhi 1965d: 62).[12] Gandhi himself designed the Gandiva charkha after making improvements to the Magan charkha (Gandhi 1966a: 499). However, he preferred the Punjab charkha, which he thought was ideal. Unlike popular perception, we should keep in mind that Gandhi was never against machines or science and technology. Shambu Prasad has argued that:

> Though a great believer in science, he (Gandhi) was clear of its role in the cosmos. Science to him was not above truth and ahimsa, which were 'truer' than many so-called scientific facts. They were however difficult to put into practice and only with 'proper previous preparation' could be rendered possible and easy .... If the pursuit of science through instrumental rationality led to the Weberian position of 'a disenchantment with the world', Gandhi's non-violent science argued that the combination of faith and reason could lead to territories hitherto unexplored by science. (Prasad 2001: 3732)

Prasad has shown the centrality of quest and the spirit of experimentation in Gandhi, who emphasised the unity of mind, body and spirt in exploring the relationship between nature, man and God. Gandhi emphasised the significance of body-labour and critiqued Rabindranath Tagore who had established spinning as an 'anti-intellectual activity' (Gandhi 1966b: 373). The ethical dimension was deeply ingrained in his concept of science, and thus for Gandhi, the machines or the improvements should suit the needs of the country and lend themselves to use in one's homes. Gandhi's understanding of the scientific method is perhaps best summarised in his own words on khadi:

> It must be borne in mind that to make the spinners self-reliant and through their activity to achieve India's freedom is, and ought to be, the Association's goal. That we may not reach that goal should not cause undue worry. It is enough for us to know that it is the correct goal and, having started the activity, we have to correct our mistakes and go forward. That is the essence of the scientific method. No science has dropped from the skies in a perfect form. All sciences develop and are built up through experience. Perfection is not an attribute of science. Absolute perfection is not possible either for man or for the science that he creates. (Prasad 2001: 3732)

The centrality of experience as the guiding spirt of any scientific experiment is one of the distinguishing features of the Gandhian framework on science and progress, and even a cursory glance through the manuals and pamphlets clearly shows a genre produced to disseminate both the ideas and the science of spinning. *Desi Kargha arthat Charkha-Kargha Shikshak* is one such example of a very detailed manual explaining the terms, objects and processes used in weaving and spinning (Khatri 1921). We also have manuals like Pattabhi Sitaramayya's *I Too Have Spun* (Sitaramayya 1946; Vijaydev 1960). A particular mention, however, must be made of *The Takli Teacher* by Richard B. Gregg and Maganlal Gandhi (1926), *Charkha Shastra* by Maganlal Gandhi (1924) and *Economics of Khaddar* by Richard B. Gregg (1928).

The response of the khadi movement to colonialism was thus both cultural and technological. It had its own way of popularising this indigenous technology. As stated before, Maganlal and later Gregg were concerned about research and other aspects of resistance to Western science and knowledge in this field. Maganlal related the death of fine cotton growing in India to the extinction of the fine art of spinning. What is interesting in these arguments is not only the content but also the style in which they have been put forward, and the claims of Western sciences negated. The *Charkha Shastra* provides one good example of the ways in which the whole discourse functioned (Gandhi 1924).

The book begins by narrating the usefulness and availability of cookery books in Europe and highlights the lack of such books in India. The author explains this as quite obvious since people in India did not dine out much. So, cooking was a part of our lifestyle and we did not need to learn it from any book. He then equates this with the pathetic condition of native cloth culture. This treatise on cotton cultivation very clearly specifies its objectives, but it also carries information on the Gandhian experience of cultivation and other related aspects of life (e.g., cleanliness, use of human waste, etc.). In this way, preaching the minute details of life in the Gandhian literature not only disseminated the ideals of living patterns, but by providing a functioning model (of the life of 'ashram'), it also tries to shape mentalities in a particular direction. The author writes,

> The special object aimed at preparing these pages has been to show that just as the key to perfect health, cleanliness, nourishment of the body and the happiness that results there from lies in manipulating all the processes from cleaning and grinding of wheat to the preparation of wholesome nourishing food at home; similarly the only way of obtaining and retaining freedom is to manage all the processes involved in the manufacture of finished cloth out of seed cotton in our homes; and that all this is perfectly possible to do. A mere perusal of the book however will not lead to a mastery of the subject. *Some of the processes cannot be learnt without actual, first hand observation.* These articles will serve to show where and to what extent the help of the teacher is necessary. (ibid.; emphasis mine)

Here, in *Charkha Shastra*, what is significant is the equation between mundane day-to-day activities and the threat posed to them by colonialism. These treaties, broadly structured in the Gandhian framework, did not lay claim to the authenticity of their words on the basis of any scientific inheritance of knowledge; rather, their claims were based on simple observation techniques which anybody could test personally. They invited readers to observe first-hand and only then believe the written word. The reference points of these treaties often come from the narration of daily life and its requirements.

These literatures can be accepted as a parody of modernity, as Gandhi himself was somehow a parody of Enlightenment rationalism. The

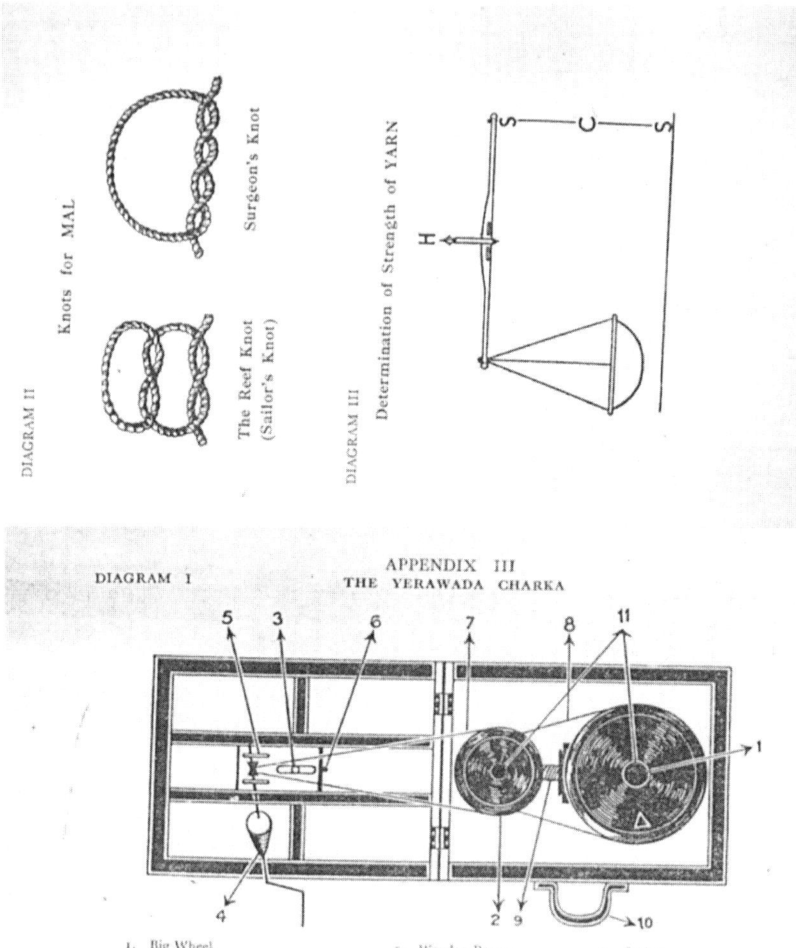

Figure 1: Yerawada charkha

Note: From an extremely lucid yet detailed manual on spinning and the spinning wheel by Pattabhi Sitaramayya, *I Too Have Spun* (1946, Appendix III). These manuals owe a lot to the efforts of Maganlal Gandhi and Richard B. Gregg for elaborating the functional aspects of the spinning wheel.

equation of modernisation with the displacement of our own traditional lifestyle is a warning about the inevitability of more disruptions in the near future if we went along with modern Western science. In such a scenario, *Charkha Shastra* warns its readers that they would have to depend on 'supplied knowledge' even for 'basic needs' like cloth and food. Thus, on the one hand, the book laughs at the validity of a particular hegemonic form of knowledge (the Western post-Enlightenment knowledge forms, which depend more on the written word than on daily observations and ignore the grassroots realities of the Indian way of life) and negates their utility at the level of innocence.[13] On the other hand, the book also plays with the fear of the future. By inviting its readers to judge the validity of claims in their own life, the book (and this is also applied to Gandhian literature in general) opens up an undreamed of field of imagination to interpret the meanings of the written words in their own desired ways, further enhancing the claims of the author. This invitation to test the validity of authorial claims further legitimises such claims. For this purpose, Gandhi used a whole network of signs, metaphors, concepts, etc., and presented very abstract philosophical thoughts in very innocent ways. Here 'a certain affinity between the speaker's mind and the supposed muddleheadedness of his listeners should not be discounted' (Adorno 2000: 29). This perspective suggests that the significance of the charkha or the khadi movement cannot be understood in isolation. Their importance can only be realised by placing them in the midst of Gandhian metaphors and Gandhi's economic philosophy. As one strategy of colonial dominance cannot be separated from another, one face of Gandhian metaphor cannot be analysed in isolation.

Conclusion: Experience and Techne

Let me reiterate a less repeated point: Gandhi was not against science (Prasad 2001). There is ample evidence to suggest that the contrast created by the binary of the saint versus the scientist is hugely simplistic and misleading. Gandhi was against a specific mode of science. However, here, I refrain from demonstrating Gandhi's views on science. What I find quite interesting in Gandhi's references to science is his complete adoration of the figure of the scientist. Gandhi also coined the word 'satyagrahi scientist'.

He once wrote, 'I have nothing but praise for the zeal, industry and sacrifice that have animated the modern scientists in pursuit after truth'.[14] He was also not against speed, a point which may not be palatable to Gandhi's critics. Gandhi once wrote, 'But, the village movement, as I conceive it, does not discount speed or efficiency of production' (Gandhi 1976: 210). His appreciation and craving for speed leading to production growth can be easily noticed in the history of the experiments carried out in the ashram under the diligent managerial eyes of Maganlal and, subsequently, in the growth of the Amber charkha.

Such a history then leaves us with a twofold question: What do Gandhi's scientists like Maganlal or Richard Gregg (who worked closely with Maganlal) offer us in the history of the charkha? Second, what was the nature of Gandhi's engagement with science and technology? Let us narrow down the question further to technology: What insights do we get from harping on this history of technology in the Gandhian investment in the spinning wheel?

The question of Gandhi's technological investment in the charkha leads us to the history of spinning technology in India's past. In terms of historical documentation, there is a debate on the emergence of the spinning wheel. If we agree with Irfan Habib, we find that the important mechanical device of the spinning wheel is referred to in India for the first time in Ishami's *Futuh-s-Salatin* (1350), as an instrument to which women should apply themselves. As pointed out by Lynn White Jr., the spinning wheel was unknown in ancient India. It is probably certain that the spinning wheel came to India from China through Iran or central Asia, possibly in the thirteenth century (Habib 2007: 371). However, I must confess that the scope of this chapter does not permit me to venture into the pre-colonial historical trajectories of the spinning wheel, no matter how enticing and rewarding such a journey might be. Instead, I am keen to ask how Gandhi, in his investment in the charkha, enables us to think about technology differently. For this purpose, I find Heidegger's question on technology quite insightful.

Heidegger suggests that we move away from a technical understanding of technology as that will only lead to an instrumental understanding of the term. For him, technology is no mere means. It 'is a mode of revealing. Technology comes to presence in the realm where revealing and unconcealment take place, where aletheia, truth happens'. In its ambit, 'techne is the name not only for the activities and skill of the craftsman, but also for the arts of the mind and fine arts. Techne belongs to bringing-forth, to poiesis; it is something poetic' (Heidegger 1977: 13). However, he differentiates between technology and modern technology. 'The revealing that rules in modern technology is a challenging [*Herausfordern*] which puts to nature the unreasonable demand that it supply energy that can be extracted and stored as such' (ibid.: 14). In this way '[m]odern technology as an ordering revealing is, then, no merely human doing' (ibid.: 19).

The coming together of techne and poiesis in Heidegger's formulation also paves the way for bringing in Gandhi's spinning wheel and folksayings and songs related to the charkha, some of which are mentioned in this chapter. In both cases, experience comes before us as a connecting thread. To appreciate this linkage, we need to recall Jean-Francois Lyotard's critique of the authority of the scientific truth when he mobilises the episteme of the narratives (Lyotard 1992: 27–37). Lyotard argues,

> Consider the form of popular sayings, proverbs, and maxims: they are like little splinters of potential narratives, or molds of old ones, which have continued to circulate on certain levels of the contemporary social edifice. In their prosody can be recognised the mark of that strange temporalization that jars the golden rule of our knowledge: 'never forget'. (ibid.: 21–22)

Unlike scientific knowledge, in the proverbs, couplets and folk forms of knowledge, the reliance has been on the experiences which keep the poetic (poesis of Heidegger) alive and circulating. Kabir's poetry can be quite illustrative of this connection: *Charkha chalai surat birhin ka. Kaya nagari bani ati sundar, mahal bana chetan ka* ('A birhin [one who is longing for her beloved] is plying the spinning wheel. The city has taken a beautiful form, where consciousness is the palace.') (Dwivedi 1995: 218; author's translation).

In another popular poem, Kabir says: *Jhini jhini bini chadariya ... Ingla pingla taanaa bharani, Sukhman taar se bini chadariya, Aath kamal dal charkha dole, paanch lat gun bini chadariya*' ('Delicately and in slow pace, he weaves the spread ... *Ingla pingla* [names of two nerves] as warp, sukhman [another nerve] as the thread, with a spinning wheel on the eight lotuses, with five senses and three gunas [essential properties], he thus weaves the spread') (author's translation).

Here, in Kabir's poetry, with all the symbolism and metaphors of weaving, the technology of spinning is embedded in the experiential landscape; and techne, in such embedded occurrences, is not merely about the knowledge of spinning which can be reproduced outside this specific milieu. This poetry (poesis), this technology (of spinning and weaving), the language and this experience all are essentially coordinated in and through an economy of the human body. It is this body which alone gives meaning to each of these elements in this web.

Scholars have shown that weaving, weavers' looms or the weaving techniques are not merely modes of cloth production. Roy Dilley, in his study of the Tukolor loom of Senegal, has shown the interplay of myths, traditional beliefs and rituals at work in the weaving space, the weaver's loom (Dilley 1987). In the Indian context, Deepak Mehta, in his study of the community of Muslim weavers of Barabanki (Uttar Pradesh), has analysed that 'the technique of making cloth and quilts is constituted within a semiotic system' (1997: 3). He explores the body of the weaver as the site where both verbal and non-verbal actions are embodied and disembodied. On the other hand, Kathryn S. March, in her study of the Tamang culture of Nepal, compares the cultural act of weaving with that of writing. She tells us that,

> [f]or the Tamang, weaving and writing are not only technical skills but dense symbols of gender. They are gender symbols not only because they tell the Tamang about the separate roles of the sexes, but because they are about what transpires between the sexes as each defines the other. Two opposing conceptions of the world emerge as Tamang men and women view one another. (March 1984: 729)

Returning to Mahatma Gandhi's mobilisation of the spinning wheel, we find that like Kabir's poetic rendering, the Mahatma's usage of spinning is not detached from other experiences. It is central to his overall anchorage of the truth as revealed in and through one's own experience/experiment. Hence, an experiment with truth. It is only in this embeddedness that truth is revealed. In both Gandhi and the philosopher Heidegger, therefore, technology has to be about the revelation of its connectedness with the human body. It is in this revelation that the knowledge of spinning, of technology and the science of spinning remains essentially corpothetic in nature. It is here that the body can never be separated from the knowledge of either spinning or its ultimate objective, i.e., satyagraha and swaraj. Therefore, here we are once again reminded of Heidegger's proposition that 'manufacture' implies surfacing and technology is not merely a means or a tool. It has to serve the purpose of revelation in one form or another. Similarly, in Gandhi, one cannot separate means and ends, process and outcome, the experiment and the knowledge. At another level, when Heidegger harps upon the *poesis* (poetic), one can read it as an incitement to critique the language of the science which takes its legitimacy from being non-poetic, precise and unambiguous. Similarly, Gandhi's weaving of the politics of the spinning wheel comes before us not through a separation of science and art, economics and ethics, scientists and satyagrahis, and knowledge and experience. It is in their embedding of one in another, in giving primacy to experience over knowledge backed by the specific history of science that Gandhi spins truth and the politics of knowledge.

Notes

1. By July 1917, seven looms were working in the ashram and five more under its supervision. The total capital expenditure involved was Rs 300 and, by this time, cloth worth Rs 500 had been sold. Four families (who had given up weaving earlier), altogether 17 people, made their living from weaving. The monthly expenditure on weaving was Rs 100. See 'Circular Letter for Funds for Ashram' in Gandhi (1964: 455–58).

2. Established on Vaisakh Vad 6, Thursday, 20 May 1915, the ashram was initially accommodated in two houses on the banks of the Sabarmati river at Ahmedabad on the road to Sarakhej across Ellis bridge. Later, in July 1917, it was moved to its current spacious location. The ashram consisted of three groups of people: controllers, novitiates (those desirous of following the programme but unable to take the necessary vows immediately) and students (any children above four years of age, including grown-ups admitted in the ashram). See 'Draft Constitution for the Ashram', before 20 May 1915 (ibid.: 91–98).

3. 'The controllers believe that one of the chief causes of poverty in the land is the virtual disappearance of spinning wheels and handlooms. They will therefore, make every effort to revive this industry by themselves weaving cloth on handlooms'. See 'Draft Constitution for the Ashram', before 20 May 1915 (ibid.).

4. See 'The Birth of Khadi', in Gandhi (1970: 390).

5. Gandhi said: 'The Poet lives in a magnificent world of his own creation—his world of ideas. I am a slave of some body else's creation—the spinning wheel' (Gandhi, 'The Poet and the Charkha', *Young India*, 5 November 1925, in Bhattacharya [1997: 122–26]).

6. 'Is it [Charkha] really so big as all that? .... Can it then be expected that in the shrine of swaraj, the charkha goddess will attract to herself alone the offerings of every devotee? Surely such expectation amounts to a distrust of human nature, a disrespect for India's people.' See Rabindranath Tagore's 'The Cult of Charkha', *Modern Review*, September 1925, in Bhattacharya (1997: 99–112).

7. Within a short span of less than two years, by August 1919, Gandhi proudly wrote that 125 women were spinning under the leadership of Gangabehn Majumdar in Vijapur (Gandhi 1965b: 8). Here, one must not accept these figures in literal terms as Gandhi had a very strange relationship with numerical figures—a theme so far not addressed by Gandhian scholars. Four days after the abovementioned letter, the number increased to 150 women (ibid.: 21).

8. On earning from the spinning wheel, Gandhi wrote: 'The man who spins earns three annas daily, but the man who weaves earns eight annas. Talking to the weavers of Madanwadi in Bombay, I came to know that many of them earned as much as one rupee, even two rupees daily' (*Indian Opinion*, 10 October 1919, in ibid.: 18–22). Along with widows (very much at the centre of Gandhi's appeal), he wanted to incorporate even the big mass of mendicants in this task of spinning. Gandhi wrote that there were 56,000 sadhus in India who lived entirely on begging—'tempt these sadhus out of their idleness and to persuade them to employ themselves in spinning and weaving' (Speech at the opening of Shudha Swadeshi Vastra Bhandar, 18 June 1919, in Gandhi [1965a: 378–81]).

9. In his long piece on the 'Use of Khadi', Gandhi wrote, 'Hundreds of women have started spinning in this way but we do not get enough men and women to wear the cloth produced. A year ago, Khadi was not available in sufficient quantity. A spun yarn was quite difficult to come by in the beginning. Now, after one year, I am offered so much of hand-spun yarn that I can not take it all. The stocks of Khadi with me have grown so large that the quantities cleared are inadequate' (Gandhi 1965c: 339).

10. On Maganlal's birthday, Gandhi wrote to him from Motihari, 'You are all that I have and all I desire' ('Letter to Maganlal', Shravan Sud 5, 1973 [24 July 1917], in Gandhi [1964: 475]). The term 'satyagraha' is a revised form of 'sadagraha' which was suggested by Maganlal when a small prize was announced in *Indian Opinion* seeking the best designation for the Indian struggle in leiu of 'passive resistance' (Iyer 2000: 269).

11. The model was to reach Satyagraha Ashram by 1 January 1920 (Gandhi 1965b: 217–18). The competition for this prize was held at Ahmedabad on 31 March 1920.

12. This euphoric outburst, however, did not survive long and by October 1920 we find a public statement that the model was found unsatisfactory (Gandhi 1965d: 59, fn. 2).

13. Lyotard has discussed this aspect of the legitimacy of knowledge in scientific and narrative forms of knowledge (Lyotard 1992: 27–37).

14. Gandhi's speech at the opening of Tibbi College in Delhi (Gandhi 1966a: 357–58).

References

Adorno, T. W. 2000. *The Psychological Technique of Martin Luther Thomas' Radio Addresses*. California: Stanford University Press.

Amin, S. 1995. *Event Metaphor, Memory: Chauri Chaura 1922–92*. New Delhi: Oxford University Press.

Bagchi, A. K. 1976. 'Deindustrialisation in Gangetic Bihar, 1809–1901'. In *Essays in Honour of Prof. S. C. Sarkar*, ed. B. De, 499–522. Delhi: People's Publishing House.

Bayly, C. A. 1998. *Origins of Nationality in South Asia: Patriotism and Ethical Government in the Making of Modern India*. New Delhi: Oxford University Press.

Bean, S. 1980. 'Gandhi and Khadi, the Fabric of Indian Independence'. In *Cloth and Human Experience*, ed. A. B. Weiner and J. Schneider, 355–76. Washington, D.C.: Smithsonian Institution Press.

Bhattacharya, S., ed. 1997. *The Mahatma and the Poet*. New Delhi: National Book Trust.

Cohn, Bernard S. 1996. *Colonialism and its Forms of Knowledge: The British in India*. Princeton: Princeton University Press.

Crooke, William. 1972. *Things Indian: Being Discursive Notes on Various Subjects Connected with India*. Delhi: Oriental Books Reprint Cooperation.

Dilley, Roy. 1987. 'Myth and Meaning and the Tukolor Loom'. *Man* 22 (2): 256-66.

Dwivedi, H. 1995. *Kabir*. New Delhi: Rajkamal.

Freitag, S. 1980. 'Sacred Symbol as Mobilising Ideology: North Indian Search for a "Hindu" Community'. *Comparative Studies in Society and History* 22 (4): 597–625.

Gandhi, M. 1924. *Charkha Shastra*. Sabarmati: All India Khadi Information Bureau.

Gandhi, M. K. 1922. 'Economic vs. Moral Progress'. In *Speeches and Writings of M. K. Gandhi*. With an introduction by C. F. Andrews, 286–93. Madras: G. A. Natesan & Co.

——. 1964. *The Collected Works of Mahatma Gandhi*. Vol. 13. New Delhi: The Publications Division, Ministry of Information and Broadcasting, Government of India.

——. 1965a. *The Collected Works of Mahatma Gandhi*. Vol. 15. New Delhi: The Publications Division, Ministry of Information and Broadcasting, Government of India.

——. 1965b. *The Collected Works of Mahatma Gandhi*. Vol. 16. New Delhi: The Publications Division, Ministry of Information and Broadcasting, Government of India.

——. 1965c. *The Collected Works of Mahatma Gandhi*. Vol. 17. New Delhi: The Publications Division, Ministry of Information and Broadcasting, Government of India.

——. 1965d. *The Collected Works of Mahatma Gandhi*. Vol. 18. New Delhi: The Publications Division, Ministry of Information and Broadcasting, Government of India.

——. 1966a. *The Collected Works of Mahatma Gandhi*. Vol. 19. New Delhi: The Publications Division, Ministry of Information and Broadcasting, Government of India.

——. 1966b. *The Collected Works of Mahatma Gandhi*. Vol. 21. New Delhi: The Publications Division, Ministry of Information and Broadcasting, Government of India.

——. 1967a. *The Collected Works of Mahatma Gandhi*. Vol. 25. New Delhi: The Publications Division, Ministry of Information and Broadcasting, Government of India.

——. 1967b. *The Collected Works of Mahatma Gandhi*. Vol. 26. New Delhi: The Publications Division, Ministry of Information and Broadcasting, Government of India.

——. 1970. *The Collected Works of Mahatma Gandhi*. Vol. 39. New Delhi: The Publications Division, Ministry of Information and Broadcasting, Government of India.

——. 1976. 'The Reed v. The Fountain-Pen'. In *The Collected Works of Mahatma Gandhi*. Vol. 65. New Delhi: The Publications Division, Ministry of Information and Broadcasting, Government of India.

——. 1991. *The Collected Works of Mahatma Gandhi, Supplementary Volume II (1929–1934)*. Vol. 92. New Delhi: The Publications Division, Ministry of Information and Broadcasting, Government of India.

Gregg, R. B. 1928. *Economics of Khaddar*. Madras: S. Ganesan.

Gregg, R. B., and M. Gandhi. 1926. *The Takli Teacher*. Sabarmati: Technical Department, All India Spinners' Association.

Grierson, G. A. 1885. *Bihar Peasant Life: Being a Discursive Catalogue of the People of that Province*. Calcutta: The Bengal Secretariat Press.

Habib, I. 2007. *Essays in Indian History: Towards a Marxist Perspective*. New Delhi: Tulika Books.

Hamara Charkha. n.d. Proscribed literature. Delhi: Nehru Memorial Museum and Library.

Heidegger, M. 1977. *The Question Concerning Technology and Other Essays*. Translated and with an introduction by William Lovitt. New York and London: Garland Publishing.

Huq, A. M. 1985. 'The Economics of Growth and Employment: The Gandhian Approach'. In *Essays in Gandhian Economics*, ed. R. Diwan and M. Lutz, 158–65. New Delhi: Gandhi Peace Foundation.

Iyer, R. N. 2000. *The Moral and Political Thought of Mahatma Gandhi*. New Delhi: Oxford University Press.

Jha, S. 2004. 'Charkha, "Dear Forgotten Friend" of Widows: Reading the Erasures of a Symbol'. *Economic and Political Weekly* 39 (28): 3113–20.

Khatri, T. P. 1921. *Desi Kargha arthat Charkha-Kargha Shikshak*. Banaras: Munnilal Gujarati.

Kripalani, J. B. 1946. *Politics of Charkha*. Bombay: Vora & Co.

Lyotard, J. F. 1992. *The Postmodern Condition: A Report on Knowledge*. Manchester: Manchester University Press.

March, K. S. 1984. 'Weaving, Writing and Gender'. *Man* (New Series) 18: 729–44.

Mehta, D. 1997. *Work, Ritual, Biography: A Muslim Community in North India*. New Delhi: Oxford University Press.

Mishra, S. K., comp. and ed. 1998. *Azadi ki Shikhayan*. New Delhi: Indian Fertilisers Co-operative Ltd.

Pande, B. N. 1994. 'Gandhi ji Early Encounter with Economists'. *Yojana* 38 (18): 4–11.

Pandey, G. 1983a. 'Economic Dislocation in Nineteenth-century Eastern Utter Pradesh: Some Implications of the Decline of Artisanal Industry in Colonial India'. In *Rural South Asia: Linkages, Change and Development*, ed. P. Robb, 89–129. Delhi: Segment Book Distributors.

——. 1983b. 'Rallying Round the Cow: Sectarian Strife in the Bhojpur Region, c. 1880–1917'. In *Subaltern Studies*, Vol. II, ed. R. Guha, 60–129. Delhi: Oxford University Press.

Parel, A. J., ed. 1997. *Hind Swaraj and Other Writings*. New Delhi: Cambridge University Press.

Prasad, C. S. 1999. 'Suicide Deaths and Quality of Indian Cotton: Perspectives from History of Technology and Khadi Movement'. *Economic and Political Weekly* 34 (5): PE-12–21.

——. 2001. 'Towards an Understanding of Gandhi's Views on Science'. *Economic and Political Weekly* 36 (39): 3721–32.

Roy, T. 2000. *The Economic History of India, 1857–1947*. New Delhi: Oxford University Press.

Sitaramayya, P. 1946. *I Too Have Spun*. Bombay: Hind Kitab Limited.

Tarlo, E. 1995. *Clothing Matters: Dress in India*. New Delhi: Viking.

Trivedi, L. N. 2003. 'Visually Mapping the "Nation": Swadeshi Politics in Nationalist India, 1920–1930'. *The Journal of Asian Studies* 62 (1): 11–41.

Vicziany, M. 1986. 'Imperialism, Botany and Statistics in Early Nineteenth Century India: The Surveys of Francis Buchanan (1762–1829)'. *Modern Asian Studies* 20 (4): 625–60.

Vijayadev. 1960. *Ambar Charkha: The Silent Revolutionary*. Bombay: United Asia Publications.

Yang, A. A. 1980. 'Sacred Symbol and Sacred Space in Rural India: Community Mobilization in the "Anti-Cow Killing" Riot of 1893'. *Comparative Studies in Society and History* 22 (4): 576–96.

Seven

Swaraj and *Nai Talim*
Notes on Self-sufficiency

Deeptha Achar

I can only think of national education in terms of swaraj.
—M. K. Gandhi, 1924

In many ways, this chapter is about the demand for compulsory education in India. I focus here on the 1930s, when popular aspiration for education found its way into public policy. What is particularly significant about this demand at this time is the manner in which it was manifested in the Wardha Resolution of 1937. It was in this influential resolution on education that a new category was deployed in the national debate on schooling: that of craft. Clearly, this category was in itself not new; indeed, it was a keyword in other discourses, other disciplines, and implicated in the making of nationalist art history. What was novel, perhaps radical, was its entry into the discourse on education in India.

The demand for free, compulsory primary education emerged in the first decade of the twentieth century, precisely at the time when Ananda Coomaraswamy was writing works such as *The Indian Craftsman* (1909) and the *Arts and Crafts of India and Ceylon* (1913). G. K. Gokhale had moved a resolution for compulsory free education in 1910, which he withdrew on the assurance that the colonial government would examine the question thoroughly. He reintroduced the Bill in the Imperial Legislative Assembly, but it was defeated in 1912. The idea of setting up a state-wide scheme for compulsory education was not, however, new. Sayajirao Gaekwad III had put in place a compulsory education programme in Baroda State, first conducting a pilot study in Amreli district in the 1890s, and then extending it to the whole state in 1906. By the time Gandhi took up the question of an education for the nation, key elements in the discourse on education had already been put in place.

Gandhi's intervention in the debate in 1936, it can be argued, was not unexpected. He had consistently written on education—a chapter in *Hind Swaraj* is focused on education—and, in Tolstoy Farm, he had sought to work out a new kind of education where manual labour was centrally placed. This chapter attempts to examine the way the idea of *swaraj* or self-rule is built into the Gandhian scheme of education and its implications for the way the nation is imagined.

I

It is commonplace today to argue that the key elements of Gandhian thought were forged in South Africa and that the ideas of swaraj and *satyagraha* (truth force) shaped Gandhi's political and social thought. In *Satyagraha in South Africa*, Gandhi positioned the satyagraha practised in South Africa as the first instance of and as parallel to 'all our experiences in the present struggle to date' (Gandhi 1972: xiv). Swaraj, too, was conceptualised in a South African context. His reconceptualisation of swaraj away from 'English rule without the Englishman' (Gandhi 1938: 25) to 'It is Swaraj when we learn to rule ourselves' (ibid.: 60) famously shifted the field of government from the state to the self. Reimagining swaraj as self-government placed a new emphasis on the body, for where else can the self be housed? The body, then, becomes the site where practices of self-government are put in place. The Gandhian stress on diet and *brahmacharya* (control of the senses in thought, word and deed) is an index to the new value of the body. In some ways, the interest in diet was in place even when Vivekananda is famously supposed to have declared that the salvation of Hindus depended on the three Bs: beef, biceps and the *Bhagavad Gita* (Gandhi 2006: 209; Nandy 2009: Ch. 1). This is not, however, to suggest that there were no pre-colonial engagements with the body in relation to food and sex; with colonialism, though, this interest took a quite different trajectory.

Gandhi established these regimes of bodily control in the interest of a new self-fashioning characterised by a sacrifice of the self that is at the same time a realisation of manhood.[1] The recurrence of manhood, being a man, as tropes in his writings on swaraj and satyagraha, gestures to the impossibility of extricating the body from the self. Gandhi, in his initial speech about the 'new principle' of satyagraha that he recounted in *Satyagraha in South Africa*, repeatedly referred to an individual's manhood being at stake if that individual breaks the *satyagrahi's* pledge: 'Personally I hold that a man, who deliberately and intelligently takes a pledge and then breaks it, forfeits his manhood' (Gandhi 1972: 97). Elsewhere in the book he refers to the community 'manfully' standing the test as satyagrahis (ibid.: 99).[2] By the end of the book, Gandhi can confidently say: 'Satyagraha is a priceless and matchless weapon, and ... those who wield it are strangers to disappointment and defeat', their 'manhood' forged by passing 'through the fire of Satyagraha' (ibid.: 307). Gandhi's argument around education in *Hind Swaraj* too states that 'whether you take elementary education or higher education, it is not required for the main thing. It does not make men of us' (Gandhi 1938: 83). These ideas were still in play by the time Gandhi presented his vision of *Nai Talim* (basic education/new education).

The Wardha Resolution of 1937 was a moment when popular aspiration for education found its way into public policy. It is not as if the question of primary education had not been the subject of debate in colonial India. Indeed, colonial education was a site of debate and discussion from its very inception. What marks the 1937 resolution as particularly significant is the fact that the popularly elected, largely Congress, government in the Provincial Legislative Assemblies sought to write these aspirations into a policy and a programme.[3]

The All India Educational Conference was held in Wardha in October 1937, under the leadership of Gandhi. The following four resolutions passed at the conference succinctly represent the alternative educational paradigm, which it was hoped would shape the national educational system of independent India.

1. That, in the opinion of this conference, free and compulsory education be provided for seven years on a nation-wide scale.
2. That the medium of instruction be the mother tongue.
3. That the Conference endorses the proposal, made by Mahatma Gandhi, that the process of education throughout this period should centre round some productive form of manual work, and that all other abilities to be developed or training to be given should, as far as possible, be integrally related to the central handicraft chosen with due regard to the environment of the child.
4. That the Conference expects that the system of education will gradually be able to cover the remuneration of the teachers.[4]

The report of the Committee appointed by the Wardha Conference to prepare a detailed educational scheme based on these principles was presented to the Indian National Congress (INC) at the Haripura session (the annual session of the INC) of 1938. Except for the last resolution concerning the economic self-sufficiency of educational institutions, the Wardha Scheme was accepted. The concept of Basic Education, or Nai Talim, as it was called, became the guiding principle of the Provincial Legislative Assemblies, as well as the cornerstone for educational thinking in a newly independent India.

The first two resolutions are not particularly novel. In fact, compulsory education had been introduced by Sayajirao Gaekwad III in 1906.[5] The debate on mother tongue versus English as a medium of instruction had been raging for a good part of the nineteenth century.[6] Far more radical are the last two resolutions regarding work and self-sufficiency. The craft-based education proposed by Gandhi, and elaborated in the *Report of the Zakir Husain Committee*, envisaged a mass education system organised around manual work embodied as craft. The report argued that

> Socially considered, the introduction of such practical productive work in education, to be participated in by all the children of the nation, will tend to breakdown the existing barriers of prejudice between manual and intellectual workers, harmful alike for both. It will also cultivate in the only possible way a true sense of dignity of labour and of human solidarity—an ethical and moral gain of incalculable significance. (Aggarwal 1992: 59)

Quite clearly, the Wardha Scheme was a product of Gandhi's thought.[7] Glyn Richards has traced the Gandhian emphasis on craft and self-reliance back to the early 1920s; he finds no significant shift in Gandhian thinking on education. He notes that Gandhi 'favored the correlation of handicrafts and literacy in the field of primary education, because it cultivated the creative instincts, promoted self-reliance and encouraged self-sufficiency' (Richards 2001: 33). As early as 1921, Gandhi had argued that '[t]he introduction of manual training will serve a double purpose in a poor country like ours. It will pay for the education of our children and teach them an occupation on which they can fall back in afterlife' (Gandhi 2012: 45). His 1936 Wardha Scheme was in line with his vision of a thriving self-sufficient rural economy, and was consistent with his efforts to provide alternatives to 'Western' conceptual models. Working away from the Western model of childhood which saw childhood increasingly defined away from the public sphere and located across the worlds of education and leisure, the Gandhian model saw childhood as firmly situated within the economics of the nation. Indeed, he characterised training in manual work as a key function of national education, as it was this that could equip most of the agrarian population with ability and pride in work.

The idea of a national education system that could run independently without external funding went against everything known about national education systems. The main reason for opposition to Gokhale's Education Bill was that a national system would cost a lot of money. Further, it rescued national education from being tainted by 'drink revenue'. Gandhi declared:

> We shall deserve the curse of posterity if we do not wisely decide to stop the drink evil, even though we may have to sacrifice the education of our children. But we need not. I know many of you have laughed at the idea of making education self-supporting by introducing spinning in our schools and colleges. I assure you that it solves the problem of education as nothing else can. (Gandhi 2012: 44)

To that extent, Gandhi's plan extricated the system of national education from that of the national economy by means of putting the child to work. This move could be made only through the radical re-visioning of the very structure of modern childhood, which was premised upon the separation of childhood from paid work. Gandhi said:

> I fancy that even under an ideal system of government, we shall not be able to devote two thousand million rupees which we should require for finding education for all the children of school going age. It follows, therefore, that our children must be made to pay in *labour* partly or wholly for all the education they receive. (ibid.: 45; emphasis in the original)

The transfer of the cost of education onto its recipients makes education reach all, but does so through the alienation of the labour of the child.

In many ways, Gandhi's idea, bypassed in contemporary India, that mass education should be given through village crafts like spinning and weaving and not through books, that children should actually produce articles that are marketable, and that these should be sold to make education self-supporting went against the nationalist line.[8] Even national leaders did not feel too comfortable with this scheme, evident in Gandhi's reassurance to Madan Mohan Malviya 'saying that there was nothing final about the Conference as it was a Conference of seekers and everyone was invited to offer suggestions and criticisms. He never had the idea of carrying through anything by storm' (Gandhi 1976: 273). Indeed, the opposition to this clause was so strong that despite Gandhi's charisma, it was dropped at the INC's Haripura session in 1938.

However, Gandhi argued:

> It is my belief that a craft which immediately suggests itself for making primary schools self-sufficient is spinning and allied processes. This includes all the processes from picking cotton to weaving intricate designs into khadi .... While teaching the crafts, subjects like history, geography and arithmetic would be partially or wholly covered. Language and grammar as part of it, and also correct pronunciation would be naturally included.[9]

Craft, here, is a democratic principle that 'breaks down existing barriers of prejudice', as also an ideal fusion of intellectual progress woven around traditional technical skill that could inculcate a 'true sense of dignity of labour and of human solidarity'. In this model, manual work disciplines the body and trains the mind. At the centre of primary education, it stands as a counter to a mere literary education and equips the child for life after school. It addresses questions of livelihood and employment. 'If a barber or shoemaker attends college, he ought not to abandon the profession of a barber or shoemaker', Gandhi had argued in 1921 (Gandhi 2012: 40–41).

This move to institute work at the heart of mass education was truly radical. Pedagogically, it offered an alternative to the compartmentalisation between subjects, to the separation of physical and intellectual activity in schools. Ideologically, such a move was productive at a number of levels: it countered colonialist ideas which conceived childhood as radically separate from the sphere of work. Focusing on village craft, it displaced the urban-centredness of modern systems of education even as it privileged working-class competencies over dominant-class book learning. In fact, the *Report of the Zakir Husain Committee* suggests that craft-based productive learning worked against the separation of life and education, work and learning, outside world and school, on which Western education is structured in order to construct a holistic model of the self through which 'the highest development of the mind and soul is possible'.

By situating manual work at the heart of national education, Gandhi fixed the labouring body of the child at its centre. This was the body that would house the self which was to be governed by the principles of swaraj, the body that would contain soul-force enough to offer satyagraha. Its labour would allow national education to be self-sufficient through training that would render the child able to earn a livelihood, making him able to govern his own self. Stephen A. Marglin's distinction between the knowledge systems 'techne' and 'episteme' would help to elucidate the radical possibilities that such a scheme of national education could have had (Marglin 1990). Marglin argues that the twentieth century has been marked by the rise of the episteme, which is structured by instrumental reason; it is 'purely cerebral, disembedded from the body, and indeed from particular contexts; episteme produces universal knowledge' (ibid.: 36). He suggests that '[e]pistemic rules for transmission and innovation are highly individualistic; in principle epistemic knowledge is an open book which anyone can read', in contrast to techne.

> [Techne] has a very different epistemology, emphasizing a variety of sources which range from intuition to authority. It is knowledge embedded in practice, often implicit in nature, indeed often tacit knowledge literally embedded in the body, as the knowledge of a wheelwright, surgeon, or pianist is embedded in the hands as well as in the mind. It is, in a word, non dualistic. (ibid.)

Such an understanding of knowledge systems surely is indicative of the possibilities of seeing craft-as-education in a non-dualistic form that refuses the colonial emphasis on the episteme.

The basic crafts proposed for study in the *Report of the Zakir Husain Committee* were defined as follows:

> The Basic Craft: Such reasonable skill should be attained in the handicrafts chosen, as would enable the pupil to pursue it as an occupation after finishing his full course.
>
> The following may be chosen as basic crafts in various schools:
>
> (a) Spinning and weaving
> (b) Carpentry

> (c) Agriculture
> (d) Fruit and vegetable gardening
> (e) Leather work
> (f) Any other craft for which local and geographical conditions are favorable and which satisfies the conditions mentioned above.
>
> Even where an industry other than spinning and weaving or agriculture is the basic craft, the pupils will be expected to attain a minimum knowledge of carding and spinning with the *takli*, and a practical acquaintance of elementary agricultural work in the local area. (Aggarwal 1992: 61)

This list offers us an insight into the manner in which the policy acquires a critical charge. A careful examination of these craft categories shows a remarkable coincidence of these categories with artisanal work performed by 'lower'-caste groups. This has been noted by Glyn Richards, who comments that 'Gandhi was proposing something quite revolutionary when he referred to the sacramental nature of manual labour, by means of which we were identifying ourselves with the lower strata of society' (Richards 2001: 31). Indeed, Gandhi declared,

> Your suggestion for different schools for different classes—weavers, spinners, carpenters and so on—would not answer my purpose. For I want to bring about an equalization of status. The working classes have all these centuries been isolated and relegated to a lower status. They have been Shudras, and the word has been interpreted to mean an inferior status. I want to allow no differentiation between the sons of a weaver, of an agriculturist and of a schoolmaster. (Gandhi 1976: 341)

The offer of an accessible education to 'lower' castes is a radical offer of a new—indeed, modern—equality. Quite clearly, it is craft that could overturn an urban-centric book-centred educational system through the emphasis on the manual, productive labour that structured 'lower'-caste life. The celebration of craft, in a sense, worked against a nationalist art historiography which endorsed art at the expense of the manual-productive dimension of craft, and, again, unlike early Indian art history, the Wardha Scheme acknowledges the material conditions of caste in which craft is born. Nevertheless, the scheme which sought to equalise the life chances of all castes ended up teaching the oppressed castes what they know already and enabled them to pursue occupations that are anyway their lot. In fact, the *Report of the Zakir Husain Committee* explicitly states: 'Economically considered, carried out intelligently and efficiently, the scheme will increase the productive capacity of *our workers* and will also enable them to utilize their leisure advantageously' (Aggarwal 1992: 59; emphasis added).

II

It is, of course, a moot point whether such a national scheme of education could offer a way out of traditional roles and traditional occupations. In fact, Gandhi was ambivalently placed in relation to the radical possibilities of educational opportunity, which offer the chance of breaking out of oppressive structures. Although Gandhi carefully separated caste from *varna* (the four traditional social classes) by arguing that, unlike varna, caste is a custom that has nothing to do with religion, he finds no difficulty in advocating 'the law of *varna* [which] teaches us that we have each one of us to earn [our] bread by following the ancestral calling' (Ambedkar 1990: 108). According to varna, 'there is no calling too low and none too high. All are good, lawful and equal in status' (ibid.). However, his careful separation of caste and varna collapses precisely because he goes along with the idea of 'ancestral calling' or occupation determined by birth. Ambedkar writes: 'As defined by the Mahatma varna becomes merely a different name for caste, for the simple reason that it is the same in essence—namely, pursuit of one's ancestral calling' (ibid.: 125). One can see the homology between Gandhi's espousal of varna and his scheme of education that envisaged teaching the potter, the weaver and the farmer the very occupations they were born into. Craft, tied to occupation, clearly emerges as a category of caste. Craft-centred education does not offer a radical way out of caste oppression in the manner that Ambedkar envisaged because it fails to examine its caste dimensions. Particularly, it does not construe oppression in terms of the fixity or the limited horizons of life opportunities determined solely by birth. It is this to which Ambedkar draws attention when he argues: 'When can a calling be deemed to have become an ancestral calling so as to make it binding on a man? Must a man follow his ancestral calling even if it does not suit his capacities, even when it has ceased to be profitable?' (ibid.: 120). It seems clear, therefore, that craft in India is tied to occupation determined by caste.

Independent of Ambedkar's more general critique of the Gandhian position on caste, attempts to implement Nai Talim quickly recognised the caste implications of the scheme. C. Rajagopalachari's endorsement of the scheme both before and after Independence is a case in point. As the elected premier of the Madras Presidency, he partially introduced Nai Talim in the Madras province in 1939, giving it a decidedly gendered structure. It was put in place for female students of Classes 3 to 5 only. They were supposed to attend school for three hours and were asked to help with cooking and other domestic work, learning from their mothers, during the rest of the day (the second shift). Later, as the chief minister of Tamil Nadu, Rajagopalachari introduced the Modified Scheme of Elementary Education or New Scheme of Elementary Education in 1953 that drew heavily from his earlier attempt to introduce Nai Talim and which continued to work with a gendered organisation of education. It required that rural children attend school in two shifts, as in the earlier scheme: in the first shift they would attend school for three hours, and in the second shift they would go home, where the boys would learn their father's (caste-based) occupation, and girls, domestic work and cooking. The opposition parties called it *Kula Kalvi Thittam* (Hereditary Education Policy) or Acharyar Education Scheme (Brahminical Education Policy), resulting in public protest, the fall of his government and the replacement of the policy with another scheme when K. Kamaraj succeeded Rajagopalachari as chief minister.

It is significant, and in line with the economic position held by Gandhi, that the key arguments made by the Rajagopalachari government in favour of the Modified Scheme of Elementary Education were also economic. In the policy document published by the Director of Information and Publicity of Madras State, the central justification for the scheme is made in financial terms; it argued that the cost of educating all children in the 6–12 age group, setting up infrastructure for schools and hiring teachers to enhance the poor student-teacher ratio would be enormous in the context of the financial limitations faced by the government (Madras State Education Department 1953). However, although the scheme was laid out in alignment with the Directive Principles of State Policy of the Indian Constitution, which required the Indian state to provide education to all citizens and on the basis of fiscal prudence and viability, the caste contours of the scheme were unmistakable. Indeed, Rajagopalachari himself was quite open about this. He noted:

> The food is grown, the cloth is woven, the sheep are shorn, the shoes are stitched, the scavenging is done, the cartwheels and the ploughs are built and repaired because, thank God, the respective castes are still there and the homes are trade schools as well and the parents are masters as well, to whom the children are automatically apprenticed. (Gandhi 1997: 348)

Periyar opposed the scheme in sharp terms. In *Viduthalai*,[10] 17–18 November 1953, he wrote:

> As soon as Comrade Rajaji introduced the hereditary educational policy, only I said at first 'This educational policy is a casteist educational policy. This has to be opposed and abolished.' ...
>
> What is this scheme? What do you think is the basis for this scheme? Is this educational scheme not a reconstruction and protection of varnashrama?
>
> According to this educational scheme, every child should study for sometime every day and the rest of the time they should practice their hereditary caste occupation. Who physically labours and slaves in the name of caste? Only we, who are called sudras.[11]

Thus, Nai Talim, in this modulated policy and practice, could not evade charges of casteism that haunted it from the very outset. The Gandhian idea of Nai Talim did put in place a critically new idea of education that inverts colonial notions about childhood, the administration of national systems of education, schooling, curriculum and pedagogy, while also setting up a critique of a dominant-caste distaste for manual work. But by being blind to the caste dimensions of craft-based occupation, and thus the body of caste, the scheme of education faltered in its ambition to forge a radical national system of education for India.

Notes

1. For a sharply argued account of Gandhi's vegetarianism, the body and the colony, see Amarendra Pandey's chapter, 'Vegetarianism and the National Self: Gandhi's Food as the Site of Anti-Colonial Struggle', in Pandey (2015).

2. I have commented on the Gandhian engagement with manliness in my study of Gandhi's *Satyagraha in South Africa*. See Achar (2010).

3. For an earlier version of a discussion of Gandhian Nai Talim, in which I have engaged some of the arguments discussed here with the colonial craft question, see Achar (2003).

4. See *Report of the Zakir Husain Committee*, 1938 in Aggarwal (1992: 57).

5. Gandhi did not have a high opinion on Sayajirao Gaekwad's introduction of compulsory primary education in Baroda State. He considered it a mere replication of the English system of national education. He said: 'The fact is the education in Baroda is an almost slavish imitation of the British type' (*Young India*, 21 January 1926, in Gandhi [2012: 4]); still, he considered Sayajirao Gaekwad's motives 'perfectly pure' (M. K. Gandhi 1938: 82).

6. See Boman-Behram (1943) for a detailed account of the medium of instruction debate.

7. Gandhi himself traced his ideas on education based on craft to his experience of education through craft in Tolstoy Farm in South Africa, where Hermann Kallenbach taught him shoemaking. See Gandhi's 'Speech at Educational Conference, October 22 1937', in M. K. Gandhi (1976: 263).

8. For a sense of the pedagogic outcry, see Gandhi's 'Some Criticism Answered' in M. K. Gandhi (1976: 238–41).

9. See 'To National Teachers' (M. K. Gandhi 1976: 150). Although Gandhi favoured spinning, he also included crafts such as tailoring, embroidery, paper-making, cutting, bookbinding, cabinet-making, toy-making, and *gur*-making, which could 'easily be learnt and handled without much capital outlay' (ibid.: 195).

10. *Viduthalai* was a bi-weekly newspaper initially, before becoming a daily.

11. Kandasamy, et al. (2005: 262). Periyar E. V. Ramasamy was the founder of the Self-Respect Movement and Dravidar Kazhagam and a significant anti-caste thinker.

References

Achar, D. 2003. 'Crafting Education: Caste, Work and the Wardha Resolution of 1937'. In *Towards a New Art History: Studies in Indian Art*, ed. S. K. Panikkar, P. D. Mukherji and D. Achar, 385–93. New Delhi: DK Printworld.

——. 2010. 'Attaining Majority: With Gandhi in South Africa'. In *Discourse, Democracy and Difference: Perspectives on Community, Politics, and Culture*, ed. M. T. Ansari and D. Achar, 342–59. New Delhi: Sahitya Akademi.

Aggarwal, J. C., ed. 1992. *Documents on Primary Education in India, 1792–1992*. Delhi: Doaba House.

Ambedkar, B. R. 1990. *Annihilation of Caste*. Ed. M. R. Anand. New Delhi: Arnold.

Boman-Behram, B. K. 1943. *Educational Controversies in India: The Cultural Conquest of India under British Imperialism*. Parts I and II. Bombay: D. B. Taraporevala Sons & Co.

Gandhi, L. 2006. *Affective Communities: Anticolonial Thought, Fin-de-Siècle Radicalism, and the Politics of Friendship*. Durham and London: Duke University Press.

Gandhi, M. K. 1938. *Hind Swaraj or Indian Home Rule*. Ahmedabad: Navajivan Publishing House.

——. 1972. *Satyagraha in South Africa*. Trans. G. Desai. Ahmedabad: Navajivan Publishing House.

——. 1976. *The Collected Works of Mahatma Gandhi*. Vol. 66. New Delhi: Publications Division, Ministry of Information and Broadcasting, Government of India.

——. 2012. *Towards New Education*. Ed. B. Kumarappa. Ahmedabad: Navjivan Publishing House.

Gandhi, R. 1997. *Rajaji: A Life*. Gurgaon: Penguin India.

Kandasamy, W. B. Vasantha, F. Smarandache and K. Kandasamy. 2005. *Fuzzy and Neutrosophic Analysis of Periyar's Views on Untouchability*. Translation of the speeches and writings of Periyar from Tamil by M. Kandasamy. Phoenix, Arizona: Hexis.

Marglin, S. A. 1990. 'Sustainable Development: A Systems of Knowledge Approach'. *The Black Scholar* 21 (1): 35–42.

Madras State Education Department. 1953. *The Modified Scheme of Elementary Education: A Guide Book*. Madras: Director of Information and Publicity.

Nandy, A. 2009. *The Intimate Enemy: Loss and Recovery of Self Under Colonialism*. New Delhi: Oxford University Press.

Pandey, A. 2015. 'Writing Travel and the Question of the National Subject'. Unpublished Doctoral Thesis, Department of English, The Maharaja Sayajirao University of Baroda.

Richards, G. 2001. *Gandhi's Philosophy of Education*. New Delhi: Oxford University Press.

Eight

Reading Texts and Traditions

The Ambedkar–Gandhi Debate*

Valerian Rodrigues

While inter-subjectivity may mark all human understanding, certain conjunctures draw attention to it much more sharply than others when the criteria employed for the endeavour, its need and consequences are subjected to a reflective focus. The nationalist movement in India was one such moment when, among other things, questions came to be raised about the nature and process of understanding itself and, consequently, of the status of truth and knowledge. Among other things, it resulted in a struggle for and against texts and traditions with regard to their authenticity and authority to speak for truth and knowledge. It was a specific point in time when colonial knowledge, India's complex traditions and present practices, as well as anticipated futures, were closely subjected to critical scrutiny by a body of thinkers in the context of an emerging public.

Seized with the complexity of their endeavour, these thinkers advanced distinct conceptions of the public, often at odds with one another. They deployed their fervour to suggest specific imaginings of the self, society and the world. There were among them some who attempted to construct an alternative vision in opposition to the colonial dispensation, such as Bankim Chandra Chattopadhyay, Swami Vivekananda, Dadabhai Naoroji and Muhammad Iqbal; some who sought engagement with modernity *sans* colonialism and dominance, such as Pandita Ramabai, Justice Ranade, Sir Syed Ahmad Khan and Ramaswami Naicker; some who wished to factor in diversity and multiple sites of exclusion and domination, such as Kamaladevi Chattopadhyay, Jyotiba Phule, Jaipal Singh, Iyothee Thass and Abul Kalam Azad; a few such as Aurobindo Ghose and Ananda Coomaraswamy thought that the nationalist movement was a unique opportunity for India to make its distinct presence in the world; and

*Originally published in *Economic and Politically Weekly* 46 (2), 8 January 2011.

the occasional few such as Rabindranath Tagore, who thought that the moment was germane with possibilities both for degradation and new creative relationships founded on authenticity (Bevir 2010: 690–99).

Needless to say, these thinkers were complex and cannot be quarantined into neat pigeonholes. At the same time, there was a discernible slope visible in their writings and speeches in favour of one particular perspective. Bhimrao Ambedkar too struggled to suggest a new world and is deep in the hermeneutic venture in his major writings. Certain texts like *The Buddha and His Dhamma* (Ambedkar 1957) dwell at length on what constitutes a valid hermeneutic perspective. There is broad scholarly agreement today on how M. K. Gandhi revisited the tradition very differently from the way he himself was inserted into it; subjecting modernity, including its colonial avatar, to intimate and searching scrutiny and, through the churnings of the Indian national movement, he envisaged a future not merely for India but for the rest of the world which was markedly different from most of his articulate contemporaries and epigones. At the same time, Ambedkar and Gandhi are in contention over the way in which they read texts and traditions and chartered futures for themselves and others. They differed in their understanding of modernity, in assessing traditions and in proposing options for India and the world. However, across their disagreements, there was much that united them, not merely on issues and concerns, but on substantive positions as well. Their hermeneutic engagement provides a privileged site to highlight the reasons that kept them apart and concerns that brought them together. It also demonstrates why they left behind a differing but lasting impact on the constituencies and issues they addressed.

Ambedkar's readings and perceptions were not innocent, and were not a mere distillation of the conditions of degradation and exclusion that he suffered, although a negative setting of belonging that placed 'untouchables' outside the matrix of culture left him with few honourable options. There was a conceptual framework, supple and open-ended, that he carried enthusiastically and he was deeply aware of and committed to it. The context is intimately woven with the way Gandhi approached and read the texts. He was constantly asked to mark his positions from that of others and to formulate his own in a context where the ravages of colonial modernity were visible for all to see. He thought that it was essential to recapture another vision of the world and not merely strive to form another national unit. At the risk of simplification, let me reconstruct the frameworks that more or less remained invariant in their respective hermeneutic endeavours.

Ambedkar's Conceptual Framework

The moral and political framework that Ambedkar enthusiastically adopted owed much to the European Enlightenment paradigm (Goldman 1968; Habermas 1987). Although he made significant changes in it over time, particularly after his encounter with Gandhi (Rodrigues 1994) and attunement with Buddhism, this referential and evaluative framework remained substantially intact. The following elements were central to this framework.

The Modern as the Triumph of Reason

Ambedkar subscribed to a specific historiography: he sharply demarcated the modern era from the earlier epochs. A characteristic marker of the modern was the triumph of rationality (Ambedkar 1987c), under which human reason came into its own and extricated itself from its servitude to myths, customs and religious ideologies. The relationship between reason on the one hand and myths and traditions on the other was radically altered in a reversal of their mutual roles. The Greeks upheld reason. But reason in their case could not undermine the customs and hallowed ways of life. In medieval Europe, reason was at the service of religion, expressed in the famous dictum of Aquinas, 'philosophy is the handmaiden of theology'. The modern reversal involved the contention that customs and traditions and religion and theology are valid to the extent that they are reasonable. It is not that every value, religious tenet or way of life has to be rejected; however, they are not tenable if they are not compatible with reason (Sen 2009: 45). Ambedkar also associated reason with human dignity. The human person is specifically endowed with the capacity for reason, which entitles him to a unique dignity. Further, he saw knowledge as eminently practical rather than speculative and esoteric. He felt that speculative knowledge divorced from active engagement with practice led to priestcraft and speculation.

Radical Secularity

Ambedkar argued that the world and man could be explained by human reason and endeavour. You do not need to invoke the supernatural to explain them. In fact, the supernatural itself is the product of weak human capacities or an underdeveloped state of affairs when man himself did not have the ability to explain and control nature or even society. Ambedkar's perspective, therefore, saw the world—to use Weber's charming metaphor—as 'disenchanted'. This radical secularity went along with the assertion of the autonomy of man. The need of a transcendental power to regulate the affairs of man and his world was, he felt, an affront to human reason, a slight to human dignity and an effective denial of freedom.

His attitude towards religion, however, remained ambivalent. While he was suspicious of a belief in a personal god and revelation, with their inevitable fallouts of priestcraft and superstition, he at the same time felt that religion is required for it elevates baser orientation and provides a perspective to resolve conflicts of interests (Ambedkar 1979a). It upholds altruism, making us reach out to others. It binds people in love, solidarity and concern. It nurtures and cares. It is oriented towards service and militates against injustice and wrongdoing. It teaches respect towards the human person so as to not make him the instrument of the purposes of others. It thereby constitutes, in a way, the grid and an evaluative standpoint for the exercise of reason and choice. Religion 'upholds' the world in the true sense and invests man with this responsibility. These characteristics also mark good religion from bad and advance the criteria to retrieve the right elements from existing religions.[1] Therefore, religious formations are susceptible to pruning and shaping through human endeavour while they shape human conduct in turn. Ambedkar's argument is caught in a circular web while stipulating such connections: religion makes man truly human; man has to propose and choose a religion that can make mankind human.

This engagement with religion in spite of the avowal of radical secularity continues to be a recurrent theme in Ambedkar. It has few parallels elsewhere (Robb 1993; Ryan 1995).[2] The context of nationalist discourse, particularly the Gandhian interlude and the options it set for the Dalits, did impart a great deal of urgency to such considerations. This position recognised that modern reason alone cannot beget virtue. However, virtue has to be reasonable and reason has to be cultivated virtuously. Such a religion, by definition, cannot be doctrinaire or ritualistic.

Centrality of Human Agency

Even if religion is seen as the moral basis of social and personal life, how does one ensure that a religion claiming the moral province would not be deployed to serve partisan ends? How does one rescue religion from falling prey to authoritarianism, subordination and privileging one section over the others? There needs to be certain criteria by which one could distinguish true religion from false. Besides, if there are conflicts, there need to be standards to solve and negotiate them across time. Ambedkar felt that in the existing perspectives, such as liberalism, the link between the moral domain and rights on the one hand and rights and interests on the other was far too weak, and he set himself to reformulate them afresh.

While Ambedkar admitted the power of structures and relations to subdue and discipline human agency, he refused to admit that the entire spectrum of the operation of human agency could be wholly subdued by factors outside it. Whenever structures and relations do not intimidate its expression, human agency stands for freedom, equality and fraternity. Ambedkar saw these threefold values not merely as slogans of the modern era, but as its motor force. They constitute the criteria to judge prevailing social relations as well as lay down benchmarks for social practices in the present. They define the parameters of the good life one should strive towards and Ambedkar employed them devastatingly not only to critique India's social institutions, but also colonial modernity, liberal democracy and the socialist promise. A recurring statement in his writings is: 'My ideal society would be a society based on liberty, equality and fraternity' (Ambedkar 1968: 54). He called them 'valuable ends' (Ambedkar 1979a: 452). However, exclusive emphasis on any one of them, such as freedom or equality, could violate other claims. Stress on freedom of choice alone without the resources and opportunities to exercise such a choice, and without respect for the similar claims of others, would make a travesty of it.

Foregrounding these values, Ambedkar formulated a series of rights that he considered their specification. However, here Ambedkar's arguments seem to move in a vicious circle. Conflict among right-claims can be resolved only by appeal to the moral basis of society and the moral basis of society can be tested to the extent that it upholds rights. Ambedkar rarely attempted to probe the conundrum that such counterpositions led to. He did not see rights as socially sanctioned claims to possessive individualism. In fact, he saw them as criteria to constitute social relations and the measure to adjudge social relations and social systems. He was emphatic on the need to sustain an ambience of rights. He also felt that the claim of rights could be deceptive if the means of production were concentrated in a few hands. Rights need to be expressed as a way of life and sustained by a communitarian ethos. Thereby, rights can be ordered on a scale of priority, with the necessary trade-off across them.

Ambedkar viewed the nation as a cultural grouping defensible in terms of rights. Therefore, where rights are violated or perceived as violated, a hitherto unified cultural group may give way to diverse cultural identities, including the demand for self-determination. Similarly, the existence of rights enables groups to relate to other groups in myriad ways, thereby forging shared ground. Following John Dewey, he called this process social endosmosis.

In spite of the significant changes that Ambedkar's thought marks across the years, these three elements remain invariant, although new nuances and emphases tend to appear continuously. They are also constantly invoked to upbraid, explore, explain, approve and adjudge. They make him the principal interlocutor of the Indian tradition as a whole and someone who proposes a distinct vision for India and the world. We need to consider Ambedkar's intellectual and political positions on the basis of the paradigm constituted of these elements.

Interrogating the Cultural Sphere

For Ambedkar, the given values of a culture cannot constitute moral imperatives and they cannot elicit allegiance on that basis alone. In fact, domination and subordination are built into most of the cultures, albeit to differing extents. The cultural sphere remains the terrain of contestation. Only those cultural contexts that uphold reason and rights can be defended.

Cultural worlds are therefore susceptible to constant reconfigurations. Ambedkar sees culture as referring primarily to as the character of a historical community in common usage. Such a character is expressed in language, history, values, ways of life and standards of valuation. Although cultural structures are attributed a certain invariance and permanence, cultural communities can alter them by reviewing and reformulating earlier ways of life without necessarily abdicating their cultures. He therefore rejected any essentialist conception of culture. He was also aware that certain interests tended to essentialise culture (Kymlicka 1989). In his own work, Ambedkar resorted to a symptomatic (*Young India*, 23 April 1923) retrieval of culture, tested on the criteria of reason, secularity and respect for human agency.

Certain scholars like Eleanor Zelliot, who have been involved in lifelong work on Ambedkar and the Dalit movement, demarcate his sociopolitical engagement into three phases. The first phase sought to reform Hinduism; the second attempted to carve out an autonomous political constituency for Dalits; and, in the third phase, disenchanted with mere political pursuit, Ambedkar sought an alternative in Buddhism and attempted to redraw the boundaries of political action by founding the Republican Party of India (Zelliot 1986: 161–75). Without commenting on the appropriateness of this distinction, one can say that across the phases, one of Ambedkar's major attempts seemed to be to define a national cultural community on the criteria outlined above. The deputations before the official committees, the Mahad Satyagraha, the temple-entry movements and particularly the text in *Annihilation of Caste* illustrate the same during the first phase. These efforts primarily involved claims such as equal access to common resources, freedom of worship and conscience, respect towards a human person, and so on, calling upon the remaining concerned people to recognise and stand by such claims. Their claim to be a nation along with the depressed classes depended upon the extent to which such belonging and recognition is mutually accorded. His suggestions in *Annihilation of Caste* to reform Hinduism through inter-caste marriage and allowing Dalits the option to become priests were also steps in the same direction. However, the prevailing usages and valuations proved intractable, in spite of considered and sustained endeavour to transform them. Groups closed in on themselves and refused to engage with one another through the threefold values of liberty, equality and fraternity. Culture became a hurdle of sorts in the way of rights. Any attempt to term such a dispensation as a national-cultural community would, he argued, inevitably install orthodoxy in power.

In the second phase, Ambedkar's attempt was to construct a state which would embody reason, secularity and rights. He thought that such a state would be able to make deep inroads into society by cultivating civic virtues based on rights. Usages and valuations contrary to rights would have to give way and those practices and valuations which were not contrary to rights would survive, developing over time a complex culture and giving expression to rights and consonant customs. Ambedkar's experience of state intervention in this direction, however, convinced him that this was not the strategic way to seek a relationship between culture and rights. He saw resistance to the Hindu Code Bill as one such indicator. The other subaltern traditions, such as those to which the great Mahar saint Chokhamela belonged, might seem to enlarge the context of choice. However, Ambedkar saw them as having a highly limited conception of rights and their non-engagement with secularity made them irrelevant to social and political destinies. He saw Buddhism alone as amenable to symptomatic reconstruction around reason, secularity and rights, towards which he tended, in the third phase, to reconstruct the popular national agenda.

The Gandhian Paradigm

In Gandhi's structure of thought, beliefs and practices, as available to us today, the following elements recur constantly and their significance is repeatedly restated. While relations across these elements, and even their substantive connotations, underwent some changes, the frame indicating the place and significance of these elements persisted over time.[3]

Idea of the Self and Transcendence

After a period of consideration in South Africa, Gandhi came to subscribe to the view, central to mainstream Hindu tradition, that man was essentially spiritual and the cosmic spirit informed and pervaded the whole universe. In spite of the autonomy of domains and even of discrete entities, the whole universe was an organically interdependent system and a coherent whole. It was a partnership and no one can make an exclusive claim over it. While everyone can access all that they need, they cannot do violence to the integrity and harmony of the order of beings. By respecting the rhythm and harmony of the cosmos, man enabled the conditions of his own reproduction. Man is also the deputy of the cosmic spirit, a partner in his design. According to Gandhi, 'Absolute Truth has no power unless incarnated in human beings' (Gandhi 1966: 108).

Gandhi distinguished between the *atman* (soul) and the self, while avoiding to the extent possible the intricacies through which different philosophical schools spelt out this relationship. Every man is unique and self-made, of distinct dispositions, propensities and temperaments inherited from birth. This self is the seat of desires and wants, projected in time and sustained through those desires and wants. It has a history encompassing several lifespans. Every man is solely responsible for what he is. At the same time, man is also an atman, which is nothing but the cosmic spirit manifest in him. While the self is the basis of individuality and personal identity, the atman is the same for all. Men are also bodies and as such are constituted of elements common across them. While human fulfilment lies in overcoming the sense of discreteness and in unity with the cosmic spirit, the diverse aims and purposes of human existence have a bearing on people and have to be necessarily attended to.[4] The final human realisation is moksha, liberation from samsara or the cycles of births and rebirths. Moksha consisted in dissolving the identity of self, as well as that of the other, by attaining total identification 'with the limitless ocean of life' (Gandhi 1969: 150).

Being a unique self, every individual perceives the world and lives his life in his own way. He has to work out his moksha following the path best suited to him. While the goal is the same, paths vary. Man is the architect of his own self and responsible for his own actions. While men can be persuaded out of their beliefs, their integrity and choices have to be respected, unless their choices threaten the social order or undermine the context of choice itself. Mankind itself is an organic whole and men are necessarily interdependent. Therefore, every action is both self- and other-regarding. No man can brutalise or degrade another without inflicting it on himself. In harming others, men harm themselves. Gandhi revisited the traditional doctrines of *varnashrama* (fourfold hierarchical division in Hinduism based on social class) and *Karma Siddhanta* (law of karma or action) and considered them the bearers of the principles of interdependence, responsibility and freedom.

Religion and Morality

For Gandhi, religion encompassed the practices that disposed a person towards the cosmic spirit, including prayer, fasting, penance, meditation, etc., and morality stipulated relationships across human beings. While the spirit is impersonal and unfathomable to the human mind, the latter tends to conceive it in personal and moral terms. Religion represents the way man conceives of and relates himself to god. Since there are plural ways of such pursuits, there are and necessarily will be a plurality of religions and no religion can claim that it alone is true. If anyone does so, they do it out of sheer arrogance, reducing the cosmic truth to the limited truth of one's life. Religions have also worked out distinct ways of reaching out to god and therefore dialogue across religions can be an immensely enriching experience. While 'truth' is infinite and human understanding of it is limited, respect towards other truth seekers and towards cultures and traditions is integral to the very search for truth. At the same time, one cannot be anything other than what one is, and respect for one's moral integrity requires that every individual should live by the truth as they see it. Mutual respect, curiosity and dialogue, therefore, are integral to the search for truth.

Tradition as *parampara* and *achar*, i.e., beliefs, practices and institutions, handed down over generations as salutary and enjoying widespread acceptance, has had an important place in informing and directing social practices in India. Gandhi's attitude towards tradition, not merely in India but elsewhere as well, was deeply ambivalent. His experience demonstrated that traditions sometimes can and in fact do undermine principles, as his encounter with the priests at the Vaikom Temple showed.[5] In his own life, Gandhi resorted to few practices which could be construed as authoritatively handed down from generation to generation. Gandhi identified several practices in the traditions of India that were not defensible and were sometimes outright immoral, such as those associated with untouchability, child marriage, polyandry, sacrificial violence and temple prostitution.

> At the same time, 'For Gandhi the basic values and insights of a tradition were "valid" and binding, not because of their age or certification by an individual, but because they had survived the rigorous test of lived experience and the scrutiny of their critics' (Parekh 1999: 1). Gandhi made the distinction between 'basic values and insights', the central organising principles of a tradition which have an enduring value, and 'beliefs and practices' which were subject to constant revision, and one owed loyalty to the former rather than the latter. For Gandhi, this was particularly the case with Hinduism because '[u]nlike many traditions, it was based not on divine self-revelation placed in the charge of an accredited organisation but on unconscious collective experience regularly fertilised and enriched by the moral and spiritual experiments of its great sages'. (ibid.: 24)

While an individual remained free to revise traditional values, they had to do so only 'after making a "respectful" study of them and giving them the benefit of the doubt' (ibid.: 29).

While every religion is unique, Gandhi believed that comparisons across religions were possible on several grounds: religion is ultimately how one lives rather than what one believes in; since all religions grasp an aspect of the ultimate truth, religions that are open and tolerant and disposed to dialogue are better; each individual is unique and relates to god in their own way and therefore religions that provide greater scope for self-expression are better; a religion that subscribes to compassion, i.e., unity of men and all life, is better. While Gandhi respected all religions, he believed Hinduism to have an edge over other religions on all four counts (Parekh 1989: 82–83).

Gandhi argued that love was the only way of identifying oneself with other living beings, involving absolute openness to others, breaking down the barriers between the self and others, and filling one's being with the deepest concern for the well-being of others. At the same time, he upheld the ideal of detachment and saw its relation to love as complementary. In the process, love became not merely a specific bonding but a disposition that took its context seriously. Thereby, it took on an activist posture and connoted service, love in action. It became not a demarcated or specific state and activity, but informed everything that one did. In the modern age, Gandhi saw politics as the central focus of service. Pursuit of *artha* (wealth and power) in the form of politics was integrally bound with the search for moksha (*Young India*, 22 July 1920, 18 August 1920).

The Modern World and its Other

While Gandhi's conception of *dharma* (ethics and religion) inevitably drew him to engage with the world, his aims and beliefs gave specific attenuation to this engagement. For Gandhi and several of his contemporaries, modernity was closely linked to colonial domination, although they drew different inferences from it. Gandhi understood that much of the British claim to rule India came from their being the bearers of modern civilisation. This claim affected all domains of social life: in the economic sphere, it assigned primacy to production and consumption and an incessant search for markets. It assumed a conception of man as the creature of infinite desires and wants. In the political sphere, it undermined traditions and lived ways of life and subjected man to a mode of regimen that he had little control over. Colonial modernity as culture destroyed the integrity and identity of Indian culture.

But Gandhi also understood that colonial modernity was integrally bound with mainstream modernity. He saw it as ceaseless activity aimed at the annihilation of time and space itself (Appadurai 1976: 5). It undermined man's relationship with his environment and other fellow beings and destroyed stable communities. It had a flawed theory of man focused on his body and materialist strivings. It promoted selfishness an and 'infinite multiplicity of wants' without giving him a scale to choose from. It was deeply caught up in violence and stressed on power. It was not self-determining moral agents that were its priority, but rather the satisfaction of externally induced wants. It led to mechanisation for its own sake, breeding fetishism. Under it, the bond between men was based on a 'set of self-consciously followed and externally legislated impersonal rules. He (Man) lived outside himself and exhausted himself physically and spiritually' (Parel 1997: 37). It involved violence against oneself and against other men, a violence that was ultimately institutionalised by the state and under which the state became the sole font of moral order. The institutions of modernity, such as medicine and law, attempted to subject men to passivity.

Gandhi thought that imperialism was the natural continuation of this civilisation. He thought that a civilisation needs to be measured by the criteria of certain distinct human powers such as self-determination, autonomy, self-knowledge, self-discipline and social cooperation. Modernity fell far short. Unlike many of his contemporaries, Gandhi did not position himself against Western civilisation; it was modern civilisation that he opposed. There was 'no such thing as western or European civilisation, but there is a modern civilisation' (Iyer 1986: 293). He thought, by the way modernity marked its trajectory, that it was self-destructive.

Gandhi, however, was appreciative of some of the contributions of modernity: it fostered a scientific spirit of enquiry, which for him meant 'the spirit of search for the truth in place of being satisfied with tradition without question, and implied intellectual curiosity, rigorous pursuit of truth and critical examination of established beliefs' (Parekh 1989: 31). Further, modernity has developed our understanding of the natural world and brought it under greater human control, although it has often been deployed for ill-suited ends. Technology and machines have a place in life and if appropriately employed, contribute a great deal to enhancing the quality of life. Besides, modern civilisation has contributed to the organisational side of life through the cultivation of civic virtues, respect for rules, public morality, mutual respect and punctuality.

What was Gandhi's alternative to the depredations of modern civilisation? He formulated them in the concepts of *swadeshi* (self-sufficiency) and *swaraj* (self-rule). Much of his appreciation of modernity was made integral to these concepts. The spirit of swadeshi is the way a person responds to his *desh* (*swa* means one's own; desh is one's natural and cultural setting). *Swadesh* was a territorial unit that denoted a way of life and a belonging and was not necessarily coextensive with polity or state. For him, it was a kin concept alongside tradition, culture and community, with much in common across them. One owed one's specific humanity to swadesh and the latter cast a duty on its members to nourish it. One's self-respect, courage and independence were closely bound up with swadesh. Gandhi's constructive programmes such as Hindu-Muslim unity, removal of untouchability, ban on alcohol, use of *khadi*, development of village industries, craft-based education, use of indigenous languages, etc., were geared towards building up swadesh as much as the nation.

Swaraj was both self-government (*prajarajya*) and self-rule. He also called it dharma or *Ramarajya* (Gandhi 1969: 489). While as self-government it connoted national independence and organisation of the polity in a specific way, clearly it meant much more to him. Swaraj is the capacity to give purpose to oneself and the ability to carry that purpose through. Gandhi associated it with a certain character nurtured through temperance (*brahmacharya*), truthfulness, courage, absence of greed, and love of justice and freedom. He related it to the ideal of *sthithaprajna* (in a state of equanimity) (Gandhi 1968: 316). He associated swaraj with moral development. True swaraj for him 'was the acquisition of the capacity by all to resist authority when it is abused' (*Harijan*, 1 September 1940). He thought that it is the citizens who ultimately enforced moral responsibility on the state. He argued that when a law was just, a citizen had a sacred duty to give it his fullest cooperation and willing and spontaneous obedience. Everyone had a moral duty to support something good and as a citizen, he had the duty to sustain communities. If a law is unjust and morally unacceptable, he had the duty not to cooperate with it. Such an understanding of swaraj became foundational to his conception of democracy. Under a democracy, men as self-determining moral agents and as the source of all political power were fully capable of regulating their personal and common affairs. It was not so much a complex of institutions as a way of life to develop and actualise popular power.

Gandhi thought that India would be the battleground of an epochal battle between modern civilisation and a civilisation grounded in swaraj and he saw a number of conducive conditions for this. In India, the impact of and reception to modernity was feeble and limited, and a long civilisation and religious cultivation had left behind enduring legacies. Hinduism for Gandhi never set up an absolute gulf between reason and faith as Christianity or Islam did, and therefore could set up a different relationship with modernity. The *swarajist* perspective would necessarily deploy the contributions of modernity and make them integral to the 'basic values and insights' of tradition. It will nurture a civilisational perspective that is deeply diverse and plural, while at the same time bonding with other societies and cultures through numerous ties.

Reason and Action

If every self is differently constituted, and if a life of truth is to examine one's sincerely held beliefs and act accordingly, how do selves otherwise differently constituted cooperate with each other in social action? And if there are differences, how does one resolve them? As suggested earlier, Gandhi saw a deep bond between human beings that cut across traditions, cultures and nations. This bond had its foundations in a shared humanity, which, in turn, related it to nature and the universe as a whole. Further interactions across cultures and civilisations through time and space had reinforced this bond through numerous ties, although it might have given rise to new cleavages. Such bonds, however, were much stronger among people belonging to the same culture and traditions. Given these bonds, much of the communication across human beings in context is 'pre-discursive',[6] although the term is by itself inadequate to handle hard cases and particularly when communities and traditions revolving around distinct ways of life have to live together. In all later instances, Gandhi thought that rational discussion and persuasion was the principal way to pursue cooperative action and deal with conflict.

A rational course of action involved looking at an issue from each other's point of view, appreciating the force of each other's arguments, deliberating over its different aspects and formulating a mode of action based on such a process. It is quite possible that this process may not lend itself to agreement on some aspects. But the channels of communication need to be kept open to be renewed with vigour whenever the occasion demanded it. No one could possess the absolute truth; each one may access some aspects of it and that too faintly. Reason, therefore, becomes the principal bond that unites relevant communities and groups into action and justifies one course of action over another. If there are serious disagreements, reason is an aid to knowing why each party saw 'truth' significantly differently. Reason also suggests that certain dispositions are essential to arrive at shared ends: there are certain principles, such as fairness and rules of the game, to initiate a reasonable encounter. One cannot harbour ill-will to others or be selfish or conceited. One cannot set out to reason with a gun in hand. Truth requires an open mind and an 'open heart'.

Gandhi, however, was acutely aware that reasonable agreements were difficult to come by, that interests lurked deep behind the talk of reason and good reasons did not necessarily find public approval or even attention. Sometimes, the context of reasoning and the modes employed for the purpose themselves could be exclusionary. Power and domination did not merely set terms for what is reasonable, but often pre-empted the outcomes themselves. Reason finds itself helpless, sometimes against entrenched interests and prejudice. Therefore, there could be a gap between what appeared to be a sound reason and moral claims. Limitations of rationality, therefore, often led people to resort to violence and defend their action in the language of morality. Gandhi was opposed to such an early exit from reason by taking shelter under a moral halo.

For Gandhi, resorting to violence denied its targets the capacity to evaluate and re-evaluate their lives, while arrogating to its proponents such a capacity in ample measure. It also denied the essential unity of mankind, and the respect that one owed to another. Such a view did not take into account the fact that men perceive the truth differently and that those who attempt to set standards consider themselves privy to truth and infallible. Gandhi also thought that those resorting to violence in the name of establishing a morally desirable order did not realise that often, its consequences were irreversible; while violence forced the opponent to work against his beliefs and convictions, it rarely changed them, and experience showed that violence rarely achieved its intended results. To the contrary, violence often spiralled out of control. It put people on guard and led to social closure, surveillance and suspicion. Non-violence was therefore central to most of his key concerns. It was both the approach and measure for social relations. Little wonder, then, that he called *ahimsa parmo dharma* (non-violence as the most profound dharma).

While Gandhi did not see an alternative to reasoned engagement, he was, at the same time, deeply conscious that ignoring its limitations could lead people to acquiesce to untruth or make resorting to violence attractive. He thought that *satyagraha* (truth force) was a way out of this impasse. He saw satyagraha as the 'surgery of the soul' to weed out distortions begotten by hatred and narrow self-interest, enabling a person to recognise the other human being as a fellow man. It involved non-violent non-cooperation with what one regarded as evil. One voluntarily accepted condign punishment due to the act or acts. A *satyagrahi* (one who practises satyagraha) refused to take the bait and engaged with his adversary as a moral being. He accepted whatever punishment was meted out to him and did not try to embarrass, harass, anger or frighten his opponent. Satyagraha for Gandhi was 'suffering love'. It was an attempt to persuade others to one's point of view and to understand that of others. Through it, a satyagrahi attempted to generate in his opponent a process of self-examination and review of the initial terms of engagement. Over the years, Gandhi also became deeply aware that satyagraha as 'suffering love', as action for social transformation, had its limitations. He often found the need to mobilise strategic social groups in favour of satyagraha and added to his armoury such weapons as social and economic boycott, civil disobedience, non-payment of taxes, non-violent raids, strikes and other forms of non-cooperation, none of which rested merely upon 'suffering love'.

For Gandhi, a regime of oppression was sustained by the cooperation of the oppressed. Both oppressor and oppressed believed that all power lay with the former. It made the oppressor act confidently and decisively while turning the oppressed into supplicants. The belief that the oppressor had all the power was of course incorrect, but to the extent that it was taken as true, it worked. Such a belief 'veiled the *satya* that the oppressor had no power save what his victims chose to give him' (Parekh 1989: 155). For Gandhi, the key to the salvation of the oppressed was in their very hands. Therefore, those interested in fighting against oppression must instil courage and confidence in the victim and remove the illusion of powerlessness. Satyagraha was meant to achieve such a purpose. It demystified the system, built up the power of the oppressed and demanded that the system be accountable. Satyagraha facilitated the process of reasoning.

While reason shored by satyagraha was the predominant basis of public action, Gandhi thought that it was not an adequate or even the most desirable mode of engaging with a situation under certain conditions. He saw the human mind as an 'essentially plural, federal and non-hierarchical structure of autonomous and interacting faculties, each with its distinctive mode of operation and way of knowing the world' (ibid.: 74). Reason laid down the minimum and not the maximum criteria, 'what men may not believe, not what they must believe' (ibid.). He therefore often resorted or appealed to other capacities and dispositions, such as friendship, compassion, faith, companionship and, particularly, love.

Beyond Reason

A framework made of the above fourfold elements made Gandhi reach out to specific concerns and issues in his own distinct way. A political order had to be judged by the extent to which it contributed to the bonding of and concern for people and sustained an interdependent world; the extent to which it sustained self-rule and autonomy and reduced dependence and domination; the state of swaraj and swadesh; the respect it owed to people as persons, and the extent to which non-violence, reason and love become the arbiters of social relations. If these elements foreground institutions and relations, then a plurality of sociopolitical arrangements can be possible. He personally thought that a decentralised panchayat system has more to offer than a centralised polity. He rejected both capitalism and communism. While every social order was essentially a cooperative enterprise involving a spirit of sharing, mutual concern, self-sacrifice and the best that one could offer to collective well-being, capitalism paid little heed to them. The institution of private property, central to capitalism, stressed on selfishness, aggression, exclusive ownership, narrow individualism, etc. It dehumanised both the workers and the capitalists and set a standard for human existence that could hardly be called human. No man could degrade another without degrading himself. On the other hand, communism was based on the materialist view of man and did not represent a new and higher civilisation. It was a statist approach to problems, which impoverished individuals and dried up local sources of initiative and energy. Against them, Gandhi suggested a mode of organisation of economy foregrounded on essentially human aspects of man's relation to other men and to the world. Work became both a right and a duty and was foundational to developing essential human virtues such as self-respect, dignity, self-discipline, etc. These principles determined the nature and pace of the economy. Inequalities of income and wealth were acceptable insofar as they served these ends. He thought that the scheme of trusteeship was conducive to such an end.

Gandhi deployed several facets of the 'other' of modernity (Parel 2006: 68–84) to rebuild a vision for man and his world by marrying them with the core aspects of tradition. Some of the terms of his discourse were very clear while others were rhetorical, and were constantly formulated in the course of the encounter in question. He also sought an engagement with the world and bodily concerns, rarely heard before (Brown 1989: 85–86, 92–94). There was a robust engagement with the body and concern to keep it fit for the tasks at hand. He was also deeply concerned with the degradation of social life and public virtues in India, against which modernity still looked attractive. Overall, Gandhi thought that he had an alternative to offer which could debunk the attractions and trappings of modernity. In many ways, his was a call to affirm the world and return to civilised ways of existence.

Gandhi–Ambedkar Hermeneutic Engagement

For both Gandhi and Ambedkar, hallowed texts were very important. Such texts advanced normative designs for their believers, justified one set of actions rather than another, kept communities together by making them feel distinct and of worth, imparted a sense of continuity and belonging to people, and often provided substantive guidance for action. While a tradition might acknowledge several texts, some were more important, although such valuations were susceptible to change and re-evaluation. When there is an established authority, there is an authoritative guidance in this regard, including in the interpretation of the text. Both of them agreed that all authoritative interpretations were ultimately caught in contestation. However, given their differing frameworks, they viewed and assessed texts and traditions differently, imparting a specific hermeneutic thrust to their readings. Methodologically, we will dwell on this interface as well as confrontation by making Ambedkar an interlocutor and Gandhi the proponent. There is no discursive or historical precedent implied here and the roles could be easily reversed.[7]

Both Ambedkar and Gandhi agreed that texts do not speak by themselves. We read them through the perspectives that we are heavily influenced by. We carry our frameworks into the experience of our reading. Ambedkar, for instance, charged both orientalist scholars and their Indian counterparts for carrying, too enthusiastically, their distinct perspectives into the reading of texts. He found that much of the orientalist reading of Buddhism saw its principal teachings as *samadhi* (condition of mental concentration) and *vipassana* (a form of mediation to help grasp authentic insight), and extolled its esoteric and mystical character (Ambedkar 1957: 201). He often found Indian writers pushing back the age of a text vis-à-vis Western writers on a theme (Ambedkar 1979b: 371–80). Gandhi too found that most Indian thinkers tended to read their favourite theories back into a text (Parel 2006: 182–83).[8]

Both Ambedkar and Gandhi admitted that many concerns of contemporary life had no explanation or parallel in the hallowed texts, and which could, at the most, only provide some guidance on how to negotiate such concerns. Both admitted that authoritative readings of a text appropriately institutionalised, such as the reading of the Bible in the Catholic church, help in standardising a text and its interpretation, but such readings could be deeply bound with interests and power relations, often eschewing all creativity. They could also sustain priestcraft and obscurantist interests.

We do not merely interpret but also act on the interpretations of hallowed texts, and in the process change and transform their meaning and orientation and their significance for us. Therefore, interpretation is also action that affects a text intimately. Gandhi and Ambedkar are in agreement on this issue, although they differed on its consequences. Gandhi therefore often asked the basic question: Who can interpret a text and who is the best interpreter? Ambedkar thought that all texts should be available for critical scrutiny and, eventually, have to defend themselves in the battlefield of ideas.

What is striking, however, are the disagreements between the two and the range of the texts and traditions they read:

(i) Gandhi felt that the outcome of interpretation is indelibly linked with the hermeneutic criteria employed. If the paradigms are markedly different and opposed, the grasp of reality and reading of texts and contexts would be varied too. However, fundamental differences in outlook and frameworks need not preclude dialogue, so long as one does not close oneself to an encounter with the truth and cease to be a *jigyasu* (curious). Ambedkar agreed that frameworks of understanding indelibly mark our interpretation, but the way out of this trap of incommensurability is to give up and combat shoddy thinking, identify the prejudices and interests that vitiate our thinking and subject our very framework of understanding to critical scrutiny. Calling for an early dialogue without such hard enquiry and appropriate moral disposition would be akin to the blind leading the blind (Ambedkar 1957: 201–02). In this regard, while Gandhi's overall emphasis was on disposition, Ambedkar was on the side of scientific understanding.

(ii) Gandhi argued that the whole should not be condemned for the defects of the parts. The Hindu scriptures, taken as a whole, have the capacity to lead humanity to genuine holiness. Here, learning needs to be combined with holiness while reading such texts. It is also important to see how a reader who has read a text engages with it. The author of the Gita, for instance, was showing people how to change the meaning of terms to fit the needs of his day. A present-day interpreter of the word has to show the same capacity. It has to become a 'living faith speaking like a mother to her aching child' (ibid.). Ambedkar saw this as a tunnelled argument, which already assumed the truth of something that was contested. He wanted to know why defects were so overwhelming and moral rectitude and sense of elevation so rare and confined in instances of this kind.

(iii) Gandhi argued that it is important to know the form of a text before we interpret it. The *Mahabharata*, for instance, was not historical writing but an allegory that dwelt on man's internal struggles, presented in a quasi-historical form (*Harijan*, 3 October 1936). The Gita, for instance, is not a historical work. It was not an aphoristic work like the *Brahmasutra*. It was primarily a poetic rendering (Gandhi 1970: 100). A poet's meaning required reinterpretation across time. Ambedkar regarded the form as important but insisted on not ignoring the central arguments, omissions and emphasis, and substantive orientation of texts. The positions of *Manudharmashastra*, for instance, cannot be simply collapsed to the form of this literature (Ambedkar 1979b: 332–56).

(iv) For Gandhi, ahimsa was 'parmo dharma', an integral element of his paradigm. Therefore, for him, morals constituted the first premise of epistemology and human practice. One has to engage with and support the other in spite of basic differences. While Ambedkar agreed with Gandhi about the need to engage with opponents, he insisted on taking into account experience which would significantly affect the initial terms of engagement. Historical and material dimensions need to be taken into account too.

Besides, morals are not merely an attitude, a substantive content underwrites that attitude, i.e., whether one treats the other as equal, free, rational, and so on. Further, partisan interests may also take the form of morals. Ambedkar felt that Gandhi was himself a victim of such a malaise. The latter was of course a practical and not a hermeneutical judgement.

(v) Generally, Gandhi argued that reason and enlightened conscience remained the *sine qua non* for any understanding of the sacred scriptures. In 1920, he had clashed in this regard with the Vaishnava Maharajashri (a high priest in the Vaishnava tradition), to whom the adherents of the sect had gone, demanding that a directive be issued prohibiting the *Antyaja*s (untouchables) from attending school with their children. Against the argument of the Maharajashri, that in the interpretation of the shastras reason has no scope (a reiteration of Manu's injunction), Gandhi argued that which reason could not understand and that which the heart does not accept cannot be shastras and anybody who wanted to follow dharma cannot but admit this principle. Otherwise, one would even endorse violence in instances such as 'Rama killing Ravana', or consider eating meat as sanctioned by the shastras (*Navjivan*, 12 December 1920), positions which, according to him, went against the very fundamentals of Hinduism.

In fact, from the traditional criteria of authoritative understanding based on *sruti* (heard), *smriti* (remembered), *achar* (allowed practice) and the understanding of *sadvipra* (righteous person), Gandhi eliminates the first three by the law of lapse (principle of decay or depreciation), and retains only the last in the form of righteous person. Sruti, smriti and achar are now internal to sadvipra as informing and constituting him and not independent of him or prior to him.

Ambedkar did not contest the criteria that Gandhi employed directly, although he did say that they could be merely procedural but lacking in practice. How does one know that a conscience is enlightened? It could be highly prejudiced. In such a case, we will be left with nothing but personal testimony without any objective criteria of validation. Ambedkar thought that there were few believing Hindus who were prepared to give up the textual authority of the shastras just because a 'mahatma' tells them that religious authority rests in the mode of one's life. Besides, in a context like that of India, there were many who hailed from traditional strata and claimed good reason and enlightened conscience for their stances, although they were refurbished versions of orthodoxy.

(vi) Gandhi argued that when we interpret a text, we should first be able to establish that what it said is the same as what we understand in the present. Ambedkar broadly agreed on this issue, but was deeply uncomfortable with the argument. There were the methodological problems of adequate evidence regarding the past (Ambedkar 1948: i–viii), but more than that there were the epistemological problems of access from the boundedness of the present to the past. Ambedkar thought that the past could always be accessed from the present, and was not independent of the latter. We highlight those issues which mean something to us in the present. However, with these qualifications, it was Ambedkar meticulously sought all the conceivable historical evidence on an issue, as can be seen in all his writings.

(vii) Gandhi felt that while interpreting the shastras, one has to distinguish between the essence of dharma which is universal and social arrangements, which are contingent (Gandhi 1970: 100). Formally, Ambedkar does not seem to have much of a problem with this criterion, as can be seen in his masterpiece, *The Buddha and His Dhamma*. But he raised several queries: How does one distinguish the essential from the inessential, particularly when one does not have a validated set of beliefs and no established authority for the purpose? What if social arrangements endure rather than remain contingent, as in the case of untouchability? What if a large number of people believe that behind social arrangements is *dharmic* (relating to or practising dharma) sanction?

(viii) Much of the confrontation between Gandhi and Ambedkar on interpretation was occasioned by their approach to the shastras. Gandhi argued that the interpretation of the shastras must be in tune with the fundamental principles of a belief system. With respect to Hinduism, he said that such fundamental principles are *satyameva jayate* (truth alone triumphs), 'ahimsa parmo dharma', etc. However, Ambedkar felt that when there is grave doubt about foundational beliefs, even of the so-called revealed religions, then there can be little consensus regarding Hinduism. Here, he pointed to and questioned the very principles that Gandhi considered foundational.

(ix) Gandhi believed that one has to take into consideration 'the differences of opinion' with regard to the 'meaning' of an issue and what constitutes a difference. Differences regarding meaning may not constitute a disagreement with the issue itself. For instance, while the acharyas disagree on the relationship between the atman and *Brahman* (universal, divine reality), they do not deny the existence or significance of either.[9] Ambedkar did not directly comment on this problem. However, he argued that one has to see differences on an issue and differences in the meaning of an issue in context, rather than formally. While under certain contexts differences may not lead to a parting of ways, in other contexts even differences of meaning may do so.

(x) With regard to the relationship between principles and customs and codes of conduct, Gandhi felt that 'religious codes are contingent'. With knowledge and 'the spirit of liberalism' they 'will change from age to age'. 'The practices and modes of conduct' advocated in the religious books were 'the best in those times and those lands'. If our reason cannot accept them in this age, then it is our dharma to change them or abandon them altogether. As for customs and practices, words and their meanings do undergo a change: 'Words certainly have a meaning but there are ebbs and flows in the meaning of words if they had a life of their own' (Iyer 1986: 84–88). I do not think Ambedkar disagreed much on this count, except that he did not see concepts and meaning as independent of words as much as Gandhi did. He felt that meanings are intimately bound up with words. Besides, there are those who set themselves up as guardians of words and meanings and monopolise the latter as personal estate and resource. Ambedkar pointed to the power wielded by the Brahmins in India through the control of such an estate, even though economically they could be very poor.

(xi) Gandhi argued that there cannot be any plain or simple reading of texts and their central thrust and objective has to be kept in view always. For instance, he said,

> The *Mahabharata* is not to me a historical record. It is hopeless as a history. But it deals with eternal verities in allegorical fashion.... It takes up historical personages and events and transforms them into angels or devils as it suits the purpose of the poet whose theme is the eternal duel between good and evil, spirit and matter. (ibid.: 183)

Again, Ambedkar did not disagree with Gandhi's argument here. For Ambedkar, the questions were: Who decides the central thrust and objective of a text? What are the different interests at work which seem to silence certain parts and project certain other parts of the text? If every reader decides what is central to a text, then does this not lead to a cacophony of readings and relativism?

(xii) Sometimes, Gandhi argued that an overall perspective is essential before one attempts to interpret a text. With respect to Hinduism, Gandhi laid down his own perspective in a language full of evocative similes. He felt that Hinduism is

> one and indivisible at the root (although) it has grown into a vast tree with innumerable branches. The changes in season affect it. It has its autumn and summer, its winter and spring. The rains nourish and fructify it too. It is and is not based on scriptures. It does not derive its authority from one book. The *Gita* is universally accepted but even then it only shows the way. It has hardly any effect on custom. Hinduism is like the *Ganges*, pure and unsullied at its source but taking in its course the impurities on the way. It takes provincial form in every province but the substance is retained everywhere. (*Young India*, 8 April 1926)

Insisting on keeping the perspective in view, Gandhi disagreed with those who wanted to see a message in the Gita to justify violence (Parekh 1999: 152–54). He considered *Anasaktiyoga*[10] as its 'natural and logical interpretation'. While Ambedkar agreed on the need for an overall perspective, he did not agree with Gandhi on his reading of the overall perspective of Hinduism. He saw Gandhi reading Hinduism in his own way, with little correspondence with established practices. Therefore, Gandhi's position will not help in altering those practices which are obnoxious, but which people consider religiously sanctioned. Ambedkar did not see the sociology of Hinduism in the way Gandhi saw it either. Gandhi, for instance, argued that there was no basis for untouchability in the Hindu shastras (*Young India*, 20 October 1920, 29 December 1920). At the same time, he thought that Hinduism could not have given rise to and sustained a social evil as abhorrent as untouchability. While Ambedkar found little evidence of the origins of untouchability in the texts, he drew on a great deal of circumstantial, comparative and inferential evidence (Ambedkar 1948) instead and argued that the books were suffused with ideology conducive to untouchability. Ambedkar also argued, against Gandhi, that the principles of purity and pollution central to the caste system are integral to the practices of untouchability.

(xiii) In 1925, Gandhi observed that the sacred interpretation of the texts must be based on a well-cultivated moral sensibility and experience in the practice of their truths. Interpreters of these texts should have observed the prescribed disciplines in their lives and cannot be opposed to truth; the interpreters should observe *tapascharya* (practice of penance) and the context and spirit of the text has to be kept in mind (*Navjivan*, 11 October 1975). Ambedkar could not have disagreed more. He saw Gandhi as defending privileged access beyond the brief of reason. Those conditions reproduce the privileges of the existing elites, as they alone could claim and be recognised as possessing such qualities. Ambedkar of course conceded that any understanding requires certain conceptual and technical competence. But these conditions were different from the kind of requirements that Gandhi upheld. He felt that under the Gandhian stipulations, one is already routed through the course rather than having the critical independence to adjudge.

(xiv) One of Gandhi's major interpretative interventions was with respect to Ambedkar's paper 'Annihilation of Caste' where Ambedkar argued how reason and morality cannot be reconciled with Hinduism. In this context, Gandhi brought in the factor of interpolations. He said, 'the scriptures properly so-called can only be concerned with eternal verities and must appeal to any conscience whose eyes of understanding are opened'. If they do not, they constitute interpolations. Then he repeated the criteria that we have traced above: 'Nothing can be accepted as the word of God which cannot be tested by

> reason or be capable of being spiritually experienced. And even when you have an expurgated edition of the scriptures, you will need this interpretation. Who is the best interpreter?' (*Harijan*, 15 August 1936).

Gandhi felt that when religious judgements are made, the court of appeal is not the worst but the best that a religion has produced. Ambedkar admitted that there are interpolations which distort a text and behind interpolations lurk interests of various kinds. However, he felt that the major texts of Hinduism and their central characters uphold inequality and other indefensible positions. If they all had to be rejected as interpolations, then nothing would be left to be upheld at all. What does one do if the best specimens themselves show a careless disregard for the social evils and concerns of this world, or if they were far too few? Further, against the word of the saint he upheld a rational critical attitude towards the sacred scriptures, and against Gandhi he defended his interpretation, which was sourced from a critical study of the texts.

> The saints have never according to my study carried on a campaign against caste and untouchability. They were not concerned with the struggle between men ... they did not preach that all men are equal. They preached that all men were equal in the eyes of God ... the masses have been taught that a saint might break caste but the common man must not .... Thus it can be a matter of no consolation that there were saints or that there is a Mahatma who understands the shastras differently from the learned few or ignorant many. (Gandhi 1976: 339)

Conclusions

Is there a coherent theory of interpretation that one can attribute to either of these proponents? While there is no substantial body of reflective thought regarding the interpretation they left behind, there seems to be a consistent application of a body of ideas that they employed while reading texts and traditions. Besides, their application of the ideas regarding the reading of texts and traditions seems richer in comparison to their deliberate reflections. The paradigms that we suggested in the earlier part of this chapter acted as the anchors for their respective positions.

Is the paradigm of interpretation connected to the traditional mode of interpretation in India? There has been an argument that Ambedkar's reading of Buddhism 'goes well with a tradition in which philosophical innovations were introduced by authors mostly under the garb of discovering the hidden meanings of the original texts' (Gokhale 2004: 121). We have argued that Ambedkar definitely does not insert himself into any such tradition and even Gandhi distances himself from being incorporated into *a* tradition, although he claims to belong to an inclusive tradition. What we find in both Gandhi and Ambedkar is an attempt to break new ground through their modes of interpretation and reaching out to the past selectively.

Ambedkar employed a mode of interpretation that did not tie him down to context and tradition. While Gandhi was not always consistent on this count, he was calling for greater sensitivity to tradition, context and culture. Gandhi's inconsistency has little to do with philosophical lapse, but related to the complex framework of understanding that he was enthusiastic about. For Ambedkar, *The Buddha and His Dhamma* became the great laboratory for reading a text and tradition, while for Gandhi it was the Gita.

Ambedkar did not wholly reject all of Gandhi's yardsticks of interpretation but demonstrated their weakness in order to advance his own paradigmatic and methodological project. Beyond the immediate combatants, there was the audience to be won over. There was also much rhetoric throughout their encounter. With respect to Hindu scriptures, when Ambedkar explored their weaknesses through the lens of his paradigm, he arrived at an entirely different conclusion from Gandhi. Similarly, he found Islam and Christianity wanting (Ambedkar 1950). However, he deployed his paradigm and interpretative criteria for a different reading of Buddhism. Given their respective paradigms, Gandhi's and Ambedkar's engagement could have spilled over to many other texts and traditions. That it did not, is largely incidental. While their reading of tradition and texts remained markedly distinct, they were at the same time available to each other for reasonable contestation and engagement. In fact, it was the orthodoxy which characterised their respective readings as illegitimate.

Ambedkar's hermeneutic engagement upholds a partisanship that constructs emancipatory spaces. Ambedkar recognises too that hermeneutics is a double-edged sword that could be deployed, and has been ably deployed, to defend and promote vested interests. But he thought that there are certain criteria on the basis of which the legitimate deployment of hermeneutics can be separated from its use as a tool to defend vested interests. His conceptual framework provided him with the formidable resources required for the same. Eventually, he thought, the public domain of a modern democracy becomes the final arbiter of deciding what is a legitimate reading and what is not so legitimate, although such judgements themselves were subject to re-evaluation.

Notes

1. Initially, Ambedkar felt that Hinduism too could be reformed in a similar vein. The Mahad Satyagraha in 1927 and the temple entry movements were attempts in that direction. However, by 1936, when he came to write *The Annihilation of Caste*, he had lost all hope in this direction.

2. There are the secularising versions of Christianity in Saint-Simon and Auguste Comte. However, it is quite plausible that Ambedkar fell back on his own reading of Buddhism for the purpose. See Rodrigues (1993) and, particularly, the formulations of John Dewey in this regard. For a lucid formulation of Dewey's ideas, see Ryan (1995), particularly Chapter 7.

3. Everyone has their favourite Gandhi. Gandhi's uneasy and complex relationship to a tradition of thought, and even belief, makes him a shopping mall for distinct intellectual persuasions. While such a charge can be levelled against the framework employed here too, it might hold good only against the substantive elaborations that we have resorted to and probably not to the elements that we consider as central to his paradigm.

4. Recently, Anthony Parel has argued that the *purusharthas*, *artha* (wealth and power), *dharma* (ethics and religion), *kama* (pleasure) and *moksha* (liberation from *samsara*, the cycle of birth, death and rebirth) is the grid through which Gandhi has to be read. According to him, they exemplify the fourfold way in which reason constitutes our humanity. While each purushartha has its own 'specific autonomy', it is at the same time 'oriented to the others'. There is no radical separation between moksha and the other three orientations. Parel's conclusion is, 'the coordinated pursuit of all the purusharthas constitutes the new Gandhian

paradigm'. Parel, therefore, argues that Gandhi wanted to build a strong economy and state-power in India, had a positive disposition towards religion, including practices associated with it, although unlike the Western model which privileged artha, Gandhi wanted to build an organic link between all the four purusharthas (Parel 2006: 12–13).

5. Indanturuttil Nambiatiri, the head priest, quoting tradition, refused the passage to the Vaikom Temple to be thrown open to the untouchables. For details, see Ravindran (1980).

6. Sudipta Kaviraj uses this term to denote Gandhi's mode of communication to the masses, by inserting himself into a world shared in common. Gandhi's critique and challenge also became something internal, often reinforcing those oppositional stances that already existed within popular understanding. See Kaviraj (1986: 226).

7. A substantial number of these criteria are elaborated in Gandhi's rejoinder to Ambedkar's *Annihilation of Caste* (1968) and the latter's subsequent reactions to it.

8. For instance, he charged Tilak, Aurobindo, etc., with importing their favourite readings into the *Bhagavad Gita*: see Gandhi (1967: 179, 1970: 91). Also see Parel (2006).

9. The three important systems concerned with this relationship are the *Advaita, Vishishtadvaita* and *Dvaita*.

10. Principles of detachment and selflessness in action.

References

Ambedkar, B. R. 1948. '*The Untouchables: Who Were They and Why They Became Untouchables?* New Delhi: Amrit Book Co.

——. 1950. 'Buddha and the Future of His Religion'. *The Maha-Bodhi* 58: 117–18, 199–206.

——. 1957. *The Buddha and His Dhamma*. Bombay: Siddhartha College.

——. 1968. *Annihilation of Caste with a Reply to Mahatma Gandhi: And Castes in India, Their Mechanisms, Genesis and Development*. Jullunder: Bheem Patrika.

——. 1979a. 'Buddha or Karl Marx'. In *Dr Babasaheb Ambedkar Writings and Speeches*. Vol. 3. Ed. and comp. V. Moon, 439–62. Bombay: Education Department, Government of Maharashtra.

——. 1979b. 'India and Pre-requisites of Communism'. In *Dr Babasaheb Ambedkar Writings and Speeches*. Vol. 3. Ed. and comp. V. Moon, 93–440. Bombay: Education Department, Government of Maharashtra.

Ambedkar, B. R. 1979c. 'Riddles in Hinduism: An Exposition to Enlighten the Masses'. In *Dr Babasaheb Ambedkar Writings and Speeches*. Vol. 4. Comp. V. Moon. Bombay: Education Department, Government of Maharashtra.

Appadurai, A., ed. 1976. *Documents on Political Thought in Modern India*. Vol. II. New Delhi: Oxford University Press.

Bevir, M., ed. 2010. *Encyclopedia of Political Theory*. Vol. 2. California: Sage Publications.

Brown, J. M. 1989. *Gandhi, Prisoner of Hope*. New Haven and London: Yale University Press.

Gandhi, M. K. 1966. *The Collected Works of Mahatma Gandhi*. Vol. 22. New Delhi: Ministry of Information and Broadcasting, Publications Division

——. 1967. *The Collected Works of Mahatma Gandhi*. Vol. 23. New Delhi: Ministry of Information and Broadcasting, Publications Division.

——. 1968. *The Collected Works of Mahatma Gandhi*. Vol. 28. New Delhi: Ministry of Information and Broadcasting, Publications Division.

——. 1969. *The Collected Works of Mahatma Gandhi*. Vol. 32. New Delhi: Ministry of Information and Broadcasting, Publications Division.

——. 1970. *The Collected Works of Mahatma Gandhi*. Vol. 41. New Delhi: Ministry of Information and Broadcasting, Publications Division.

——. 1976. *The Collected Works of Mahatma Gandhi*. Vol. 63. New Delhi: Ministry of Information and Broadcasting, Publications Division.

Gokhale, P. P. 2004. 'Universal Consequentialism: A Note on B. R. Ambedkar's Reconstruction of Buddhism with Special Reference to Religion, Morality and Spirituality'. In *Reconstructing the World: B. R. Ambedkar and Buddhism in India*, ed. S. Jondhale and J. Beltz, 120–31. New Delhi: Oxford University Press.

Goldmann, L. 1968. *The Philosophy of the Enlightenment: The Christian Burgess and the Enlightenment*. London: Routledge and Kegan Paul.

Habermas, J. 1987. *The Philosophical Discourse of Modernity: Twelve Lectures*. Trans. F. Lawrence. Cambridge, M.A.: The MIT Press.

Iyer, R. 1986. *The Moral and Political Writings of Mahatma Gandhi*. Vol 1. Oxford: Oxford University Press.

Kaviraj, S. 1986. 'The Heteronomous Radicalism of M. N. Roy'. In *Political Thought in Modern India*, ed. T. Pantham and K. L. Deutsch, 209–35. New Delhi: Sage Publications.

Kymlicka, W. 1989. *Liberalism, Community and Culture*. Oxford: Clarendon Press.

Parekh, B. 1989. *Gandhi's Political Philosophy: A Critical Examination*. London: Macmillan.

——. 1999. *Colonialism, Tradition and Reform: An Analysis of Gandhi's Political Discourse*. New Delhi: Sage Publications.

Parel, A. J., ed. 1997. *Hind Swaraj and Other Writings*. Cambridge: Cambridge University Press.

——. 2006. *Gandhi's Philosophy and the Quest for Harmony*. Cambridge: Cambridge University Press.

Ravindran, T. K. 1980. *Eight Furlongs of Freedom*. Madras: Light and Life Publishers.

Robb, P., ed. 1993. *Dalit and Labour Movement in India*. New Delhi: Oxford University Press.

Rodrigues, V. 1993. 'Making a Tradition Critical: Ambedkar's Reading of Buddhism'. In *Dalit Movement and the Meaning of Labour in India*, ed. P. Robb, 299–338. New Delhi: Oxford University Press.

——. 1994. 'Between Tradition and Modernity: The Gandhi-Ambedkar Debate'. In *Dr Ambedkar, Buddhism and Social Change*, ed. A. K. Narain and D. C. Ahir, 137–61. New Delhi: B. R. Publishing.

Ryan, A. 1995. *John Dewey and the High Tide of American Liberalism*. New York: W. W. Norton and Company.

Sen, A. 2009. *The Idea of Justice*. London: Penguin.

Zelliot, E. 1986. 'The Social and Political Thought of B. R. Ambedkar'. In *Political Thought in Modern India*, ed. T. Pantham and K. L. Deutsch, 161–75. New Delhi: Sage Publications.

Notes on the Contributors

Deeptha Achar is Professor at the Department of English, Faculty of Arts, Maharaja Sayajirao University of Baroda, Gujarat. She has co-edited *Towards New Art History: Studies in Indian Art* (2003), *Discourse, Democracy and Difference: Perspectives on Community, Politics and Culture* (2010), and *Articulating Resistance: Art and Activism* (2012), and *Nation, Region Modernity: The Art of K. Venkatappa* (2025). She is the series editor of *Different Tales*, a multi-language series of illustrated children's books that thematise marginalised childhoods and contexts. Her research interests include visual culture studies and childhood studies.

Akeel Bilgrami has held the Johnsonian Professorship of Philosophy and holds the Sidney Morgenbesser Chair of Philosophy at Columbia University, where he is also a Professor on the Committee on Global Thought. He has been the Director of the Heyman Centre for the Humanities as well as the South Asian Institute at Columbia. His publications include *Self-Knowledge and Resentment* (2006), *Secularism, Identity and Enchantment* (2014), *Nature and Value* (2020, edited), and *Capital, Culture and the Commons* (2022). His long-term work is on the relations between agency, value, and practical reason.

Sudarshan Iyengar is former Vice-Chancellor, Gujarat Vidyapith, Ahmedabad. He was also Chair Professor of Gandhian Philosophy at IIT, Mumbai (2016–18). He worked to rehabilitate tribal families displaced by the Narmada Dam project in Gujarat (1989–94) and undertook relief work during the Kachchh earthquake of 2001. He is one of the Directors at Gandhi Research Foundation, Jalgaon.

Sadan Jha is an Associate Professor at the Centre for Social Studies, Surat. His research interests lie in the domains of the history of visuality and contemporary urban society. He has worked on symbols and icons like the spinning wheel, Bharat Mata, partition violence, Hindi literature, history of colours, neighbourhoods, streets, and migration. Sadan's publications include *Social City: Urban Experience and the Question of Belonging* (2022), *The Social Life of Streets in India: Histories, Contestations,*

Subjectivities (2022), *Neighbourhoods in Urban India: In Between Home and the City* (edited, 2021), and *Home, Belonging and Memory in Migration: Leaving and Living* (edited, 2021).

Prabhat Patnaik has taught at the University of Cambridge, UK, and at Jawaharlal Nehru University, New Delhi, where he currently holds the title of Professor Emeritus. His publications include *The Value of Money* (2008), *Re-envisioning Socialism* (2011), *A Theory of Imperialism* (with Utsa Patnaik, 2016), *Capital and Imperialism* (with Utsa Patnaik, 2021) and *Beyond Liberalism* (2024).

Dhananjay Rai is the Head of Department and Associate Professor at the Department of Gandhian Thought and Peace Studies, School of Social Sciences, Central University of Gujarat, Vadodara. His recent books include *Hind Swaraj* (2024), *Poorna Swaraj* (2023), and *Contested Representation: Dalits, Popular Hindi Cinema, and Public Sphere* (2022).

Valerian Rodrigues has taught at Mangalore University, Karnataka (1982–2003) and Jawaharlal Nehru University, New Delhi (2003–15). He has been a Visiting Scholar/Professor at Erfurt University (2012), Wuerzburg University (2011 and 2015), Simon Fraser University (2019), and Fellow of St. Antony's College, Oxford University (1989–91), Indian Institute of Advanced Study, Simla (1999–2001) and Max Weber College, Erfurt (2012). His publications include *The Indian Parliament: A Democracy at Work* (co-authored, 2011), *Speaking for Karnataka (co-authored*, 2018) and *Ambedkar's Political Philosophy: A Grammar of Public Life from Social Margins* (2024).

Anuradha Veeravalli is former Assistant Professor at the Department of Philosophy, University of Delhi. She is the author of *Gandhi in Political Theory: Truth, Law and Experiment* (2014). Her long-standing research focus has been on issues concerning the relationship between science, religion, and politics from the point of view of epistemology and philosophy of language. Her forthcoming title is *What's in a Name? A Grammar of Pluralism and Foundations of the Vernacular* (2025).

Index